A QUALITATIVE STANCE

A QUALITATIVE STANCE

In memory of Steinar Kvale, 1938-2008

Edited by
Klaus Nielsen, Svend Brinkmann, Claus Elmholdt,
Lene Tanggaard, Peter Musaeus & Gerda Kraft

Aarhus Universitetsforlag |

Cover: Jørgen Sparre

Painting used on cover: Hans-Peter Eder, www.ederart.dk

Typeface: Indigo

Printed by Narayana Press, Gylling

Printed in Denmark 2008

ISBN 978-87-793-4414-3

Published with the financial support of

Aarhus Universitets Forskningsfond

Studienævnet for Psykologi og Musikterapi, Aalborg Universitet

Lillian og Dan Finks Fond

Udviklingskonsulenterne Aps

Aarhus University Press

Langelandsgade 177

DK-8200 Århus N

www.unipress.dk

White Cross Mills

Hightown, Lancaster, LA1 4XS

United Kingdom

www.gazellebookservices.co.uk

PO Box 511

Oakwille, CT 06779

USA

www.oxbowbooks.com

Steinar Kvale passed away on 12th March 2008. He had the opportunity to read through the manuscript for this book, and he highly appreciated all the contributions.

CONTENTS

INTRODUCING THE QUALITATIVE STANCE

Qualitative research methods are endemic to many research and practice traditions such as education, psychology, anthropology, sociology, human geography, marketing, business, and nursing science. Behind the increasing popularity of qualitative methods stands what may be characterized as a qualitative stance. From this point of departure, the world – its processes and phenomena – are (or should be) described before they are theorized, understood before they are explained, and seen as concrete qualities rather than abstract quantities. This qualitative stance does not eschew concepts or theories, but it insists that description is not the same as theory, and that in order to understand the intricate phenomena of today's world, we do well to start with precise descriptions of the concrete. This does not favor any one method a priori (participant observation, open-ended interviews etc.). What the qualitative stance opens up for is that researchers go about seeing, telling, imagining etc. what people do in order to deliver descriptions of the concrete rather than abstract qualities or quantities of the social world. A qualitative stance involves focusing on the cultural, everyday, and situated aspects of human thinking, learning, knowing, acting, and ways of under-standing ourselves as persons while at the same time striving to be scientific. In the present book, all the contributors make an effort in different ways to advance such a qualitative stance to social science research.

Since this qualitative stance speaks to a multitude of meanings, it is the possession neither of a single research discipline nor of a single author, al-though we will mention one person in particular: Steinar Kvale. The book is written in honor of Professor Steinar Kvale. Kvale is most widely known for his book on qualitative research interviews, *InterViews: An Introduction* to *Qualitative Research Interviewing*, (Kvale, 1996), but his interests span a much broader range of topics such as qualitative, psychological, and educational research. The present book attests to the inspiration that scholars from around the world have drawn from his writings. Kvale's work has pioneered a qualitative stance that draws from psychoanalysis when studying the therapeutic interview, from Maoism when pondering dialectics, from hermeneutics and phenomenology when understanding the nature of learning, and from history when uncovering the impact of the Church in contemporary psychology.

In Kvale's works we significantly find a critical exposition of the self-understanding and the ways of thinking that are displayed in some modern educational and psychological institutions, not least that they embrace a problematic kind of advanced and complex rationality. Most pointedly, this critique is formulated in the account of psychology as a child of modernism (Kvale, 1992). Contrary to psychology's modern self-understanding, Kvale's works emphasize that in such institutional formations, power and dominance structures are concealed and will not appear in the self-understandings of the institutions. Kvale stresses this point when he argues that the prevailing thinking of education is formulated not on the basis of pedagogical/philosophical thinking, but rather on the basis of the bureaucratic organization forms widespread in the world of industry and business (Kvale, 1976, 1977).

In several of his works, Kvale has formulated constructive alternatives to the thinking hidden in modern psychological and educational institutions. This search for alternatives is rooted in what may be termed a phenomenology of everyday life, arguing that the basis for our analyses of pedagogical and psychological issues is to be found in actual descriptions of people's ways of acting in daily life situations. Kvale has tried in particular to establish an alternative to the technologization of human relations by stressing the importance of founding educational and psychological research on the experience of what is meaningful in practical everyday life. This is displayed for instance in his works on apprenticeship, which is regarded as an alternative to technologized and subjectivized forms of educational thinking, where the contents of learning are separated from the form of learning. What has emerged from the different directions that Kvale's work has taken is a distinct qualitative stance, which implies a commitment to study people's everyday lives, as they experience, learn, and act in the world, and opposes "technified" approaches to the study of human lives in any form.

The book's chapters illustrate and advance this qualitative stance in different ways. Three distinct themes stand out as pivotal points in the book. The first theme centers around qualitative studies on learning. In the respective chapters, learning is studied as a social ontological phenomenon concerning human change in changing social practices. The second theme concerns critiques of current educational practices and the postmodern consumer society. This critique is arrived at through careful descriptions of subjectivity and contemporary social relations. The third theme is about the development of new ways of thinking about qualitative inquiry. Within these respective themes, many chapters address the relations between qualitative social research and the ethical and political presuppositions and implications for knowledge, identity, and learning. In what follows, we give a brief overview of the chapters that make up this book.

I. Understanding Learning

JEAN LAVE & MARTIN PACKER set the stage with a chapter outlining a social ontology of learning. The chapter explores the concept of "the everyday", which is popular in a variety of theoretical arenas at the present time, but remains mostly unanalyzed. Lave & Packer propose that a view of the everyday is implicit in all theories of learning. However, they argue for the need for an explicit conception of the everyday social character of the politics and epistemology of learning: that learning is ubiquitous in ongoing social activity.

KLAUS NIELSEN differentiates in his chapter between a narrow perspective and an expanded perspective on learning. In pursuing the expanded perspective, Nielsen applies the metaphor of a learning landscape, which was originally developed together with Steinar Kvale. The metaphor of a learning landscape emphasizes the learning resources of everyday practice. The chapter illustrates the expanded perspective on learning through two studies on the concrete everyday practices involved in the process of becoming either a pianist or a baker.

PETER MUSAEUS focuses on learning and identity, a great concern in contemporary educational research as well as the classical Bildungsroman, being interrelated with space and time. The essay explores the extent to which Bakhtin's concept of chronotope can serve as an analytical tool to analyze dialogic notions of identity. The chapter is a case study of an eminent guitar luthier and it explores the significance of the chance encounter, the threshold and the road to identity formation in being an informal apprentice and a journeyman seeking out the influence of foreign guitar luthier masters.

In his chapter, CLAUS ELMHOLDT explores how identity dilemmas of belonging and becoming may become barriers to learning. The chapter takes its point of departure in a case study of an ethnic migrant girl's negotiation of identity across the cultural communities of home and school/work. According to Elmholdt, the girl's participation across contexts enacts an identity dilemma of learning to be a good girl (adopting the traditional religious lifestyle as recommended by her parents), or learning to be a learner (adopting the modern urban individualized reflexive lifestyle as required by school and workplaces). Elmholdt argue that the described identity dilemma of belonging and becoming is also a dilemma of learning in fundamental ways.

OLE DREIER investigates situated learning and persons moving around in social practice in the pursuit of learning. On the surface, the article looks at institutionally arranged ways that affect the opportunities and nature of learning processes; but at a deeper level, the article challenges psychology to develop a conception of structures of social practice. The article uses illustrations from empirical research on studying changes and learning taking place in people when they attend therapy sessions as a secluded part of their everyday lives in structures of social practice.

The central theme in TONE SAUGSTAD's chapter about the knowledge society is the clash between scholastic versus non-scholastic learning that stems from a poor understanding of the field of practice and a one-dimensional understanding of knowledge. Using Aristotle's categorization of knowledge, the paper concludes that some forms of knowledge are acquired in practical life, while other knowledge forms are acquired in school through the use of analytical and systematic principles of learning.

HUBERT & STUART DREYFUS present their five stages for the acquisition of professional skills from novice to expert. In this paper, the conditions for a sixth stage denoting the step from expertise to mastery is introduced. Generally the advancement from one step to the next is characterized by a decreasing dependence on instruction and context-free rules and features, and an increasing experience-based awareness of subtle contextual features crucial to the task at hand. A core notion in identifying progress in professional skills is "intuitive expertise", signifying a capacity to encompass multiple aspects of a given situation. What finally distinguishes a master from an expert is the capacity, the courage, and the willingness to enlarge the repertoire of perspectives and the accompanying actions. The precondition for this development is, it is argued, an exceptional motivation and dedication to the profession.

KENNETH & MARY GERGEN extend the implications of one of Kvale's catalytic proposals, namely that "the conversation may be conceived of as a basic mode of knowing". They do so in order to broaden our conceptions of educational practice from being seen as a means of enhancing individual competence to being increasingly collaborative. In the view of Gergen and Gergen, educational practices for the future develop skills in effective dialogue and link scholarly understanding to broader contexts of practice. It is proposed in the chapter that educational programs for the future develop curricula that recognize multiple constructions of the world, that confront important conflicts in value, and that cultivate appreciation for ambiguity over certainty.

LENE TANGGAARD pays attention to the looping effects of the post-modern and very popular concept of life-long learning. She does so inspired by Steinar Kvale's idea of the ideological function of learning theories. Looping effects occur when people actively take upon themselves the ideologies implied in what they read or hear. In the chapter, the possible looping effects involved in the present shift in our assumptions about learning, in the change from modernity and to postmodernity, are analyzed. The chapter addresses some of the effects this may have on our self-understanding in post-modernity when learning is said to be a process happening everywhere, or at least as being a process out of the teachers' control.

II. Critiquing Theory

AMEDEO GIORGI sets his focus on the prevailing experimental and objectivistic trend in mainstream (American) psychology. This trend, he argues, still dominates psychological research even though scholars have tried for half a century to pose the question of its methodological presuppositions and its consequences. The problematic effect of this attitude is that a crucial part of psychology's subject-matter is neglected or strictly devalued, namely subjective experience. Giorgi questions the usefulness of experimental procedures when it comes to understanding research findings. A precondition for understanding the meaning of data is the inclusion of experiential categories in research. His aim is a clarification of the question of what it means for subjective phenomena to be objective.

In his chapter, IAN PARKER highlights a connection in the discipline of psychology between qualitative research and psychoanalysis. According to Parker, this connection consists of dialectical materialism as laid out by Chairman Mao. Parker argues that the dialectical materialist conception of contradiction and change can energize and politicize both qualitative research and psychoanalysis by showing how and why they must confront a common enemy, namely mainstream "metaphysical" psychology.

SVEND BRINKMANN takes a classic paper by Kvale and Grenness from 1967 (on B.F. Skinner and J.-P. Sartre) as the starting point for a critique of the current psychologized image of man in the social sciences. By drawing on the classical positivism of Auguste Comte, as well as the "literary sociology" of Michel Houellebecq, Brinkmann further develops an analysis of human life in postmodern consumer societies, which demonstrates a productive role for literary works in qualitative social science discussions.

III. Challenging Qualitative Research

DONALD POLKINGHORNE addresses the ethics of interviewing and presents the thoughts of the philosopher Emmanuel Levinas as an alternative frame of reference for ethical thinking in qualitative interviewing. Levinas holds that the place of the ethical is located in the face-to-face encounter with another person. His ideas of the Face, the Said and Saying, and Desire are explored. The chapter concludes with a discussion of the implications of Levinas' ethics for qualitative interviewers.

JULIANNE CHEEK focuses on qualitative research and inquiry in particular and the wider political context in which qualitative research is conducted and in which qualitative researchers are embedded. The chapter develops a notion of both inter-view and inter-viewing as craft, thus highlighting the need to consider the interconnectedness of theory and method, the inter-view as a metaphor for the relationship between research context and research method/ design and the relationship between the researcher and the researched.

In his chapter, NORMAN DENZIN criticizes the ethical standards of Institutional Review Boards (IRBs) as being based on a bio-medical, ethical model resulting in disciplining qualitative research. Consequently, qualitative researchers are in danger of being marginalized both in relation to public forums and in relation to defining the field of scientific research. Alternatively, Denzin suggests viewing ethics as pedagogies of practice, grounding qualitative inquiries in research communities where ethical and scientific values are integrated into daily practices fostering an integrated ethical qualitative behavior.

CARSTEN ØSTERLUND lets Steinar Kvale have the final word by reporting an interview with Steinar Kvale about advising, and, in particular, the advising of qualitative research projects carried out by graduate students. In the interview, Østerlund explores how Kvale's own work on evaluation, dialogue, qualitative interviews, and apprenticeship influences his advising practices. Furthermore, the interview pursues issues such as the selection of PhD students, navigating institutional requirements, helping students build and conduct qualitative research, the advising dialogue and power dynamics.

*****

The editors would like to thank Lone Hansen, secretary at the Department of Psychology, University of Aarhus, for all her help and careful editing of this manuscript. In addition we thank the donors that made this book possible: The Aarhus University Research Foundation, Lillian & Dan Finks Fond, The Board of Studies for Psychology and Music Therapy at Aalborg University, and funds provided by Udviklingskonsulenterne for Claus Elmholdt.

UNDERSTANDING LEARNING

Jean Lave   *Martin Packer*
University of California, Berkeley *Duquesne University*

TOWARDS A SOCIAL ONTOLOGY OF LEARNING

Introduction

Recent attempts to develop social or cultural theories of learning assume, often unreflectively, that the lived experience so addressed is "everyday" in character. There is movement in this direction in linguistics (e.g. around issues of pragmatics, deixis, sociolinguistics, language use as social practice) as well as in other disciplinary contexts (psychology, education, sociology, and cultural studies). These attempts include discussions of socially shared cognition, cultural psychology, cognition in practice, situated activity, learning in practice, and arguments about culture, praxis, pragmatics and social practice. "Everyday life" has taken on new salience, a new popularity, in these efforts to develop more socially grounded approaches to cognition, thinking, and speaking, and in anthropological studies of social practice. The latter assert that everyday life is the site of central sociocultural, historical processes that should be the object of our study.

What are we to make of the pivotal, but mostly unanalyzed, popular conception of "the everyday" and its vague but recurring place in academic discourse? "The everyday" has a variety of related meanings: life experience that is mundane, prosaic, humdrum, boring, or that which recurs, the routine, the unchanging, the ordinary and expected, perhaps inescapable, round. It is sometimes equated with culture, the customary, and the commonplace; sometimes with the fabric of belief, value and lived experience, or with the site of praxis, pragmatics, and social practice. If anything, these various interpretations sustain the vague and open sense of the term. We might expect, then, that the problem with "the everyday" would turn out to be its lack of specific meaning in fields of endeavor in which its pivotal role should recommend a more searching acquaintance. But in fact the problem is just the opposite: the "everyday" has a longer history and a more broadly shared, more narrowly constrained meaning than the users of the term are generally aware of. For example, The Critical Theory Program at the University of California, Davis sponsored a conference in the mid-1990s entitled "Problematics of Daily Life."[1] Speakers began in similar ways, with a disclaimer: none of them felt that they had any idea what a conference on the everyday might be about; then they went on to discuss a surprisingly closely related set of issues. All of them claimed dissatisfaction with some well-known ways of conceiving of the everyday (ways to which we shall have occasion to return). And all of them took the matter at hand to be a question of how and what people *know* under ordinary circumstances. This convergence of approaches and foci deserves attention. And given that everyday life is such a key conception in such a variety of theoretical arenas at the present time, and that it has a history of which its friendly users seem unaware, the topic is worth exploring further.

Furthermore, we will propose that a view of the everyday is implicit in theories of learning which make no explicit mention of it. This assertion may seem surprising. After all, we can talk about problem solving, meta-cognition, analytic skills, and problem spaces, apparently without reference to an everyday world. But that should not be taken at face value. In fact, the vast majority of contemporary theories of learning presume and rest upon a polar opposition: their key notion is always one of moving toward scientific knowledge, and implied in this is always the movement away from the opposite pole, one of everyday life. We propose that this and related and unquestioned dualistic oppositions have held studies of learning to ransom. If these oppositions are to be resolved and the dualisms overcome, explicit and careful attention must be paid to the realm of the "everyday," to everyday practice and learning. But a cognitive theory of the everyday mechanisms of learning, knowing, and problem solving will not help, for reasons we will describe.[2]

Embedded in, and central to, the polar opposition between the scientific and the everyday in conventional learning theory is a political-social dimension that generally goes unrecognized, one that has a narrowly epistemological (and individual, ahistorical, rationalistic) character. We shall try to propose a different view of the politics and epistemology of "everyday learning." A more complete understanding of the quotidian brings with it an alternative understanding of learning: that learning is ubiquitous in ongoing social activity. It is a mistake to think of learning as a special kind of activity, taking place only at particular times in special places arranged for it. This view of learning raises its own questions, of course (Lave & Wenger, 1991; Chaiklin & Lave, 1993).

In the following section we will briefly characterize two theories of learning (in cognitive science, in the work of Piaget) in comparative terms, and describe their common assumptions. Proponents of each of these theories consider the other to be very different from, even opposed to, their own. They may make strange bedfellows.[3] But their comparison leads us to a level of underlying assumptions at which there turn out to be fundamental similarities. These assumptions need to be questioned if we are to recognize and move beyond the shortcomings of these theories. The most significant shortcomings may be summed up in what we have come to call a Refined/ Crude model of learning (and of the world that it implies). Learning is assumed, without question, to involve processes of "refinement. In Section III we characterize a strategy that has been employed in recent discussions of situated cognition and social practice to move away from conventional theories of learning by reversing the customary value ascribed to the two poles of the Refined/Crude model, a "High-Grade Crude" strategy. Although this doesn't change the underlying assumptions, it does have the merit of focusing attention for the first time on the "everyday" pole, otherwise suppressed, as a site for learning.

We then turn to the body of philosophical/social theoretical work in the existential Marxist tradition that seems to us to have the most to say about the everyday in terms that also address the other problems we encounter in the Refined/Crude model. In Section IV we draw on two strengths of this work: its development of a social, historical ontology, and with it an emphasis on questions about being and becoming – living in the world. It seems to us that together these offer a needed framework for asking new questions about knowledge, knowing, and learning.[4]

Both of the typical accounts of learning – the Refined/Crude and the High-Grade Crude – are inadequate in so far as they are ahistorical. If we insist on the importance of historical process and historical analysis, we need to offer an account of why such a worldview is so pervasively characteristic of the Western world at the present time. In Section V we take up two historical views of everyday life (those of Georg Lukacs and Henri Lefebvre). Lukacs' theory of reification seems to provide a compelling historical explanation of contemporary theories of learning, in which these are taken to be descriptions of reified existence in which mind can be described as, and in terms of, alienated formalisms. Lefebvre's work illustrates both strengths and problems with the way in which the existential Marxist philosophers conceive of the everyday. Finally (Section VI), we consider the implications of our analysis for theorizing learning.

Typical Theories of Learning

We start by analyzing the shared assumptions that underlie the way learning is viewed in two representative theories in psychology. Our analysis attends to assumptions about the relationship between subject and world, the telos or direction in which the change that is learning takes place, and the mechanisms or processes whereby this change is accomplished. These seem to us to be the minimum components of any theory of learning worthy of the name. They provide us with a framework for comparing theories of learning.[5]

Cognitive Science

Haugeland's (1981) sympathetic overview of the program of cognitive science provides a useful text for our task. There is no explicit mention of learning per se, but Haugeland's account contains reference to each of the three components of theories of learning we have just mentioned: the relationship of subject and world; the telos; and the mechanism for change. Cognitive science aims to describe areas of human competence in terms of a formal system of rules that operate on tokens. The subject is taken to be computational in character, logically equivalent to an automated formal system. The rules of such a system are syntactical; that is to say, they require no interpretation or judgment for their application. They are like the rules of a game like chess. The tokens on which these rules operate are also formally and explicitly defined, like the arrangement of pieces on a chessboard.

In Haugeland's account it is also the case that tokens (taken now as symbols) can represent the world. "We regard interpretation as relating or connecting a formal system to the outside world (i.e., to whatever its tokens are 'about')" (p. 27). But the world that a formal system can be said to represent, as Haugeland describes it, itself stands distinct from any interpretation of it, formal or otherwise. This world is simply an objective collection of objects, states, or facts, all material and directly given. Clearly this is a dualist account of subject and object. Since a computer is a material object too, as well as being computational, Haugeland suggests that computer science is not dualistic because it avoids dividing reality into distinct mental and material realms. We disagree: there is at best a material-material dualism in cognitive science instead of a mental-material one: the two realms now are those of "inside" and "outside" the computer.

But who or what is in a position to be able to take a token as a symbol representing the world or one of its elements? Not the formal system itself, for the world is outside that system, and the rules by definition cannot operate on anything external to their scope of application. If a formal system represents the world it is unaware, so to speak, that it does so. Only someone with access to both system and world could judge the adequacy of such a representation. This bird's-eye view is usually taken, of course, by the programmer, but to acknowledge this is to see that the semantics is done by a human, not by the formal system, and that a third term is needed to overcome the dualism between the system of representations, and what is represented. Haugeland can only say, hopefully, that "the semantics takes care of itself." The persisting dualism between computational subject and material object is at the root of this difficulty. Yet semantics is one central criterion which cognitive scientists use to judge the success of their formal models: does the system make true statements about the world? A better system makes more true statements and fewer false ones.[6] In sum, then, for cognitive science, formal computational systems generate statements about an objective world that can be true or false.

Learning in cognitive science, then, is a movement towards self-contained, computational rationality (where "rationality is loosely analogous to truth-preservation in mathematical systems", 1981, p. 28). The work of interpreting real life reduces to the "systematic specification of what all the tokens of a system mean" (1981, p. 22). Ultimately, in principle, this formal rationality will encompass all domains of life. Haugeland concludes by saying "The basic suggestion [of some critics] is that those areas in which computers excel (or can be expected to excel) are all of a special sort, where the relevant considerations are comparatively few and well defined. This includes formal games (by definition) and also a number of other routine technical or micro-world tasks. But it is an open question whether the intelligence manifested in everyday life, not to mention art, invention, and discovery, [note that these are presumed to be things that everyday life is not] is of essentially this same sort (though presumably more complicated.) Cognitive science is, in effect, betting that it is ..." (1981, p. 34).

Piaget's Genetic Epistemology
A seemingly very different account of learning can be found in the work of Jean Piaget. In his 'genetic epistemology' Piaget describes the child's movement from sensori-motor intelligence to preoperational and then concrete operational thinking, as a consequence of a "reflexive abstraction" operating on the child's own actions in the physical environment. The final stage of Piaget's developmental trajectory is that of formal operational intelligence. Formal thinking is abstract, freed from the constraints of space and time that were characteristic of concrete operations and the sensori-motor stage. Its abstraction from the constraints under which action is performed means that operational thinking is reversible and atemporal. In this final stage, operations can operate recursively upon one another, and this free combination of operations makes possible the hypothetico-deductive reasoning that characterizes science. These distinct operations constitute a stage of intelligence insofar as they form a coherent, integrated system.

The developmental telos expressed here, then, is one of an abstraction that proceeds by means of the subject's reflection on his or her operations. For Piaget it is the epistemic subject that is of interest (Piaget, 1970/1988). He aimed to give a genetic account of the epistemological structures of space, time, causality and object that Kant described, in the *Critique of Pure Reason* (1787/1965), as organizing our perception of the world (Piaget, 1937/1955). This subject is a cognitive one; its conative and emotive aspects are secondary, at best viewed as subsidiary domains of intelligence.

If the subject is the focus of much attention in Piaget's work, as a system of operations that become progressively differentiated and at the same time hierarchically integrated, the world goes surprisingly unremarked. Piaget equivocated between a naive empiricism, describing the child surrounded by chairs, tables, and other "medium-sized dry goods" (to use John Austin's phrase [Austin, 1975]); at other times he talked of unstructured data impinging upon the child's intellectual schemes. The problem, of course, was that having committed himself to the view that the world cannot be known save in the subject's interactions with it, he could not fairly try to describe that world in neutral, independent terms. We are left with a detailed account of the subject, but little sense of what non-subjective reality that subject is engaged in interaction with (Piaget, 1976/1972).

This difficulty is not fatal to Piaget's scheme of things because his interest is, at bottom, how the subject represents the world, not how the world itself is actually reproduced or transformed. As the child develops, representation of action becomes, implicitly at least, more valued than action itself. Competence, especially the ability to imagine all possible ways of conducting, say, an experiment, is to Piaget more interesting and significant than the actual performance of the experiment.

The subject-world relations, telos, and mechanisms for learning in these two theoretical genres are summed up in Table 1. These theories share a common set of assumptions. First, subject and world are taken to be entities of two distinct types. The subject is a mental, cognitive entity, while the world is an array of objects with determinate properties. The subject is unquestionably a naturalized individual, while the world is an environment, with no history. Nor is this world social, much less a contradictory, politically and culturally differentiated social world. In short, each of these theories rests on a dualistic account of subject and world. Second, the relationship between these two terms is taken to be an epistemological one: learning is a matter of the subject coming to better *know* the world. Action in the world has only a derivative place, if it figures at all. Third, the direction in which learning proceeds is towards more abstract, more formal, detached and objective knowing. Fourth, the mechanism whereby this telos is achieved is one of reflection and detachment.

TABLE 1: ELEMENTS OF THE THEORIES OF LEARNING IN HAUGLAND'S COGNITIVE SCIENCE AND PIAGET'S GENETIC EPISTEMOLOGY

	COGNITIVE SCIENCE	PIAGET
SUBJECT-WORLD RELATION	SUBJECT: an automated formal system: systems of formal rules operating on tokens. WORLD: what the tokens represent. RELATIONS: representation: semantics, truth-value.	SUBJECT: Epistemic subject. OBJECT: Kantian thing-in-itself. RELATION: interaction between subject and object involves assimilation and accommodation – play + imitation.
TELOS	TRUTH: making true statements about the world. WINNING: reaching the winning positions, the goal states, of the formal system.	STAGE of formal operations. OPERATIONAL INTELLIGENCE: detached from action; reversible (not temporal); allowing hypothetic-deductive reasoning. FORMAL: abstract (not concrete). STAGE: A coherent integrated and differenttiated system.
MECHANISM	Trial and error. Being programmed better.	DISEQUILIBRIUM (logical inconsistency) motivates learning/development. REFLEXIVE ABSTRACTION: reflection on self (self as object of knowledge) + decontextualization.

From Superior Knowing to Being Everyday

Running through these theories is a notion of *refinement*, of a movement away from the messiness of practice and mundane concerns, in short, a move away from the everyday to a realm of reflection and detachment where genuine knowledge can be obtained. When we take a careful look, we see that the refined pole is associated with higher cultural forms. The word "refinement" has rich clusters of connotations: What is refined is purified, clarified, distilled, and reduced to a pure state, freed from impurities. Refinement suggests precision, exactness; it is polished and smooth. And finally, refinement is a characteristic of the elite: to be refined is to be fastidious, distinguished, cultured and cultivated, at ease, classy, gracious, stylish, subtle, and sophisticated.

A theory that posits a telos of refinement embodies, then, suppositions about unequal social categories. In the contemporary world the salient social inequalities surely include social class, ethnicity, and gender relations. These are all frequently coded in the terms of the Refined/Crude model, summed up in Table 2.[7] The realms of rationality, formal logic, distanced contemplation, knowledge production, autonomy and neutral objectivity are all assumed without question to characterize the dominant category in each case, while in contrast the everyday world of reproduction and maintenance, the ordinary, routine, the particular, intuitive and interested are assumed to characterize the dominated category.

The simple sugar cube (by no means an everyday object) provides a model of what we mean by the refined-crude axis. It is made, of course, of "refined" sugar, that is to say, sugar that has been processed to remove its contaminants and impurities. It is now pure; its grubbiness purged. It is also a precise Platonic form with the perfection of a white cube. Sugar by the spoonful rather than as a cube is a quotidian object today. But not long ago even sugar crystals were a commodity only for the wealthy elite. In 1811 Benjamin Delessert received the Cross of the Legion of Honor from Napoleon for the achievement of his factory in turning out well-crystallized beet sugar. Crystals of sugar were counted among the family jewels of a dowry or inheritance 250 years ago.

The refined-crude axiology is to be found at work across the social sciences (at least). Structural linguistics offers an instructive example, with the axiology operating at the level of method as well as theory. Data about a person's

TABLE 2: REFINED-CRUDE AXIOLOGY

	REFINED	CRUDE
SUBJECT-WORLD RELATION	Subject-world dualism. Distanced: privileged. Priority given to the knowing subject: an epistemic relationship.	Subject-world dualism. Embedded. Priority given to objects' influence on the subject.
TELOS	REFINED: i.e. Elite. Abstract. Ideal.	CRUDE: i.e. Common. Concrete. Particularistic; flawed. Non-generative; not general; routine; mechanical.
MECHANISM	ABSTRACTION; detachment; decontextualization; contemplation; reflection. Leisure: relief from cares and concerns.	LEARNING BY DOING; by rote repetition; by absorption. Learning by imitation; observation. Learning by "practicing."

"performance" is assumed to be contaminated by the influence of setting, motivation, fatigue, and even by the exigencies of speaking in "real time." In order to adequately characterize the underlying "competence," which is seen as the proper goal of the linguist, this data must first be refined: It must be abstracted from the situation in which it makes its appearance.

But the assumptions that learning is a movement toward an ideal locus, exemplified by science or philosophy, that the everyday is the locus of the mucky particularities of existence, and that there is naturally a dualistic opposition of subject and object, person and world, are widespread in the everyday beliefs and practices of Euro American culture much more broadly. (We will come back to this relation between theoretical domains and broader cultural perspectives in Section V.)

Several strategies have been employed in an effort to overturn the Refined/ Crude model, motivated variously by a search for theoretical novelty, by opposition to its embedded ideology of social inequality, or by the hope for an antidote to a theoretical position too narrow to address pressing problems about learning.[8] The first (not just first on our list, but probably also first historically in changing disciplinary knowledges) is that of trying to overturn the Refined/Crude axiology by inverting it. A "High-Grade Crude" axiology seeks to adopt the point of view of the devalued social category, to revalue the "crude," as basic, concrete, raw, sensuous, vital, earthy, and involved. In the High-Grade Crude models of learning (using the comparative terms sketched above) the telos of the Refined/Crude model – scientific expertise, pure calculation, formal operations, great chess playing – remains unaltered, but the mechanisms for learning are revalued, with an emphasis now on such considerations as the intuitive and concrete knowledge of the scientist, or an argument that scientists actually learn their "craft" through apprenticeship (but see Lave & Wenger, 1991, for a critique). Thus, learning through doing is celebrated, there are sometimes discussions of how to transfer concrete and practical learning to the classroom, and contextual relevance is seen as an antidote to decontextualized learning (but the context/decontextualization pair betrays the unchanged basic dualism, as do the "particularity" and "intuition" that stand in contrast, implicitly, to "generality" and "logical reasoning").

If reversing the axiology of the Refined/Crude model does not offer the possibility for a radical dismantling of theories of learning, the High-Grade Crude model nonetheless has the merit of drawing attention to the previously devalued category. It encourages a much-needed focus on "the everyday," and suggests the possibility of exploring everyday life as the site of learning.[9] But such a move – simply inverting the axiology of refined and crude – will fail to transform the basic theory in radical ways, because it leaves unexamined the relationship between the two poles. The distinction between the Refined and the Crude encapsulates distinctions between the mental and the manual, between thought and action, between theory and practice, between the ideal and the real, between subject and object, between elite and commonplace. While the two terms in each of these pairs can be distinguished, and emphasis can be shifted from one to the other, a serious attempt to break with the dualistic model must cope with the fact that they cannot easily and simply be separated, because they are two ends of a single axis.

The recognition of this fact motivates the quest for a further, more radical move. Both the Refined/Crude and the High-Grade Crude models, no matter which pole they give priority to, are still ahistorical, asocial, individualist, rationalist, dualistic, and disembodied theories of learning (and consequently of life). What we seek would be a historically grounded, dialectical, social, relational theory of learning, involving the transformation in activity of participants in communities of practice. It seemed clear to us that one prerequisite for understanding learning as participation in communities of (everyday) practice is a social, historical ontology. From our previous work we know that Karl Marx and his various intellectual descendents had explored the implications of reformulating in social ontological terms questions that had been confined to epistemological interrogation for much of the life of modern philosophy. Perhaps they could show us how to address questions of learning and knowing first of all as social ontological matters, and only secondarily and in a derivative manner as epistemological ones. This promised to radically shake up our understanding of the nature of learning.

Everyday Western Existential Marxism: Social, Historical Ontology

The term "Western Marxism" was coined by Merleau-Ponty (in *Adventures of the Dialectic, 1955/1974*). According to Martin Jay (1984), "Western Marxism has often been equated with Hegelian Marxism" (1984, p. 3), because proponents, e.g. "Lukacs, Gramsci Bloch and others ... insisted on the importance of Marx's debt to Hegel" (1984, p. 2).[10] "Accordingly, such terms as alienation, mediation, objectification, and reification were understood to have a special place in the lexicon of Western Marxism." Jay suggests that, "Culture, defined both widely as the realm of everyday life and narrowly as man's most noble artistic and intellectual achievements, was also a central concern of the tradition." (1984, p. 3). "[I]t can be plausibly argued that Western Marxism has enriched cultural theory more than economic or political theory" (1984, p. 9).

We have suggested that the mechanism by which knowledge is "acquired" in the dualistic, mentalist approaches to learning of the Refined/Crude and

High-Grade Crude models is abstraction, a kind of withdrawn contemplation. We also pointed out that in common connotations of "the everyday," socialization is assumed to be the mode of learning, rather than formal instruction, which is taken to be the source of refined knowledge. Both "socialization" and "formal instruction" involve extensive mythologies about the mechanisms of learning. These myths are familiar: socialization involves learning by imitation, by repetitive practice, by unreflective doing, and by mechanical reproduction of routines. Formal learning is formal[11] because it depends on teaching. It depends, likewise, on processes by which knowledge is "transmitted." Without teaching, it is assumed, there would be no motivation to learn. Transmission processes are required to get across "pre-processed abstractions," and teaching is required for learners to gain access to genuine (read 'privileged') knowledge. Thus transmitted, knowledge must be internalized, and it must be internalized in exactly the form in which it was transmitted if the resulting knowing is not to be erroneous. And, given that learning (rather than plying knowledge) is the object while teaching is the mode of transmission, there must be a means to carry new knowledge to the sites of its future use, a process known as "learning transfer."

In order to challenge the various elements in these mythologies of socialization and formal instruction, we will lay out what we take to be some of the most important contributions of existential Marxist thinkers. On the basis of these contributions it is possible to sketch the general outlines of a socially-historically grounded theory of learning, using the account of formal instruction, in particular, as the target for transformation. This will not by any means be a complete survey of the contributions of existential Marxist thinkers, but a modest attempt to read them for answers to our questions about learning and everyday life. The most important question will turn out to be: What resources does existential Marxist philosophy/social theory provide for transforming this formal view of learning so as to go beyond surface descriptions of practice of reification and the naturalization of contemporary forms of alienation?

We began our exploration of Western Marxist writings in order to better understand some of the intellectual roots of social practice theory, a literature in which we both already had strong interest. When we began, we shared some working notions, e.g. that learning is part of everyday life, part of changing communities of practice, in a changing social world. We also tried to clarify our intuitions that knowing is not a fundamental condition for acting so much as the other way around. We set out to explore a social ontology that could underpin our ideas about how to conceive of learning, one that offered an account of the way that practice and involvement are constitutive of knowing, and that acknowledged the dialectical and tension-filled relationship between doing and knowing.

Central to the work of the Western, existentialist Marxists was a rethinking of human agency and the social order. While existentialism can take the form of an appeal to radical individual freedom, and Marxism has often solidified into a story of the deterministic effects of an economic base, in combination they have provided a fertile ground for conceptions of human agency as constitutive of, and at the same time constituted by, the social and cultural order.

Marx's social ontology has been called a "philosophy of praxis" (Feenberg, 1986; cf. Gould, 1978). Marx argues that the objective world, including its "natural" parts, is socially constituted. Human beings, too, are socially produced, including even their apparently private and personal subjective, innermost consciousness. As Marx understands consciousness "it is to be understood as an aspect or moment of *praxis* itself. Furthermore, the forms that 'consciousness' takes in society are to be understood within the context of the forms of social *praxis* (Bernstein 1971, p. 43). And they produce themselves in activity in the world. To understand 'praxis' we need to reject with Marx the analytic philosophical ontological distinction between persons and things. "The object or product produced is *not* something 'merely' external to and indifferent to the nature of the producer. It is his activity in an objectified or congealed form .... Echoing the Hegelian claim that the self is what it does, Marx maintains that a [person] (is what [s]he does. Consequently the very nature or character of a [person] is determined by what [s]he does or his/her *praxis*, and his/her products are concrete embodiments of this activity (Bernstein, 1971, p. 44). (Sexist language revised.) This ontology is historical: it is an ontology of what is found in history – people, events, etc., so that any description of reality is a historical description. At the same time, it claims that all these entities are historical entities, formed and transformed by the historical practices characteristic of the epoch they existed in. Persons in practice are engaged in projects that have continuity through time; they are born, they live a short existence, they die, but their projects can outlive them. "The defining trait of philosophy of praxis … is the attempt to show that the "antinomies" of philosophy can be resolved only in history … (Feenberg, 1986, p. 5). "When philosophy of praxis contends that human action is philosophically pertinent not just in ethics or politics but in all domains generally, it is asserting a wholly original *ontological* position. For this philosophy, human action touches the substratum of being as such, and not simply those special domains we usually conceive as affected by our activities." (Feenberg, 1986, p. 6.)

The philosophy of praxis, in sum, has several crucial implications for theories of learning. The first is that the human subject is an active agent, involved with persons and artifacts in concrete settings. This subject is not a kind of entity separate from the settings in which it acts, but is one aspect of a structural whole: subject-engaged-in-situated-practice. The practice in which this subject is engaged has a temporal organization to it: it is a project; it projects forward into the future. We are always already "thrown" into a concrete situation, in a way we cannot get out of or behind, or get completely under our control. Such practical activity has direction(s), which is not the same as saying it is instrumental. Instrumental action with means-ends planning is only one kind of project. Furthermore, the lived-body is a structure of possibilities that organizes the world we live in and are engaged in. And in addition, persons in activity are differently socially located. Their embodied points of view create value in activity because of the partial, located character of such perspectives.

The (abbreviated, all too hasty) picture emerging here contrasts with the belief, widely accepted since Descartes, that the human subject is first of all mental or cognitive, an individual thinking thing, and thus has a kind of being that is distinct from that of objects in the world. The latter are material, substantial, and extended in space, the former is a realm of thought and ideas where logic rather than causality dictates operations. Everyday existence, according to existential Marxists, is quite different from this view, nor can it be derived from it. On the contrary, the image of mind and matter as distinct and different is best to be understood as a mistaken way of interpreting the relationship between human agent and world; a mistaken view that has its roots in present-day everyday life (in a way we shall describe) rather than the other way around. In rough linguistic terms, performance cannot be explained as a derivative of competence; on the contrary, the whole notion of competence arises from a misunderstanding of the character and structure of linguistic performance in real, everyday settings.

How does learning now appear? If knowing comes into being in activity, then knowledge is not to be found only inside (Refined/Crude model) or only outside (High-Grade Crude model) the head. It is always socially, historically situated. This means that the concepts of internalization and transfer can (and need) no longer be appealed to, especially as purely mental operations. Furthermore, in a dialectically structured world, persons are produced through processes of objectification. This means that subjects' understandings of themselves are mediated through other subjects and objects. Bernstein (discussing Hegel) gives an idea of what this is about: "self-consciousness exists in itself and for itself in that, and by the fact that it exists for another self consciousness" (1971, p. 24-25). People do not "take in" unmediated "knowledge" in the form of facts about an external world but, rather, relate to other persons' mediated objectifications of themselves, their own actively mediated reflections of others, of objects, and events unfolding in the world. The world and persons acting are both in and outside each other. Here is an important challenge to the concepts of internalized facts and abstract, general knowledge transmission.[12] The notion that general knowledge can be applied to separate and independent situations is no longer possible; we need to consider the constitutive relations between persons acting and ongoing activity in the world in which they are socially located, and engaged.

The historical character of Marx's and Lukacs' social ontology (cf. Lukacs, 1978a, b) takes us a step further. These writers distinguish between relations of objectification and relations of alienation. Objectification is a universal condition of human existence. Alienation, on the other hand, is the consequence of the commodification characteristic of contemporary social formations, and so is unique to the current historical epoch.[13] From an insistence on the historical character of praxis it follows that processes of objectification, knowing, and embodiment must be different in different epochs. In addition to no longer being conceived in undialectical, unmediated terms, processes of learning must change historically as well.

It seems to us that a much more serious, broad, and deep view of learning is possible when we start with the recognition that it is rooted in being-in-practice rather than knowing. We move from the old picture of unproblematic "transmission" of knowledge in a uniform world of shared values and uniform culture, to a new picture in which there are socially located people, more or less engaged in the ongoing activity in communities of practice, different from one other, in conflict and in unequal relations of power, involved in projects that cross situational boundaries. They are aiming, albeit often un-reflectively, at becoming kinds of persons, being like other kinds of persons, and mastering practices in such a fashion that the practitioner is part of the practice and the practice part of the identity of the practitioner. Given death and difference, relations between old-timers and newcomers become fraught with a need for each other, to generate continuity, while at the same time they threaten each other's existence.

We can sum up where we have come to at this point by reviewing the consequences of this view of the world for our critique of the Refined/Crude and High-Grade Crude models. There is a decided contrast with them (Table 3): Instead of an individual, mentalist, rationalist, elitist, ahistorical, acon-textual dualistic view of learning, there is a dialectical, historical, contextual understanding of learning as an aspect of the activities in which persons are constituted by, and constitute themselves in, participation in communities of practice.

TABLE 3: LEARNING IN/AS EVERYDAY PRACTICE

	LEARNING IN/AS EVERYDAY PRACTICE
SUBJECT-WORLD RELATION	Non-dualistic; transcending dualism. Situated praxis. Subject and object in dialectical relation. Being-in-the-world. Historically constituted.
TELOS	i.e. What we are proximally and for the most part. Situated. Materialist.
MECHANISM	Changing participation in communities of practice.

Everyday Life in Late Capitalism

At the end of Section II we argued that the Refined/Crude model had undesirable properties, and bent our energies to replacing this theory with another. But this begs the question raised earlier concerning the broad acceptance of the Refined/Crude model in Euro-American culture. It seems important to account in historical terms for the durable and widespread life of the model.

Lukacs (1922/trans. 1971) provides an example of such an account in his characterization of the effects of a commoditized, industrialized political economy on (and as) everyday existence. His method is an historical one: In *Reification and Class Consciousness* he retells the history of philosophy as the working out of deep cultural contradictions that are first lived in our everyday existence. These contradictions are raised to consciousness in philosophical practice, but only against the backdrop that our culture affords. In particular, the kind of practice characteristic of modern conditions of production has generated an antimony of reified subject and object which covers up the real and fundamental relationship between the two: namely that objects are produced by subjects, operating under given historical conditions, through a process of mediation and objectification that alters an object's form of objectivity in accordance with its real potentialities.

Lukacs, like Marx, draws upon the Hegelian notion that identity is forged by and through the other: that objectification is of central importance in practical activity. But in modern society objectification is predominantly in the form of the production of commodities, and human relations are structured by the phenomenon of *reification*, which has both objective and subjective aspects. Objectively, a world of objects and events is experienced as confronting us as an arrangement of independent forms that generate their own powers. These objects are in fact the products of collective human activity, but the history of their production is obliterated and we experience them as alien, quite independent of our own activity or wishes. We believe and hope that we can gradually discover the laws of this objective realm, and that the individual can profit by knowledge of these laws, but we also believe that we cannot modify the processes that underlie them through our own activity. Subjectively, activity becomes a commodity just like any other consumer article. Activity becomes less and less active, and increasingly passive and contemplative.

Each of the theories of learning we examined earlier – cognitive science and genetic epistemology – and, we would argue, many others as well, posits precisely the opposition of subject and object whose appearance Lukacs attributed to alienated practice. They describe, with minor variations, an objective, uninterpreted world of things and events, and a subject who is active intellectually but incapable in practice of transforming this world in any respect other than tinkering with its objective contiguities. Action is viewed merely as instrumental technique. Cognition is internal activity directed towards the construction of representations of the world. The world itself is to be described in its different levels by the hard sciences of physics and biology.

It is instructive to compare Lukacs and Haugeland. Lukacs begins his essay on reification in the following way: "The essence of commodity-structure has often been pointed out. Its basis is that a relation between people takes on the character of a thing and thus acquires a 'phantom objectivity', an autonomy that seems so strictly rational and all-embracing as to conceal every trace of its fundamental nature: the relation between people." (1988, p. 83). He continues "But this implies that the principle of rational mechanisation and calculability must embrace every aspect of life" (1988, p. 91). Haugeland's starting point is strikingly similar in its content, but with a quite different value attached to the observation: "'Reasoning is but reckoning,' said Hobbes, in the earliest expression of the computational view of thought. Three centuries later, with the development of electronic 'computers,' his idea finally began to catch on; and now, in three decades, it has become the single most important theoretical hypothesis in psychology (and several allied disciplines) . . . ."

Lukacs' argument may be summed up as follows: the political-economic basis of capitalist society, in which commoditization saturates the social world, leads to reification of commodities as both the objective state of the world and the subjective comprehension and mode of relating to the world. This is as true of the bourgeois specialized, contemplative intellect as it is of those directly engaged in mechanically producing commodities. A particular historical result is that theorizing about life and mind stays on the surface of contemporary existence. Skimming over the surface of appearances, it is able to describe these appearances in apparently convincing terms, but makes the mistake (a characteristically reified one) of taking as natural, universal laws of mind the rational reckoning, the alienated formalism, that in fact is the particular and peculiar effect of pervasive commoditization under industrial capitalism. It is no surprise that we have Refined/Crude theories (and High-Grade Crude theories too): they are symptomatic of the contemporary state of our world. Rather than offering adequate explanations, they themselves require explanation.

There is one further point to Lukacs' analysis of reification: his attempt to specify its limits. In the modern world bureaucracy and rationalization seem ubiquitous. But in Lukacs' view, although rationalization appears to be complete and to penetrate the depths of our physical and psychic nature, and while bureaucracy seems to have infiltrated every corner of society, they are in fact incomplete and incoherent. Because modern systems of rationality are formalistic and consequently disregard the concrete aspects of their subject matter, only the details can be effectively subjected to their laws. The systems of social thought and organization central to capitalist rationality are in fact threatened by their inability to grasp the real character of material relations. Our work and life are compartmentalized and specialized by abstract social and economic categories and institutional structures, but the spaces which are, as it were, in between these regimented regions have escaped the impositions of rationality. The deeper processes whereby social practice produces social reality have a certain immunity to bureaucracy and formal rationality.

There is, then, what one might call a *constitutive* view of "the everyday" in Lukacs' argument. The everyday is what is outside the regimes of bureaucratic rationalization; it is where a genuine cultural production takes place, one which escapes the delusions of reification. This constitutive conception of the everyday offers a basis for a new conception of learning.

Unfortunately a certain ambivalence about the nature of the everyday seems characteristic of the Western Marxists more generally. A central issue for them is the reconstitution of the relationship between philosophy as a practice and (everyday) social practice viewed as a completely general conception of lived existence in a historically constituted world. Their development of a social ontology has this relationship at its core. But rethinking the relationship between philosophy and the everyday is not easy. Even in Western Existential Marxist views, "everyday life" is often relegated to yet another dualistic contrast between what they do, philosophy, reflection, and the residual other, everyday life, which, as the object of reflection, is not itself philosophical reflection. Ironically, then, what they have to say about everyday life directly often seems mired in the dualistic epistemological project rather than escaping from it. Thus, they seem unsure about how much of what kind of culture adheres to the proletariat; sometimes they see the everyday as a domestic, or private, or as a residual kind of zone or space or period in history; and struggle (e.g. Heller) to find a generative, emancipatory principle inherent in everyday life. Lukacs describes a sort of prevolcanic network of fissures in the terrain of reified, routinized existence, through which bubble up the unrationalized, disturbing, turbulent, unreified fragments of everyday life.

Lefebvre, in three volumes on everyday life (*Critique de la vie quotidienne*: 1946, 1962, 1968), attempts to confront the contradiction between philosophy and non-philosophical everyday life, arguing that under capitalism daily life is characterized by alienation, fetishism, and the lack of human satisfaction. Everyday life (rather than philosophy or art) is the site at which one measures the progress of the dialectic of alienation and human becoming. Expressing nostalgia for a putatively more organic, peasant-like past, he argues that only when daily life becomes a festival will we be fully human. In his 1968 *Everyday Life in the Modern World*, he treats everyday life as "non-philosophical:" the everyday deals with reality, philosophy with ideality. He argues that: "We should try to overcome the limitations of ... using borrowed philosophical terminology, but directing it at the study of everyday life. The Quotidian can't be understood outside philosophy" (1968, p. 13). "The limitations of philosophy – truth without reality – always counterbalance the limitations of everyday life – reality without truth" (1968, p. 14). For Lefebvre, "everyday life consists of recurrences – gestures of labor and leisure, mechanical movements both human and properly mechanic, hours, days, weeks, months, years, linear and cyclical repetitions, natural and rational time; the study of creative activity (of *production* in its widest sense). ... This leads to the study of re-production of the conditions in which actions producing objects and labor are re-produced, re-commenced, and re-assume their component proportions or, on the contrary, undergo gradual or sudden modifications" (1968, p. 18).

Lefebvre produces brilliant, inventive, twists on old views of the everyday, yet those old views are still fundamental to his understanding. He holds onto not only an opposition between philosophy and the everyday, but also a high cultural view of modernity, that turns the everyday into low culture. (Lefebvre warns us of the ambivalence of the philosophical towards the non-philosophical,[14] vacillating between scorn and admiration.) Thus, at one point he speaks of the interdependent realities of the quotidian and the modern: "the quotidian is that which is humble, solid, taken for granted, its parts in regular recurrence, undated, and (apparently) insignificant, etc. The modern is that which is novel, brilliant, paradoxical, technical, worldly and (apparently) daring and transitory (1968, p. 24). In fact, in his accounts of "the everyday" one can find, not surprisingly, but confusingly jumbled together, Crude, High-Grade Crude and even constitutive conceptions of the everyday.

What is bothersome about these accounts is the opposition they pose between philosophy and everyday life, an opposition that sustains the dominating value of distanced contemplation. In their different ways both Heller and Lefebvre are trying to overcome the opposition, but they are only partially successful. To give up the distinction is to give up the outside, "for itself," advantage of the philosophical position. Further, the philosophy/everyday life axis sustains the view that questions about everyday life are first of all epistemological ones. It leaves philosophers caught in their own epistemological project. In section I we argued that reversing the customary relations between ontological and epistemological issues was one of the two most central issues in reformulating a theory of learning. The Western Existential Marxist work offers clues to the epistemological 'bias' of discussions of the "everyday" alongside an ontological reformulation of a problematique for everyday practice.

It should also be noted that while the imaginary "everydays" conjured up by philosophers from their intuitions, dreams and deductions may offer clues concerning ongoing social practices, they cannot claim to capture changing everyday life merely by analyzing changes they believe to be occurring in *epistemological* landscapes (Rorty, quoted in Hebdige, *Hiding in the Light* [1988]). Perhaps the very circumscribed specialization of the everyday practice of philosophy accounts for the wobbling of their *locating* of the everyday: There are three common strategies for assigning 'location' to different conceptions of the everyday. Each specifies how everyday life is conceived to be *separated* from other aspects of life. They may be placed along a continuum:

The everyday as	The everyday as	The everyday as
residual category vis-à-vis philos., high culture, science, in some sense merely a logical operator.	banal, but a form of existence with special times, places & characteristics, e.g. as private, domestic sphere.	social practice, as all of social life; culture as praxis.

The everyday as either logical operator or as a zone of social life implies that there are other aspects of life that aren't everyday. Both preserve the dualism and reify class, gender, ethnic and other sociopolitical divisions, not to mention the other divisions they also encode.

What seems wonderful about the Western Existential Marxist accounts of everyday life (at this point one may add to Lefebvre's those of Benjamin, de Certeau and others) is the imaginative, richly detailed – though definitely not ethnographically grounded – evocations of the urban postwar culture of France and possibly beyond, their very French aesthetic eroticism (as Poster observed), their speculations about the workings out of alienation in lived experience, and the modes of resistance this engenders as well. But it is not the discussions of everyday life that most immediately offer us resources for rethinking what it means to learn. They provide instead clues that push us further toward more exotic conceptions of life and learning. These clues have to do with the clearly social-historically concrete everyday world they evoke. They enlarge our project, leading us to attend to more varied dimensions of everyday lives than those encompassed in narrowly rationalistic theories of learning.

The Historical Production of Persons in Practice: A Newfangled Guide to a Maze of Moments[15]

We proposed early in this chapter that the two most important issues to address in a critique of contemporary theories of learning are the social politics hidden within these theories and their haste to circumvent important questions of being and becoming certain kinds of persons in historically constituted practices in the world. It is time to sum up how far we've come with respect to each issue. The mainstream theories of learning aren't devoid of social and political values, as they might wish to claim. Rather, these theories invite a tacit acceptance and legitimation of the contemporary social order. If one is elite (bourgeois, adult, male, civilized, white) one learns this elite stuff; if not one must stay ordinary and learn by doing, without reflection. In the conception of learning we are proposing, differences of power, conflict, struggle, and contradiction are *constitutive* of participation in social practice. Learning is an integral aspect of changing participation in changing communities of practice, and this involves a telos of changing degrees and kinds of powerfulness and powerlessness which are dialectically constitutive of each other.

We've seen that assumptions about the relationship between person and world operate, unacknowledged, in theories of formal instruction. Such theories appeal to mechanisms such as "internalization" and "transmission" because they have no place for mediation between person and social world, or between person and person. Such mechanisms are merely names for a hand-waving process whereby something that was in an 'outer' realm appears in an 'inner' realm, or vice versa.

What do we say to the account of learning as the transfer of knowledge or information from expert to novice, with consequent internalization on the part of the latter? If one adopts a non-dualist view of the relation of person and world, such as follows from attending to the dialectical structure of social practice, very different accounts of learning become possible. Most importantly, learning can be seen to be ubiquitous; to participate in practice <is> to be learning.

Turning to the issue of the problems that follow from simply equating learning with knowing, it seems to us that all of the views we have examined fall prey to the urge to transcend, and in doing so succumb to too strong a commitment to epistemological matters. In dualist rationalist theories of learning, the end point is assumed to be an 'objective' knowledge which will enable instrumental control of the world. The telos of learning is assumed to be a movement towards general, abstract knowledge. In contrast, in Marx's work the goal is a kind of revolutionary praxis that transcends capitalism and with it social class domination and reunites subject and object. The telos for knowing could be summed up in his fine, disruptive phrase, "ascending to the concrete." The goal is an historical understanding of the most general political-economic and social forces as concrete interrelations that configure human possibilities. For the Western Existential Marxist philosophers, knowing consists of raising everyday conditions to consciousness through reflection, against the present historical horizon.

It is surely a step forward to argue that there are complex, dialectical relations between the concrete and the abstract, between immediate appearances and societal, historical structuring processes, between reflection and existence. Yet all of these conceptions of learning are about knowing rather than about being in the world. They do acknowledge the communities of practice without which this knowledge could not exist. They are sometimes, but by no means always, aware of the contradictory relations and conflicting interests and reasons intrinsic to such processes.

Making over the world in the image of our own limited practice seems to us the enemy of genuine understanding and a greater challenge to future practice than exhortation to examine our individual conditions and relations of production. There are two ideas here: One is that a concern for *the general* might transmute into a focus on *the more inclusive* phenomena of collective participation in which we, our identities, products, and knowledgeabilities have their concrete existence. Second, we might try engaging in a process through which the purposes of others' practices lead us to experiment with the telos, mechanisms and subject-world relations of our own. Let our theories become the reregistration (Willis' term (1977)) of other practices.

Conclusions

We have suggested that recent theories of situated cognition and everyday learning do not successfully part company from the computational and structuralist theories of learning they are intended to supplant; more often than not they invert the hidden axiology of computational theories. The move from Refined/Crude to High-Grade Crude merely preserves an axiology in which the "everyday" is contrasted with the "refined," with all its epistemological, social, political and even ontological presuppositions. What is needed is an examination and correction of the hidden dualistic assumptions that underlie this axiology. We have proposed that the concept of the "everyday" articulated within Existential Marxism provides a more fruitful basis for an understanding of learning, largely because it replaces dualism with a powerful social and historical ontology.

Cognitivist theories of learning appeal to a teleology of movement away from the concrete, practical, informal and unreflective. We can interpret this as an implicit reference to the concept of the everyday in its negative, residual category form. Some theoretical approaches to situated learning merely reverse the value placed on this category form and valorize everyday life. The Existential Marxist project, in contrast, grasps the everyday as a region of poesis – a site of the practical reproduction of persons and society. Everyday life is a manifestation of a constitutive causality for both persons and artifacts; but at the same time it is a place and time of alienation and ideology, so that its own character is mystified.

This alienation and mystification is what gives cognitivist theories their appeal, and their apparent power. The value they place on detachment, contemplation, mental operations and formal representation reflects a politics that derides involved practical and material activity: the activity found in the workplace, the household, and on the streets.

At its best, the existential Marxist account of everyday life is one in which knowledge and being are seen as dialectically linked; where ontology and epistemology are interrelated. Agents' knowledge of the world, and of objects in the world, contains the potential to transform agents, objects, and world. How can it do this? Knowledge is understood as the articulation by situated agents of the practical circumstances of a project in a region of artifacts. Such knowledge can resolve the conflicts and contradictions that prevent the fulfillment of this project. As the project proceeds new artifacts are produced and old ones are reworked, the totality of involvements that constitutes the region is reconfigured, and agents, understood as situated and dynamic social identities, change. Learning, in the conceptualization that is made possible by notions of the constitutive everyday, is no longer viewed simply as a change in an autonomous subject's knowledge of an objective world. Learning is construed as the reconstruction of the way a subject is engaged in the world, so that the subject herself or himself is reconfigured, and at the same time there is a reconfiguration of the production and reproduction of objects, whether they be texts, other persons, social events, or institutions.

This is very abstract. Consider a classroom. The people who we find there live everyday as teacher and students in a local setting in which they have negotiated, with different degrees of status and power, routine ways of passing the hours, a customary style, and the mundane details of their tasks and responsibilities. These are components of a 'crude' everyday life; their negative connotations should not mislead us. But at the same time we can scratch the surface and find a 'constitutive' everyday life at work: the identities of 'teacher' and 'student' are continually contested and redefined; interpretations of 'work' and 'success' and 'failure' prepare students for the reproduction of the larger social world of work and consumption they will enter after school. The practical dictates of organized space and time influence the bodies of these children and the needs, desires, and appetites they experience. Consider the ontological relationships: teacher and student are relationally-defined identities; the 'quality' of classwork produced identifies the 'ability' of a student; the world of the classroom rotates around axes of 'good' and 'bad,' 'right' and 'wrong.'

In such a setting knowledge is typically misunderstood as an 'acquisition,' the property of one individual or another. It is evident that many classrooms do in fact enforce a regime of passive contemplation and consumption, in which any ontological transformation would seem to be prohibited. Yet teachers – in their everyday conversations – do in fact make frequent reference to ontological transformations in their students and themselves. Students change in ways that cannot be interpreted solely in terms of knowledge: they 'become responsible': 'really change'; 'grow up.' An adequate theory of learning in school will uncover, describe and foster the ontological work in the classroom that lies behind such changes; the *poesis* that takes place, not primarily in the academic work that is produced but in the human relations that make this academic work possible.

NOTES

1   The titles of the talks by literary, anthropological and historical critical theorists are consistent with the meaning clusters of the first paragraph: "The Rise of Sociology and the Emergence of the Concept of 'Alltagswelt,' Cartes Postales: Representing Paris 1900," "From Everyday to Election Day: the Politics of the Street in the 1870's, Historical Self-Reflexion and Amnesia: Deroutinizing Daily Life in Times of Crisis," "Tactility and Distraction: A Contribution to the Study of Pragmatism in Everyday Life in Modern Times," "Survival, the Everyday, and Social Thought," and "Everything Everywhere: The Effacement of the Scene of the Everyday."

2   This chapter grew out of a graduate seminar we taught together over a period of two years, called Learning and Everyday Life. We thank the students in that seminar for their contributions to the ideas developed in this chapter.

3   Cognitive scientists argue that Piagetians are structuralists and Piagetians that cognitive scientists are functionalists. From within, the differences between these positions are substantive, meaningful and have implications both theoretical and practical. We don't mean to deny that this is so. But whatever their persuasion, they have strong commonalities as well. Both are concerned with the means by which individuals are supposed to become rational contemplators of an objective world.

4   This project, and this chapter, are part of a larger strategy for exploring learning as social practice. Work on apprenticeship in West Africa has gradually led to an attempt to recharacterize learning in positive terms as legitimate peripheral participation in communities of practices as persons produce changing identities as practitioners – identities of membership and of nonmembership. Knowledgeability, the narrow focus of epistemologically based theories of learning, is subsumed within the production and reproduction of identities in the "lpp" view. The present project is an attempt to understand better some of the historical roots of our own grounding in social practice theory.

5   Packer's work in developing this comparative framework for parsing theories of learning is one of the crucial steps in the development of our thinking about learning. Certainly Lave had never thought about what might be needed to give a minimal account of a theory of learning until Packer raised the issue. At the same time, we do not want to reify what for us has been a heuristic device. (It seems clear, for instance, that a new theory of learning might provide a critique that would lead us to change the framework for future comparisons.)

6   An alternative criterion is one that says that a better system "wins" more trials of the "game" in which it is engaged. But what counts as a winning state is quite arbitrary as far as the

system is concerned, just like the definition of a "true" statement. Why should the mating of the king define a win in chess, and not, say, the capture of the last pawn?

7   See Durkheim & Mauss *Primitive Classification*, Levy-Bruhl *How Natives Think*, and the social Darwinists, e.g., Tylor, Spencer, Morgan (whose work considerably influenced Engels) for the supple way these social evolutionary templates were – and are – available to justify any and all forms of social inequality.

8   We will not discuss here the very simplest strategy: merely to argue that the other side of the dualism "is also" important and that hereafter it will be incorporated in research. One can, for instance, address the absence of any essential role for the social world in cognitive modeling of learning by attempting to annex the world into "socially shared cognition," or some such. A good example is experimental research on "social cognition," in which children are set to learning something together, but tested individually. This does not represent an attempt to change the basic dualistic theory (Lave, 1992). The problem is that the move is one of trying to incorporate one half of the dualism into the other half – which has been defined by its exclusion from the first. This obviously will not work.

9   However, this requires the claim that all kinds of practices, including those considered elite, are everyday practices realized in everyday lives. It also raises questions about what and how people learn in practice, what we are to make of educational institutions if learning is an aspect of all social practice, and what is the meaning of "failure" within educational institutions if it is produced as an everyday practice (Chaiklin & Lave, 1993).

10 For Jay, Western Marxists include Lukacs, Korsch, Gramsci, Bloch; Frankfurt School members Horkheimer, Adorno, and Marcuse; French Marxists Lefebvre, Goldmann, Sartre, Merleau-Ponty, and Althusser, the Italian theorists Della Volpe and Colletti, and Habermas.

11 We have been trying for years to figure out what is meant when the formal/informal dualism is invoked. Like the everyday, it goes unanalyzed while carrying all too much weight in advancing arguments about learning (note also similar debates concerning formal and informal economy in comparative economics). Our best guess at present is that a) it is a label for the *whole dualistic worldview* that characterizes modern beliefs about crucial distinctions within and between the world, persons, and their activities. At the same time, b) it points more specifically to the privileging of form over content in construing each and every one of them.

12 In a paper tracing connections between American pragmatists and Soviet activity theorists, Valsiner & Van de Veer point out that Royce, Baldwin and G.H. Mead take the internalized *other* as the basis of a consciousness that actively works over whatever mediated knowledge

derives in activity in the world. In fresh translations it has become clear that Vygotsky recognized that the child becomes conscious through the consciousness of others (cf. Holland & Lachicotte, 2007; Packer, 2008).

13 In a new introduction to *History and Class Consciousness* (1967) Lukacs notes that he made the error in the original manuscript of conflating objectification and alienation, thus, his use of another term to make plain the historically particular condition to which reification (for Marx alienation) referred.

14 Note the residual character of the everyday in this pair of expressions – that that is "not philosophy."

15 This phrase is Lefebvre's (1968, p. 25).

Klaus Nielsen
Department of Psychology, University of Aarhus

THE LEARNING LANDSCAPE OF ART AND CRAFT

In this chapter I will outline and describe how learning is embedded in social practice. Inspired by Steinar Kvale's works about learning (1976, 1977, 1993) I will differentiate between two conceptualizations of learning: a narrow perspective and an expanded perspective on learning. In the narrow perspective learning is perceived as a process of reinforcing a certain kind of behaviour, or as a person's process of internalizing and processing pieces of information into the cognitive system (see e.g. Omrod, 1999). Learning is a discrete process making it possible to research it delimited in time and space. The expanded perspective takes learning as being part of people's everyday life. It is a process of making sense, regulating and orienting oneself in a specific concrete practice not delimited to any particular space and time. Only through careful examination of people's concrete everyday life is it possible to say something about what and how they learn. In pursuit of developing a greater understanding of the expanded perspective on learning, Steinar Kvale and I have developed the metaphor of a landscape of learning (Kvale & Nielsen, 1999; Nielsen & Kvale, 2003; Nielsen & Kvale, 2006). In this paper I will pursue the notion of an expanded understanding of learning by focusing on how people learn to orient themselves in various landscapes of learning. This will be done by re-searching two studies of learning in practice which I conducted previously. One study is conducted at the Academy of Music in Aarhus, Denmark focusing on how to become a pianist, and the other study of learning is centred on the process of becoming a baker[1].

By applying the metaphor of a learning landscape[2] we wished to emphasize the learning resources of everyday practice (Nielsen & Kvale, 2006). This is a landscape in a general sense: not some national park where nature is ideally untouched by human hands, but a cultural landscape inhabited and shaped by human beings through hundreds or thousands of years. We moved our attention away from the individual inhabitants of the landscape and tried to capture the very aspects which made the landscape habitable, and the paths which the inhabitants followed through the landscape. It is worth noting that the etymological meaning of 'learning' contains spatial implications, that is, gaining experience by following a track or path – presumably for life (Nielsen, 1997). By using the metaphor of a learning landscape our attention shifted from the attributes of individual participants to the aspects of the environment which make learning possible. This decentralization implies a movement from individuals who learn in isolation to communities of practice where learning occurs. Furthermore, introducing the landscape metaphor is an attempt to move beyond a rationalistic conception of learning by instead bringing out non-scholastic modes of learning that take place without formal instruction. These modes of learning have existed for thousands of years; human beings learned to live and work before formal schools were introduced. The many subtle types of learning in the environment tend to disappear when perceived through the formal lenses of school learning. We assumed that extensive descriptions of the resources in a learning landscape and the modes of inhabiting a landscape would reduce the need to resort to inner cognitive processes in order to understand learning.

The learning landscapes point to a very important feature in processes of learning: the necessity for the participants (Gadamer, 1988; Lave & Wenger, 1991) to be able to understand what other participants in different communities of practice are doing and why. This approach marks that in order to understand processes of learning we do not begin with the single individual and theories about how he or she thinks, but with how the learning landscapes are organized and how he or she is situated in this landscape. Even though, the notion of a learning landscape is the necessary premise for understanding learning, it is not sufficient. We need to address individual learning as well by focusing on how people learn to orient themselves in various learning landscapes. As will be shown below, learning to know who does what and why is an important premise for being able to act as competent in practice. Furthermore, by using the notion learning to orient oneself I will emphasize that learning in practice means to develop new paths in the learning landscape, and often involves directing one's learning project.

In the following I will pursue and exemplify how these individual learning processes disclose themselves in practice by taking a closer look at how students learn at the Academy of Music in Aarhus, and how baker apprentices learn in various bakeries. I have done 16 interviews with piano students and piano teachers, and 19 interviews with masters, journeymen and apprentices from various bakeries. I found that when doing the interviews about learning the skills within these areas of art and craft, the interviewees seemed to talk about a lot of other things as well. They did not only talk about how they learned to play a sonata of Chopin or how to make black bread. They also described what it meant for them to be trained in this trade, what kind of future they would expect, what kind of conflicts they were involved in and so on. When analyzing my material I could have chosen to cut out these passages, which had little to do with learning the skills in a narrow sense. Or I could try to broaden the perspective, and look at the meaning that learning these skills had for the interviewees. I chose the latter. The perspective on learning introduced here has to do with practice in a broad sense of the word, which means that it has to do with how things are used and with meaning in the sense of what kind of life does this practice lead to.

The Bakery

The bakery in focus for this paper is located in Aarhus, and is part of a large supermarket (Nielsen, 2005; 2006). When entering the bakery you are confronted with the noise of machines, the music from the radio and the scent of freshly baked bread. The bakery is a small, square room with the ovens in one corner and sinks in the other. In between the long tables run all around the room. Along one wall the apprentice and journeyman work together on the dough, shaping it into loaves and placing them on the baking tray at a furious rate. With his back to the apprentice and journeyman the master prepares the cakes. The master is busy with his hands, and in no time his baking tray is filled with neat looking cream cakes ready to be baked. After observing and interviewing the master and the journeyman and apprentices, it became clear to me that learning the trade of baking was not as simple as it appeared.

On the one hand the apprentices need to learn the trade of baking. They have to learn the recipes by heart, to bake different kinds of cakes, to make them appear tempting for the customers, they have to learn how to handle the dough, to have an eye for what bread looks like when it has been baked properly etc. etc. Through numerous observations and a lot of interviews it became clear to me that there is an implicit curriculum in the bakeries. This implicit curriculum was not the same in all the bakeries; it varied from bakery to bakery. In most bakeries the apprentices began by doing simple stuff, e.g. whipping cream, fetching flour etc. After a while the apprentices worked closely together with an journeyman learning how to make white bread. After some time i.e. after mastering the bread, the apprentice would work together with the master to make the cakes. Finally, when close to being an journeyman the apprentice would be responsible for working the ovens. In the craft of baking and in other crafts as well there is an implicit curiculum of what the apprentices need to learn if they want to be considered proper bakers; however, this curriculum is often a part of practice and not made an object for deliberate reflection.

Furthermore, in order to comprehend learning in the bakery it is relevant for the apprentices to understand how the bakery is located in other social practices. To put it very simply, the bakery needs to sell bread and cakes in order to survive. Not only does the bakery make a certain amounts of pastry and bread. It also needs to make it at a specific time. The bread has to be ready at 7 a.m. otherwise the customers will buy their bread elsewhere. This structures the work in the bakery, since the first bread needs to be ready to be sold at that time. The customers' requirements and preferences have a great influence on how learning is organized for the apprentices. The apprentices begin to work with the bread where they are most needed in the daily production. For the first long period of apprenticeship the journeyman and the apprentice work closely together.

The apprentices and journeyman begin their working day at 3 a.m. preparing the bread. The master begins his day at 5 a.m., as he works primarily with the cakes and does the planning. He stays until 1 o'clock in the afternoon so he can see what has been sold in the shop and which cakes did sell and which did not. The master stays longer so he can plan the next day's baking.

One of the crucial things in the bakery is time. Time can be understood in one way as pace. The apprentices not only need to learn how to bake dough but also need to do it at a certain pace. The master, journeyman and apprentice are highly dependent on each other to make the production work, and in that sense the apprentice needs to follow the pace of the others in order not to get in their way, block the ovens and so on. To learn the right pace is crucial for the apprentices. Time can also be understood in another way. The bakery's working circle is related to the customer's wish for fresh bread. Consequently, the bread needs to be baked very early in the morning (or in the middle of the night) in order to be ready for the customers. This strains the private lives of the people working in the bakery. It is difficult to have a decent social life with friends, girlfriends etc. when you need to turn in between eight or nine every night.

So learning the craft of baking is dependent on many things. First the apprentices need to learn the trade of baking and the habits and expectations of the customers. Then they have to learn the pace of the place, and to get up in the morning and organize their private life accordingly. As argued here, to understand learning in the bakery one needs to get a grasp on how the landscape of learning is organized to begin to understand how and what the apprentices learn. Bakery apprentices need to be part of the various processes happening more or less simultaneously. They need to understand how they fit into practice, and to orient their new working life in relation to their private life. In this sense learning can't be understood as merely a process of internalization or reinforcement.

To add to the complexity, the anticipation of future participation plays an important role for most of the apprentices in relation to what they do in the bakery and after they have terminated their training. For example, one journeyman has the ambition to become a master himself one day. He has been working at several different bakeries, one of the reasons being that he wants to expand his possibilities af becoming a master with the explicit aim of owning a bakery himself. He puts it like this: *You become more and more skilled for every new place you are (...) And it is because I have this dream of getting my own bakery shop, so I have to see as many things as possible* (Nielsen, 2005, p. 29).

This journeyman has developed the strategy of working at a bakery for a year or so, then leaving the place in favour of another bakery. In order to improve his skills, and consequently obtain his own shop in the end, he has to work his way through a lot of bakeries. This journeyman gives us a fine example of how he actively organizes his learning process in relation to the practice of which he is part with regard to a future practice. One could state that this "at gå på valsen" (to go waltzing – to change your places of learning) is really a paradigmatic model for learning because the journeyman is obviously regulating his learning process in the landscape of the craft.

The Academy of Music

The Academy of Music in Aarhus is an educational institution that seeks to provide classical music in Denmark (Nielsen, 1999). The standard length of the course is five years. The students have lessons with a main teacher throughout the course. In addition they have lessons in a minor subject: for example, the student pianist has lessons in accompaniment, rehearsal and chamber music. They also have lessons in ear training and theoretical classes on musical topics. At the Academy of Music there is a structure that resembles an apprenticeship, while at the same time the Academy is an educational institution with a formal structure, rules and exams.

At the Academy of Music we find that there are several paths through the learning landscape in the sense that the music students orient themselves differently in relation to their ambitions and participation in future communities of practice. In our comprehension of the learning landscape there is a tendency to understand this as homogenous and non-conflictual setting (Nielsen & Kvale, 2006). However, as will be argued in the following, landscapes of learning can contain different and conflicting paths.

When you enter the Academy of Music through the foyer into the entrance hall, the first thing that strikes you is the different sounds of music coming from all directions. From one room, you hear someone singing scales 'do-re-mi-fa-so' etc. From another direction you hear someone on the trumpet, playing the same small piece over and over again. My first thought when entering the Academy was that as a student here, you would be confronted and perhaps inspired every day by a lot of different music wherever you turned in the building.

However, when the students enter the Academy of Music for the very first time most of them dream of becoming a new Horowitz or Richter. This makes the concert context the most important context for most of the students in the sense that all other contexts at the Academy of Music seem to be organized in relation to the concert activities. To exemplify, it is of great importance to the students that their main teacher him/herself is a performing concert pianist. Most of the students hope to follow in the footsteps of their main teacher and themselves eventually become a performing pianist. So a lot of what is done in the lessons and what the students work with when practising is related directly or indirectly to playing concerts.

However, only a few of the students at the Academy make it as a high-class performer. The concert venues and the record companies only need a few concert pianists to fill out the program. As an experienced Danish pianist said in an interview: *only every twenty years does a new talent make it.* Consequently, most of the student pianists who had the dream of becoming a high-class concert pianist end up as music teachers in a music school somewhere. The music schools are in great demand for qualified music teachers. At the Academy of Music there is a constant and free-flowing discussion among the students of what is most desirable: being a highly prestigious concert pianist or a low-status music teacher; a discussion about ambitious dreams on the one hand and having a steady job giving a decent salary on the other. One could argue that becoming a prestigious concert pianist means that the students need to take another path in the learning landscape than that, for becoming a music teacher.

Here are some examples of what the music students found meaningful to learn in relation to the different paths they can take through the learning landscape at the Academy of Music. It struck me when interviewing the students how different their life-stories were even though they were located in the same institute. I will use the cases of two students who portray accurately the differences in meaning and learning in relation to how they are situated in the learning landscape. One student has the ambition of becoming a concert pianist, while the other student has given up her dreams of becoming a concert pianist and has now settled for a career as a music teacher. They are both situated differently in the learning landscape at the Academy of Music.

Their participation in the concert activities at the Academy of Music illustrates nicely how the two students experience the meaning of these activities differently because they are situated differently in the learning landscapes at the Academy, and consequently they learn differently. The promising concert pianist student uses the word 'professional' to describe how the audience at the Academy of Music relates to his concert performances. He perceives the audience as both professional and competent. The ambitious student's description of the typical feedback from the critical audience is directed towards technical issues, for instance whether he had accompanied the singer closely enough, whether he had been a support for him or not, and so on. The ambitious student experienced the concert situation from the position of a pianist-to-be, and learns a number of important things to consider when playing concerts from the audience's feedback afterwards.

In the interview with the less ambitious student who had given up the dream of becoming a concert pianist, another perspective on playing concerts is expressed. She had the feeling that her audience was evaluating her, and she became nervous. She learns from playing and attending concerts that she is a failure as a concert pianist, that she can't control her nervousness and that her future in the social practice of classical music is primarily as a music teacher. In the concerts she experienced the student environment at the Academy as both hostile and competitive. After playing concerts she says about the audience: *I think you can see it in their faces* (Nielsen, 1999, p. 25). The student could read disapproval in their faces.

I find the same pattern when focusing on attending the lessons with the main teacher. The ambitious concert pianist uses a lot of different teachers in order to learn the skills of becoming a concert pianist. He changes his main teacher several times and travels abroad to be confronted with other teachers' way of playing music in order to improve his own music. The less ambitious student – the music-teacher-to-be – sticks to the same teacher all the way through her time at the Academy, and in the end she tries to lower her main teacher's expectations with regard to her preparation for the lessons in order to give her more time to work as a music teacher.

The point I am trying to make when approaching the expanded notion of learning is that we need to focus on aspects of meaning in relation to the various and conflicting paths going through the learning landscape at the Academy of Music and concentrate on how the participants orient themselves in this landscape. The students presented above are situated very differently in the practice of the Academy of Music, making them experience very differently what the meaning of particular events is, and consequently they learn differently at the Academy of Music.

Addressing an expanded notion of learning, one might argue that this is related both to particular modes of participation and to the process of making a meaning out of this participation. In this sense meaning can neither be reduced to the sum of particular stimuli from the different contexts the students are participating in, nor to some a-historical inner human ability to a process of internalizing, processing and storing information. Meaning is here understood as a person's combination and uniting what it means for him or her to participate differently in various paths at the Academy of Music.

Conclusion

In this chapter I have argued that in order to understand an expanded perspective on learning we need to take as a point of departure how practice is organized and how people are situated in these practices. In trying to come to terms with these issues I find the works of Steinar Kvale very important, and in this paper I have tried to push our shared understanding of an expanded learning perspective even further. This pursuit is conducted by re-searching some of the studies I have been involved in with respect to the notion of a metaphor of a learning landscape inspired by long-term corporation with Steinar Kvale. Based on the studies from the Academy of Music and a bakery, I have argued that the situation of learners in the learning landscape is important – as are the kinds of paths that are open to them when becoming a part of these landscapes. Furthermore, I argue that people make sense of their participation in different ways based on their situation in their learning landscape and stress that the issue of meaning is crucial when addressing issues of learning.

NOTES

1   By taking a broader view on learning the notion of structure becomes central. By introducing the concept of a learning landscape we would like to emphasize everyday concrete reality where other people, tools, conflicts and history mediate processes of learning. This emphasis on lived structure can be seen as an alternative to focusing either on cognitive structure

(psychological structure) or sociological structure (macro structure) when addressing issues of learning.

2   The expression "learning landscape" is borrowed from Maxine Greene's book *Landscapes of Learning* (1978). Inspired by Merleau-Ponty, she speaks of landscape in a temporal dimension, in the sense that people are founded in their personal histories. The extended use of the landscape metaphor in cultural contexts today can be seen as expressing a development from focusing on the individual and its cognitive processes to concentrating on man in a socially situated practice.

Peter Musaeus, PhD
Department of Psychology, University of Aarhus

IDENTITY AND CHRONOTOPE IN APPRENTICESHIP LEARNING

Introduction

Bakhtin pondered the ability to visualize time in everyday life: "[T]he ability to read in everything *signs that show time in its course*, beginning with nature and ending with human customs and ideas (all the way to abstract concepts)" (1986, p. 25). Bakhtin coined the term chronotope[1], defined as an interrelated space-time relationship or spatial and temporal sign expressed aesthetically in novels but also in social activities such as religion, science, philosophy etc. In this chapter I will argue that the notion of chronotope can be used to analyze apprenticeship learning and identity – the process of becoming someone – which is a central theme in contemporary education focusing on social activities of learning and the constitution of identity through narrative (Mishler, 1999; Sfard & Prusak, 2005) and Bakhtin's dialogic notion of heterogeneous voices (Holland & Lave, 2001; Wertsch, 1991). In extending the notion of the chronotope beyond literary analyses to capture activity in a case study on craft practice, I aim to contribute to an understanding of learning and identity viewed as fundamentally situated in space and time.

This case study is about Stephen Hill, a recognized guitar luthier. A luthier is someone who crafts and repairs musical string instruments. My first visit to his workshop in Lewis was in 2004, when I was a visiting scolar at University of Sussex analyzing my studies on Danish goldsmith craftsmen[2]. On my first visit to Stephen's workshop, I immediately felt at home. The beauty of the dozen or so guitars on display struck me. Two guitars were not for sale, namely the first guitars that Stephen ever built in his own workshop. They were made of wood from Spain after a journey to Cordoba, Spain when he was 20 years old. His identification with Spain has played a great role in his identity as a craftsman who combined English and Spanish guitar styles. On Stephen's workshop website, concert player Paul Gregory praises Stephen's guitars:

"Without any doubt, Stephen Hill guitars are top quality concert instruments. [...] They are a unique blend of the fine, clear, pure sound of the English School; fused with the solidity and projection more often associated with Spanish makers. A musical pleasure to own" (Gregory, 2007).

The quotation casts historical time (Spanish guitars that derive from the Renaissance craft of luthier crafting) as embodied in the present moment of a clear-sounding English guitar, which benefits from the fusion of Northern European with Mediterranean body (solidity). This fusion will be elaborated later with reference to the identity work at stake for Stephen Hill in becoming a luthier – but of course it also relates to the identity work as a journeyman wanting to sell his guitars to customers buying a certain story about the guitar.

In summary, the chapter aims to contribute primarily to notions of identity processes and the dialogic nature of human practice. The case study analyzes a qualitative interview, and unless otherwise stated quotes are verbatim transcripts of the interview with Stephen Hill[3]. The chapter analyzes identity as situated in terms of the narrative on apprenticeship and being a journeyman on the road, being and becoming someone, namely a craftsperson, through the process of telling one's craft story. To my knowledge, no prior studies on apprenticeship learning have studied the trajectory identity process (of becoming a journeyman) as wrought in terms of the chance encounter, threshold and the road viewed as important chronotopes for understanding identity processes in craft apprenticeship.

Identity
Apprenticeship is not only an important historical institution but also an analytical concept describing learning as a fundamentally situated activity (Lave & Wenger, 1991). Within a situated learning as well as a sociocultural

tradition, identity change is seen as interwoven with the person's place and participation in the social world (Lave & Wenger, 1991, p. 53). The changes of identity are set in motion in terms of dialogues understood by Bakhtin as fundamentally creative acts by humans who constantly engage in dialogic relations (Bakhtin, 1984), and personal identity is therefore linked in concrete space-time with larger wholes: "We take identity to be a central means by which selves, and the sets of actions they organize, form and re-form over personal lifetimes and in the histories of social collectives" (Holland et al., 1998, p. 270). According to this dialogic specification, identity is coupled to personal lifetime and to the grand time of social collectives.

Mishler (1999) studied the way craft artisans use narrative to produce identities. His argument is that there is an intricate relationship between identity and life stories defined as "socially situated actions; identity performances; fusions of form and content" (Mishler, 1999, p. 18). Mishler argued that people pursuing a career in crafts have been found to construct their identities both as craftspeople and artists (Mishler, 1999, p. 148). The life story of having/producing a double identity (as craftsman and artist) suggests that craft apprenticeship provides a particularly interesting social arena for studying identity change imbued within participation and struggle. Earlier I have tried to trace some of these struggles in the life stories of goldsmiths whose identity as a craftsman was charged with historical struggles of recognition related to goldsmith crafting as a social work practice (Musaeus, 2005). The point is that identities as performances, struggles, dialogues do not exist outside (publicly shared) chronotopes and social practices of apprenticeship, going on the road etc. while, at the same time, somebody's identity grows from the specific person with his specific perspective in a concrete space-time relationship that is thoroughly unique to that person in that time.

In this chapter, the point is not to analyze abstract chronotopes or identity markers (e.g. the road, exams), but to analyze the concrete life story of Stephen Hill from the theoretical perspective of chronotopes and identity. Using Bakhtin's notion of heterogeneous voices to grasp the crafting of identity (as also done by Holland & Lave, 2001), a luthier identity is conceived in terms of the way craftspeople actively adopt the socially sanctioned ways of talking about identity relations within luthier crafting. To analyze Stephen Hill's narrative, I will try to look at the way a person's life is given shape by the chronotope of luthier apprenticeship acting both as a social institution and in terms of narrative metaphors like the road.

Chronotopes in Apprenticeship

Chronotopes can be seen as time and space categories charged with emotion and value and with formative character. In other words, an apprentice's identity trajectory might become significantly altered as she encounters a given chronotope in craft practice. Bakhtin (1981) introduces the chronotopes of encounter often associated with the road passing through familiar territory to the protagonist and the chronotope of threshold (associated with staircases, front halls, corridors, the street and the public space) connected with crises or turning points in a person's life. This section will discuss 1) the chance encounter, 2) the threshold and 3) the road as examples of chronotopes that are significant in Stephen's narrative on becoming an informal luthier apprentice.

The Chance Encounter

Stephen Hill never did a formal apprenticeship as a luthier in the sense that he never served four years with a single luthier master with a signed indenture as an apprentice. His craft career started when he was offered a job that led to becoming an informal apprentice to a cabinetmaker.

Interviewer: "Just to start chronologically: when did you start your apprenticeship as a cabinetmaker?"

Stephen: "As a cabinetmaker, I started when I left school at 16, the day after I left school. I had no direction really as a result of school. They didn't really set me up with any particular vocational ... or anything that I really felt that I wanted to do. So I left school rather adrift. Then the next day someone offered me a job ... as a ... to help out in their workshop [...] I went to his workshop and then started to actually really enjoy the process [of work]. We were making very rough furniture."

When the interviewer frames the question in terms of the chronology of apprenticeship, Stephen steps back and instead frames his answer with reference to his secondary school experience, which failed to give him a sense of direction. Stephen continues by talking about a random encounter that led him into cabinet making. This exemplifies what Bakhtin (1981, p. 92) calls "random contingency", referring to a type of time in novels when the character encounters something or someone just at a particular and unique moment. In Stephen's narrative it is the cabinetmaker offering him a job which got his career moving and significantly formed his identity trajectory when he was 16 years old. Stephen enjoys the work process of cabinet making, and after a couple of months he sets up his own wood workshop in his home and is offered a job with another cabinetmaker, where he felt he could become an apprentice to a craftsman. His new job is to prepare woods for sanding etc. mainly for making and fitting kitchens. Stephen reports that the work was connoted with "quite a lot of good workshop practices. And so I was employed but in a sense he had taken me on – he had taken me on, he had seen something in me, he had taken me on in a sense as his apprentice". In conclusion, Stephen experienced (and his identity narrative constructs) two apprenticeships with cabinet makers: one thanks to what Stephen attributes to luck or the chance encounter, and the other because he had proven himself concretely to that master ("he had seen something in me").

Thresholds

This section will investigate thresholds, turning points and "spiritual awakenings" (to use Stephen's term) turning Stephen away from cabinet making towards guitar making. Stephen had been playing the guitar since he was around 8, stopped when he was 14 and resumed when he was 18 years old.

Stephen: "At the age of 18 I had quite a sort of spiritual renaissance and I discovered guitar playing again. [...] I went to the lessons with my guitar teacher and looked at his guitars and I was amazed that this was made by an English maker [...]. And I was becoming quite fascinated with wood: rosewood, cedar, ebony. [...] I was suddenly captivated by this instrument. And something sort of [snaps his fingers] clicked in me and it started the ball rolling."

Stephen was astonished by the realization that his guitar teacher's Spanish guitar was made by an English maker. The decision to stop playing guitars and then his decision to resume playing the guitar gave him the opportunity to view the instrument in new terms, and "the discovery" of the instrument and its material (types of wood) certainly "captivated" him and posed the question: How are outstanding Spanish guitars crafted in England (while remaining "Spanish" and outstanding)? He had become interested in instrument making and his use of the metaphor of a rolling ball is a chronotope that refers to an identity process: He had not yet forged the decision to become a craftsman, but he was in the making of becoming one. The decision to become a luthier came when he was listening to a lute musician on a later occasion:

Stephen: "I was absolutely transfixed by the music [...] a sort of elevation. And the sound of his instrument was so beautiful, I could hear the woods singing inside his instrument and it was like: 'That's what I want to be! I want to be a musical instrument maker'. I didn't know in what way, lutes, guitars, whatever."

Stephen decided to become an instrument maker after realizing that a classical musical instrument was the combination of sensual beauty of wood and beauty of sound. Importantly, becoming a luthier to Stephen was a revelatory ("spiritual renaissance", "something clicked in me") and aesthetic ("transfixed") experience in which sound (waves moving through space) – a phenomenon that fuses time and space – and lute music struck a chord with his developing identity.

At the age of 18, Stephen took private classes with a violin luthier and paid him "quite a lot of money to spend half a day with him". But this employer-employee relationship between apprentice and master quickly fell apart. When at the age of 19 he enrolled in a nine-day guitar-making course. His violin luthier teacher did not approve of this decision:

Stephen: "[M]y violin maker, teacher, said to me: 'Why are you doing this? You're working with me – why are you doing this? Why [...] do you want to do guitar making and not violin making?' And he said: 'If you do that and you carry on in that way you will become a jack of many trades, and you won't become a master of one.' And then the penny dropped for me and I thought: 'Mm, okay, I'm gonna be a master of one and it is going to be the guitar.' And I never finished the violin."

Though it might be an ideal to see many masters at work, having many vocations, being a jack-of-all-trades was not an ideal for either Stephen's violin master or Stephen himself. Stephen immediately decided to leave the violin luthier craft experience in order to concentrate on the guitar, and this led him on the road to Spain.

The Road

After this turning point, Stephen set up a guitar workshop in his bedroom. On several occasions he traveled to Cordoba, Spain in order to study flamenco guitar making. On his first visit, when Stephen was 20 years old, he met "Manuel Reyes, Antonio Marin Montero, Manuel Diaz and other great guitar makers." Stephen traveled to Granada for a month, where he would be a respectful guest in various guitar masters' workshops:

"I would just go in and out a little bit, I wouldn't hassle them or anything – just look and absorb information. And it was very nice, very inspiring, and the smells of the Spanish workshops are wonderful, because the heat makes the oils come out of the timber much more, so I was completely inspired, completely hooked on this thing. So eventually I made my way back to England having given up the idea of living there [in Spain], I thought I wasn't ready for that. So I came back to England and set up my first proper workshop."

Here Stephen relates the story of the wandering years (or rather months). He walks in and out of the master's workshops occupying the role of a visitor and an informal apprentice. The Garguantic odors of the Spanish workshops and the natural advantage that the Mediterranean climate offers over Northern Europe in instrument making gave him more and more appetite for Spanish guitar making that he would cultivate away from Spain.

But the road not only led to Spain; in terms of Stephen's becoming a craftsman it also led away from Spain. At the age of twenty, Stephen set up a workshop solely to produce guitars. The first two guitars that Stephen had built were, as mentioned in the introduction, on display in the workshop but not for sale. In describing the process of crafting these two guitars, Stephen says: "The wood was all bought from Granada and everything, it was very inspiring." In talking about his "own personal guitar" and the other precious one he said: "there are big memories associated with these guitars". In reflecting upon this time of his life when he was 20 and had started crafting guitars, Stephen relates:

"I had done my traveling and my sort of apprenticeships and my absorbing of information and it was now up to me just to build instruments. So I then started to build guitars and selling them little by little. [...] It was a long slow process and so from that point of coming back from Spain and starting by myself I was my own apprentice so to speak and I really had to teach myself from what I'd understood. And I would work and create something and develop a system to make something."

Here Stephen Hill finds himself at a threshold. He returned home (thus ending physically and temporally his formative journey around Spain), and took upon himself "just to build instruments." His identity was paradoxical: He became an accomplished luthier with his own workshop, yet at the same time his identity was in the making in the realization that things take time ("a long and slow process"). In the following time becomes embodied in an identity ideal of non-fixedness or fluidity.

Identity Formation: The Fluid Guitar Maker
The example of the Spanish master
In Spain, Stephen Hill had encountered Manuel Reyes, a Spanish, Granadan guitar maker who became his largest source of inspiration.

Stephen: "He didn't have any secrets, he wasn't holding anything back. Because his secret was himself and that he was able to build a guitar through his personality and through his own experience, and if someone copies his making it doesn't matter, because that is not his guitar, it's their guitar and it will be different. So he was very open and very warm. He then became my maestro [...] the person I looked up to in the guitar world."

Stephen's openness towards other craftspeople in Lewis can be read as a response to the openness of Manuel Reyes. The example of openness can be compared to Bakhtin's notion of an utterance that is never closed or sent from one participant to another for decoding, rather it links earlier utterances with future ones (Bakhtin, 1986, p. 94). Stephen links his meeting (relationship and utterances) with Manuel Reyes in Spain to his present relationships and way of behaving as a craftsman in England about two decades later.

This conception of identity views the very process of identifying with the master, his openness and warmth, as a discursive activity that consists of the collection of stories told about, to and by the master endorsing these characteristics. In this process of identification, Stephen paves a significant path for himself which has significant and reifying implications for his own apprentices and later led to the craft community of Lewis as a whole benefiting from Stephen's openness and entrepreneurship.

Stephen's striving to be a warm and welcoming master is mediated by the identity of other (Spanish) masters whose voices, ethics, bodies vibrated within communities of craft practices to which Stephen's identity and utterances were themselves reactions or answers as, for instance evident in his openness towards other masters and in his initiating the Lewis Guitar Festival. But Stephen not only responded to the heterogeneity of being exposed to different practices with warm and sharing masters like Manuel Reyes in terms of opening up for others to learn from himself; his response can also be read as congruent with good craft salesmanship offering customers an identity (who you become when you buy a Stephen Hill guitar). Communicating to the customers on his homepage that he is inspired by these Spanish masters is a way to sell an image as a guitar maker. His identity as a British-Spanish luthier craft master is cast in terms of selling guitars, but according to Bakhtin this is an ethical stance in which Stephen is authored by Manuel Reyes. Here Manuel Reyes should be seen both as a concrete person (flesh and blood) and in terms of the voices pertaining to his community of practice and Stephen's response to these voices, as he has authored several other luthier apprentices and journeymen to become craftspeople in Lewis.

Formation and ideal

Being his own apprentice, as Stephen phrased it, also helped him adjust to the role as a teacher. In his relation with (informal) apprentices and students taking a three-hour course in guitar making, Stephen impersonated the same philosophy of openness and kindness that he had learned from Manuel Reyes:

Stephen: "I decided from the beginning to be rather like Manuel Reyes, to be open and nurturing in my attitude rather than be closed and keep it to myself. Let's make it big, let's open it all up, let's share information, you know, let's make this, let us grow, this experience. And many things have come out of that, Lewis Guitar Festival, all sorts of different things, all the Lewis guitar makers and even a few workshops here and there, a lot of activity. A really good thing."

This quote about artistic influence and style stresses that the craft artisan struggles in vain to copy another master's style. Instead, the artisan might emulate a master's example and derive his own expression as an active craftsman within a concrete community of practice where you simultaneously share and develop your own perspectives on things. No one can copy the master, yet the apprentice appropriates the master's perspectives, gives them his own intonations. Stephen's gratitude towards Manuel Reyes' is not a passive transmission of value or a redoubling of Manuel Reye's stance on the world. It is an active construction on Stephen's behalf, and with Bakhtin (1993, p. 56f) we could say that Stephen's identity is called forth in this process as he goes about living his everyday life with all its concrete space-time determinations. The luthier identity in the apprentice's performing acts of perceiving the wood, reading about the history of guitars, feeling elevated by the sound of music, touching woods etc. is possible in a luthier community of practice that is unique and concrete and which makes the apprentice answerable. Neither values (e.g. of being an open, warm master) nor personal concrete identities are given but must be realized by any given apprentice. In other words, identity is both what you tell yourself or is told by others and more importantly a lived, unique and concrete experience of being committed to luthier crafting and luthier being. This lived experience and participation lead Stephen to take a volitional, emotional and moral stance: To be and every day become exactly that kind of master who is open towards other craft apprentices and journeyman.

Stephen: "I'd developed very much my own style of making, and then after a while I realized there were different ways of doing it. So I went through the process of ... rather than just copy and copy, I developed very much my own methods and styles which I then changed and tailored as I gained more understanding. And for six years that went on, I started to make a living from guitar making. And then I got fed up with working and living in the same house, I had a workshop at the end of my garden, and I decided to get out of the house, rent a workshop and go into the real world. And I thought that one way of doing that would be to teach guitar making. So I then got a big workshop in town and took my first students on. And that was a big change, a big moment. I was starting to be recognized slowly in the world of classical guitars, flamenco guitars as well."

In moving away from home and developing his own style, Stephen had become a well-known guitar maker who had been influential in making Lewis, his hometown on the South Downs into a center for instrument craftsmanship and the host of an annual guitar festival.

Developing an Identity through Teaching

Teaching also provides an important chronotope of encounter. Six years after his first visit to the Spanish masters, Stephen moved his second workshop away from his garden and set up his third workshop (in which the interview took place). Here he gave individual three-hour lessons to students of guitar making. Stephen developed a reputation as a "fluid guitar maker", a theme that links in with the theme of learning (being self-made and devising his own ways of doing things), but also with ethics and identity (being open as mentioned earlier. Reflecting upon his teaching guitar making, Stephen says:

"I had to relearn a lot of the different things and think about how I did it. [...] over the course of doing it again, bringing it out and explaining I would say: 'Well, there is a better way of doing it.' So I became known very much ... for a very fluid guitar maker: 'Let's try this now – let's try that. Rather than: This is the way to do it, and it is always done like this'. And this is how I learned it. I had already gained enough experience in learning by myself to be able to adjust to everything."

Stephen sees himself as self-made, but he was also shaped by others (Manuel Reyes, Sebastian) in achieving this autonomy. His learning, which came from his informal apprenticeship with the Spanish masters, helped him develop into a great master of the Lewis craft community, where he joined up with other craft guitar journeymen or informal apprentices who would later set up their own workshops in Lewis or nearby on the South Downs. I will end with a quote illustrating how fluidity became an identity ideal serving to renew Stephen's crafting as a perpetual process in which crafting and identity never ceased to influence each other as temporal-spatial signs by which the craftsman's production is judged by himself and others:

Stephen: "I'm always subtly changing the way I build instruments. So it is never in one completely fixed pattern. So each instrument is a draft for the next instrument, and it carries on like that, really, building one after the other."

Conclusion

This chapter has explored chronotopes as lived and analytic categories in a narrative on apprenticeship learning. The chronotopes of apprenticeship that shaped Stephen's trajectory, and in return helped him shape his own life of course, were characterized by the chance encounter, the threshold and the road to Spain. What are the advantages of understanding craft apprenticeship and identity formation through the notion of chronotopes? First it gives meaning to narratives dealing with the interconnectedness and ordering of space and time in everyday life and trajectories leading from apprentice to master. It pinpoints places where the temporal and spatial intersect: The things or artefacts of the guitar workshop and the places[4] where Stephen has set up workshops; the road to being and becoming a journeyman in England or Granada, which meets in Stephen's narrative of coming back to England. Pinpointing these places (as part of a timed trajectory to journeyman status) takes the fact that concrete analyses of the situatedness of identity are seriously warranted (Sfard & Prusak, 2005). In Stephen's trajectory there were no abstracts (like the right path, identity or curriculum or apprenticeship to choose from). Stephen Hill made up his own learning trajectory as he went along, but at the same time this path was created for him by the prevalent chronotopes in given practices like British society, secondary school experiences, craft etc. and primarily by the encounters etc. that formed him on the road.

Second a dialogic approach is reflexive in terms of questioning apprenticeship chronotopes as fixed categories (as though the threshold, the random encounter, the road are always present in narratives on becoming a craftsman or present in any other form). The formation (the wandering years) provides the journeyman not so much with fixed identity markers like the road and traveling hither and thither in foreign places, but with concrete and significant encounters with foreign masters who are not foreign as in alien but inspiring and dialogic asking the participant to answer the different rhythms, overtones, flavors, movements etc. flowing from the community of practice. This difference provides a learning opportunity for the journeyman eager to escape the confines of home (England, house) and to learn the craft from the best.

Although chronotopes can be hypothesized as organizing centers for the way interview persons relate their story and how a narrative account is constructed in qualitative research, the points raised in this chapter could be extended to a point about qualitative research calling for a fluid, emerging analysis focusing on what is there rather than on theoretically preconceived categories. The notion of chronotope both gives meaning to utterances and counteracts ideas about imposing upon apprenticeship and identity formation a chronological order[5] devoid of the situatedness of places, concrete workshops etc. On the one hand Stephen Hill's narrative has a clear chronological order: Leaving school, being offered a job as a cabinetmaker, becoming an informal apprentice to a cabinetmaker, deciding to become a luthier, breaking away from a violin luthier and deciding to become a guitar luthier. But on the other hand, this narrative only gains meaning through the concrete analysis of social relations being formed through places and encounters. This situatedness comes to the fore in the paradox that Stephen's identity is self-made and yet mediated by Spanish masters and practices; his identity is not fixed to producing in just one country (spatially) or any one way (spatially and temporally). Instead, his craft grows from adherence to English and Spanish guitar making traditions.

The guitars on display in his workshop are also imbued with a sense of the chronotopic in serving as identity markers for himself.

In conclusion, evoking the notion of the chronotope about becoming a craftsperson does not give a fixed scheme but allows for the notion of identity as a process of becoming through space-time signs that call forth the person but that the person also calls forth. In spite of the fundamental open-endedness of dialogue, this chapter closes, not coincidentally, in Granada. A few months after the interview Stephen and his family moved to Granada, where he still lives and works (in 2007) and arranges guitar courses for all interested laypersons and professionals. Today he lives and forms himself by building, improving, thinking about, playing and selling guitars that are the products of intricate space-time signs where his escape from the busy workshop in Lewis, England is only one such chronotope.

NOTES

1   As opposed to notions such as storyline and plot, chronotopes refer specifically to the melting of time and space. Bakhtin (1981, p. 84) writes: *"Time, as it were thickens, takes on flesh, becomes artistically visible; likewise, space becomes charged and responsive to the movements of time, plot and history."* And further: *"They are the organizing centers for the fundamental narrative events of the novel"* (Bakhtin, 1981, p. 250). As I read Bakhtin, and space permits this to be explicated further in this chapter, chronotopes can be understood in terms of three dialogic relationships: 1) an analytical and metaphorical concept (building on relativity theory), 2) as our everyday cognition – the immediate reality of perceiving and living in the world, and 3) as artistic expression as seen in novels on adventures and folklore.

2   Steinar Kvale was my Ph.D. supervisor. He convinced me that eminent university researchers/ masters act as role models not so much by teaching and explicit transmission of technical rationality but rather by their example and the norms enacted as part of a research apprenticeship (Kvale, 1997).

3   It was a 1.5 hour long semi-structured interview with an interview guide centred around themes about e.g. way in, apprenticeship learning and work tasks and creativity. But the interview guide was not followed slavishly, either by Stephen or by myself.

4   The first was in his bedroom, the second (that Stephen calls his first proper) was in his garden, and the third was the one in Lewis that he was still running at the time of the interview.

5   Parker (2005), who is inspired by Bakhtin, asks interview researchers to question the chronological narrative.

Claus Elmholdt
Department of Psychology, University of Aarhus

LEARNING ACROSS CULTURES
– A CASE STUDY OF AN ETHNIC MIGRANT GIRL'S DILEMMAS OF LEARNING

Introduction

This chapter employs a decentred approach to exploring learning across cultures, which is inspired by Kvale & Nielsen's (1999) metaphor of landscapes for learning. When doing my PhD research on workplace learning I recall my advisor Steinar Kvale saying repeatedly, "if you want to understand learning explore the landscape – the resources, barriers and learning situations – before turning your gaze towards the learning subjects that inhabit it". This methodological dictum captures very much the essence of the approach taken in this chapter – exploring an ethnic migrant girl's trajectory of learning in and across cultural communities of home and school.

The case study reveals how an ethnic migrant girl's participation across cultural communities of home and school over time increasingly enacts into a dilemma of learning to be a good girl (adopting the traditional religious lifestyle as recommended by her parents) or learning to be a learner (adopting the modern urban individualized reflexive lifestyle as required by school and workplaces). Through the case study the chapter illustrates how identity dilemmas of belonging and becoming may become barriers for learning.

The case study explored in this chapter represents a typical dilemma for many young ethnic migrant girls – coming from traditional backgrounds and growing up in modern societies with their multitude of lifestyle and identity options. What was previously taken for granted as the "natural" alternative in the context of modern societies is now open to choice between different alternatives. As Giddens points out, modern society is a reflexive society, where "individuals are forced to negotiate lifestyle choices among diverse options" (1991, p. 5). Hundeide (2005, p. 245) frames the identity dilemmas of young ethnic migrants as a problem of deciding where one belongs:

Whether to adopt the traditional religious lifestyle and identity as recommended by parents, or break with the traditional family network and embrace a modern urban teenage lifestyle, or find some intermediate solution with alternation between traditional values at home and modern values at school or work.

Instead of focussing on identity dilemmas as such, this chapter puts the focus on learning dilemmas generated by dilemmas of belonging and becoming. The case studied is part of an ongoing research project on marginalized youth learning and learning disabilities across contexts of school, home and work (Elmholdt, Ljung, Larsen, Madsen & Nielsen, 2006). The particular case is selected as an extreme case, which highlights the general claim of a situated perspective that "learning involves the construction of identities" (Lave & Wenger, 1991, p. 53). Packer & Goicoechea (2000, p. 227) argue that the most radical implication of the situated perspective lies in extending the discussion of learning beyond the epistemological question of changes in knowing towards entailing the broader question of changes in being. The chapter pursues this thread of situated learning theory, pointing out that changes in being mediate changes in knowing, and that we need, as Kvale advises, to carefully scrutinize the landscapes for learning before we turn to individualized explanations for learning or non-learning. An ethical reason for pursuing a decentred perspective on learning is, as pointed out by Jean Lave, that purely epistemological theories of learning "in the last instance blame marginalized people for being marginal" (Lave, 1996, p. 149).

A Situated Perspective on Identity and Learning

In situated learning theory the concept of identity is not treated simply as a self-concept, as knowledge of the self, but addresses the fluid character of human beings and the way identity is closely linked to participation and learning in and across social communities (Packer, 2001, p. 5). The transformative character of identity and learning was originally addressed by Lave and Wenger (1991) through the analytical concept of Legitimate Peripheral

Participation (LPP), which partly describes the position of newcomers in communities of practice, and partly describes the dynamic processes involved in gradual movement towards full participation. The assumption was that participation in a community of practice, with learning as a crucial incentive, gradually becomes more engaged and obtains a shared understanding of what people do and what it means to them and the community of practice. Whereas learning in a cognitive epistemological tradition can be seen as a process of moving away from the world towards increasingly abstract representations of knowledge, situated learning is about moving more intensively into social practice (Tanggaard & Elmholdt, 2007).

Research on personal trajectories of identity and learning in and across cultural communities of practice implies theoretical and empirical concern with studying how people combine, modify, and connect learning across places, and how they for example replace earlier learning by something new. The term trajectory does not imply a fixed course or a fixed destination, not a path that can be foreseen or charted but a continuous motion – people have a momentum of their own in addition to the field of influences (Wenger, 1998, p. 154). Trajectories have coherence through time that connects past, present and future. Part of developing trajectories involves the experience of changing passion, commitment and belonging in and across communities of practice – for example as illustrated below in and across diverse cultural communities at home and in school. This may elicit loyalty conflicts, which again may interfere with learning. If the obligation and demands of diverse communities of practice are highly contradictory, it may be almost impossible to combine participation across a coherent trajectory of learning. A striking example is Hundeide's research on becoming a committed insider of extreme countercultural communities (neo-nazis and child-soldiers), which emphasizes the deep commitment and emotional participation involved (Hundeide, 2003). The learning to become a neo-nazi or a child-soldier effectively rules out the possibility of simultaneously learning to become a democratic citizen – the basic values are simply too contradictory, and the demands of obedience, loyalty and subjugation are too strong to allow for multi-membership across more communities of practice. In general, extreme countercultural communities of practice demand deep commitment and loyalty, which collide with or fully impede the development of a trajectory of multimembership and a nexus identity across communities of practice, which is described by Wenger (1998, p. 158) as a characteristic pattern of living in modern western societies.

The Case Study

Empirically this article takes its point of departure in a case study, understood broadly as "a detailed examination of a single case" (Flyvbjerg, 2006, p. 220). The case in question is an open-ended interview with a young ethnic migrant girl (Sunniva). The interview which lasted 1½ hours, was extracted from a larger sample of open in-depth interviews with young people atrisk of educational and social marginalization. The case was selected strategically in order to achieve the greatest possible amount of information on the social ontological nature of human learning. Flyvbjerg points out that "when the objective is to achieve the greatest possible amount of information on a given problem or phenomenon, a representative case or a random sample may not be the most appropriate strategy" (2006, p. 229). On the contrary, the selection of an extreme case may be appropriate: "atypical or extreme cases often reveal more information because they activate more actors and more basic mechanisms in the situation studied" (Ibid. p. 229).

The interview was conducted by psychology student and research assistant Sarah Senger Madsen. The interviewee, Sunniva, was 18 years old at the time of interviewing, and the interviewer, Sarah, was 24. The interview was conducted in a meeting room at the production school where Sunniva had started as a clerk apprentice. Sunniva seemed self-confident and secure in her appearance when entering the room with a loose-leaf book under her arm containing papers on the factual details of the education. She was dressed in fashionable clothes, wearing make-up and no headscarf. The interview started quite formally, but soon Sunniva opened up for a much more intimate personal story. This dynamic of the interview process seems influenced by the fact that the interviewer was a female and relatively contemporary in age to the interviewee.

The interview was transcribed verbatim and straightened out grammatically. The interview situation is understood as an active meaning-making occasion, implying that data involves unavoidably collaborative constructions of knowledge (Holstein & Gubrium, 1997, p. 114). The active interviewer's role is to incite the interviewee's answers in order to activate narrative production, which is supposed to reflect both circumstantial and more constitutive aspects of the person's interpretive practices. Following this line of investigation, the empirical material is approached through a narrative analysis – exploring Sunniva's storytelling as a way to "find an intentional state that mitigates or at least makes comprehensible a deviation from a canonical cultural pattern" (Bruner, 1990, p. 49-50). As such, the narratives construed in the interview are seen as mediations between individual actions and social-structural conditions; "they reflect the dynamics of ongoing negotiations, interpretations, and construals just as they indicate the constraints operating in these dynamics" (Morowski, 1997, p. 675). This is not necessarily a self-conscious strategy, but a consequence of the human inclination to search for meaning and coherence in participation across contexts.

Learning Dilemmas across Divergent Cultural Communities

Sunniva arrived in Denmark as a refugee from Lebanon with her parents and two older brothers when she was only three months old. She is now 18 years old and lives with her parents and her younger sister in a block of flats in a Danish provincial town. At the time of interviewing she had started an education as a clerk assistant trainee. After completing business school she sends more than 60 applications for a trainee job without any result. She was close to dismissing the idea of becoming a clerk assistant when she was finally offered the opportunity to become a trainee in a new project on apprenticeship training for young people at risk of social marginalization.

The interview with Sunniva produced a narrative account which linked a sequence of events – from her arriving in Denmark, over the present moment, and towards her future dreams – into a structure, which may be described as her trajectory of participation and learning. Sunniva's narrative revealed a central tension between living a traditional Arab/Muslim religious lifestyle versus living a modern, urban, individualized, reflexive lifestyle. The tension between these diverse lifestyle options is reflected again and again during the interview as dilemmas of transgressing or bringing reconciliation to competing demands of belonging and becoming (learning) across the cultural communities of home and school. In the following interview passage Sunniva addresses her feelings of being divided between two divergent cultural communities.

Sunniva: I do feel Muslim in that way, that is when I am with Danes then I feel Muslim, but as soon as I am with the others Muslim girls, then I don't feel Muslim
Interviewer: I see
Sunniva: Because there I'm still, that is when I'm with Danes, there is still a difference, that there are many things you do that I don't do
Interviewer: Yes
Sunniva: Then I'm thinking it is because I'm Muslim, as soon as I'm with the other Muslim girls who are married then I'm thinking: holy shit, I'm not Muslim because there are so many things I do that they don't do
Interviewer: Oh, I see
Sunniva: A little like, you feel totally split between two cultures, that's what it is, you don't know where it is, what to do, where to feel and
Interviewer: I see so you feel like you are caught in between.
Sunniva: Yes, you feel caught in between. So I don't really know, you get really confused, what shall I do, this or that, you are totally confused.

When I'm with the Danish girls I feel Muslim, and when I'm with the other Muslim girls I feel Danish, Sunniva says, explaining her feeling of being split between two divergent cultural communities of practice. This position is experienced as an unsure identity – who am I, and where should I place my loyalty and commitment? Bauman (1991) describes it as a painful position not to be settled within a secure identity, and uses the expression ambivalence in order to portray a positioning between dominant cultural trajectories of identity and learning. He claims that unclear classification is painful – ambivalence – because it is experienced as a personal failure not to fulfil society's ideal of being a core subject – a categorical either/or – e.g. either Muslim or Christian. One solution is what Bauman (1991) terms the complete elimination of inconsistent elements in the self-narrative. The following interview passage illustrates how Sunniva 'plays' with the idea of completely eliminating the trajectory of identity and learning involved in adopting the traditional religious lifestyle as recommended by her parents:

Interviewer: What do you think you will be doing, five years from now, where do you think you will be living and what do you think will have happened in your life.

Sunniva: Well five years from now, I imagine that I've just finished my education, maybe.

Interviewer: Yes.

Sunniva: I'm married and living far away, that's far away from Aarhus in that way.

Interviewer: Okay.

Sunniva: Away from my family.

Interviewer: I see, so you would like to move far away from your family.

Sunniva: Yes, that's what I want to do.

Interviewer: Okay.

Sunniva: Move away and have a husband – it all depends on whom I'm married to.

Interviewer: Mm.

Sunniva: But just not living close to them.

Interviewer: Where could you imagine living?

Sunniva: A lot of people laugh at me but I would like to move to Løgumkloster[1], I don't know why.

Interviewer: (laughing) Okay.

Sunniva: It is a small, lovely town because I've been school camping there.

Interviewer: Okay.

Sunniva: Such a small town where there are no, no Arabs or someone you know.

Interviewer: Okay.

Sunniva: Just starting your life there, right.

Interviewer: Yes.

Sunniva: Of course it will be difficult but it's different if you had your boyfriend or husband with you that way.

Interviewer: Yes.

Sunniva: If you could get a job, just far away altogether.

Sunniva contemplates moving to another city in order to escape from the traditional religious lifestyle trajectory – leading towards arranged marriage, childbirth and housewifery. The possibility of moving to another city and starting a new life as an educated woman stands out as a tempting alternative to her current struggle of reconciling participation across the cultural communities of home and school. What may be termed the "marriage trajectory" stands out as what she wants to avoid at any price. Sunniva is aware that multimembership is highly difficult, and that fully adopting the traditional religious lifestyle trajectory most likely involves abandoning her wish to fulfil educational learning goals – something which she refuses to accept:

Sunniva: Normally at my age people get married, e.g. all my friends, they are all married, right, then people look a lot at me like why the hell isn't she.
Interviewer: Okay.
Sunniva: That's the way they look at me, and then I've had some problems with my parents, why don't you want to get married and why won't you so they've had so much – in the end I couldn't take any more and then I talked with Mie (teacher) about it, she then talked a bit with them, but she didn't talk as such about marriage with them, no, that's something I talk with her about, and tell her what's going on at home.
Interviewer: I see.
Sunniva: In such a way I've been very happy that I'm not married, and now I'm at any rate getting an education. I'm not getting married or anything because that is what I'm not, I don't want to be married now. Many of my friends and parents and family they are in job training and something like, and that's not what I want to do. Instead I want to get an education, now that I have the chance.
Interviewer: Do you have many friends who are in such arranged marriages?
Sunniva: Yeah, I have.
Interviewer: Okay.
Sunniva: I have many of those.
Interviewer: What do you think of that?
Sunniva: Poor them.

Notice how the traditional religious "marriage trajectory" is discursively split away from Sunniva's self narrative, and placed within the mind and body of the 'other' Arab/Muslim girls – representing what she is not, and what she must avoid being at any cost in order to maintain the desired educational learning goals and identity. The dissonant narrative elements are discursively split away because they represent a threat towards becoming the person she wants to become. Sunniva wants to become an educated, independent woman, and she wants her parents to accept her choice.

The Desired Object of Education and the Desire for Recognition

Education stands out as the desired object in Sunniva's narrative, and she desires approval and recognition from her parents for striving for this object, something which creates a tension in the narrative. Sunniva does not desire the object of education because of its intrinsic qualities, but because education represents an opportunity to escape the marriage trajectory – freedom to define and pursue her own trajectory of learning. The following quotation describes Sunniva's desire for education in terms of avoiding the traditional Arab/Muslim lifestyle package of (arranged) marriage, childbirth and housewifery.

Sunniva: Well, it's because when I look at the others who are married and haven't got a job in that way. The most important for me, and I think it is for everybody, is to get an education, of course, no matter if you are married or not married at all, just get an education first and then afterwards I can get married. It is very important, I think, it's the most important thing, I think, in my life now. Just to finish it and not to drop out and get a job because you can always do that (getting married).

The desired object of education represents on the one hand an opportunity for a different trajectory of learning. However, on the other hand Sunniva's strong desire for education represents a divide from her background culture – a divide which may force her to give up another desired object, namely the object of approval and recognition from her parents. As Packer and Goicoechea point out, "to become a participant in community is to be divided" (2000, p. 233). In the following passage Sunniva reflects upon a feeling of estrangement from certain cultural elements within her background culture. Moreover, she describes her desire to reconcile a personal trajectory of identity and learning across the divergent cultural communities of home and school:

Interviewer: So you aren't that happy about your background?
Sunniva: Sure, that's, of course, I'm still Muslim, but there are still so many things involved which I don't really like that much. I keep transcending those barriers because it's something I don't want, but now I'm of course brought up and raised in the Muslim faith, so I can't just convert to the Christian faith.

Interviewer: No.

Sunniva: I could care less for my parents, I could easily do, but it's now I'm Muslim, and of course I believe in this faith, but there are some things where I'm thinking, oh my god.

Interviewer: I see, what kind of things?

Sunniva: On the whole, it's some thing to do with headscarves and.

Interviewer: With headscarves, I can see that you aren't wearing a headscarf.

Sunniva: Yes, and to a large extent with the makeup, the clothing and such, you have to be completely covered and be married and all such traditional things. Such ridiculous things that Danes are looking at and thinking that is totally normal.

Interviewer: Yes, what e.g.?

Sunniva: That's e.g. sometimes, that with the clothes when they complain that you can see a little of it and wear long pants and do something with your hair.

Interviewer: What do your parents say to you not wearing a headscarf?

Sunniva: Really, they have of course said to me that now that's enough, now I was becoming far too Danish in that way. That now I should stop with all this, but it's still my life.

Interviewer: Do you want to become very Danish?

Sunniva: Yeah that's what I want, also for the future of my children. When I have children, they will not be raised at all in that way.

Interviewer: I see.

Sunniva: First they must have an education before they are allowed to get married. Education that's the first thing they should do, then afterwards they can start thinking about all the other stuff.

Interviewer: Okay, so you want to raise your children in a more Danish way.

Sunniva: More Danish, yes they should be. Of course they still have their background in the way that they should still remember that they are Muslims, Arabs so to speak, but I won't be so demanding on the traditions we have, that's not the way it should be, it shouldn't be in the way that my daughter has to keep it a secret that she has a boyfriend e.g.

"My daughter should not be forced to hide the existence of a boyfriend" Sunniva says, when reflecting on how she wants the upbringing of her own children to be different from the way her parents brought her up. Earlier in the interview Sunniva has confessed that she sees a boy without her parents knowing. Her boyfriend is a Muslim but he is not an Arab, which makes Sunniva fear that her parents will not accept their relationship. She describes herself as being in love, and says that she wants her marriage to build on romantic love rather than being arranged by her parents. Sunniva's fear of ending up in an arranged marriage is not groundless. In the interview she describes an incident six months earlier when her parents tried to arrange a marriage to an Egyptian police officer. The arrangement was avoided with the help of the school teachers, who explained to her parents the importance of finishing an education.

Generally, the interview passage reflects an increasing tension between the cultural communities of home and school, as Sunniva has "become more Danish than her parents want her to be". The parents react against this threat by trying to arrange a respectable marriage and confining her freedom to dress and move around in public – limiting her opportunities to engage in "non-Arab/Muslim" learning situations as much as possible.

Sunniva does not want to convert to Christianity. Instead, she wants to pursue a personal trajectory of learning that transgresses the dominant trajectories of home and school. However, it may be argued that such a reflexive attitude itself represents an individualized western lifestyle, and as such implies a fundamental rejection of the traditional Arab/Muslim girl trajectory. Basically, the idea of negotiating and forming a personal trajectory of identity and learning across communities of practice demands an individualized subject who is constantly reflexively engaged in self-construction (Elmholdt & Brinkmann, 2006). Seen in this perspective, Sunniva's reflexive approach towards her background cultural community can be described as a critical consumer attitude – acting as if she had a free choice to consume cultural elements in alignment with her personal taste.

The Trouble of Reconciling Identity and Learning across Cultures

The general citizen in modern western societies belongs to many different communities of practice; some past, some present, some as full members and some in more peripheral ways (Wenger, 1998, p. 158). Modern men and women are discursively set free to establish a coherent identity out of participation in and across multiple communities of practice. Sociologists such as Beck make clear that this is more of an obligation than a free choice – we are condemned to individualization (Beck, 1992). Modern, individualized society stands in contrast to archaic societies with their simple divisions of labour and little distribution of knowledge, where everyone pretty much became what they were supposed to be (Packer & Goicoechea, 2000, p. 234). All the various forms of participation in a modern life involve learning, and contribute more or less to the production of our identities. Wenger claims that identity entails (1) an experience of multi-membership, and (2) the work of reconciliation necessary in order to maintain one coherent identity across cultural communities of practice (1998, p. 158). The enactment of a coherent identity is an effort we make to overcome division across the multiple cultural communities of practice we engage in.

The case study of Sunniva's trajectory of identity and learning reveals that not all cultural communities of practice are as permissive to reconciliation as Wenger seems to suggest. The dilemma of learning to be a good girl in the religious Arab/Muslim community by adopting the traditional woman trajectory, and learning to be a learner in modern western society by adopting an individualized reflective lifestyle is not easily reconciled. However, Sunniva's story reflects an attempt to enact a coherent personal trajectory of identity and learning that transcends the dominant trajectories of identity and learning within the cultural communities she participates in and across at home and in school.

The struggle to reconcile division and obtain a coherent trajectory of identity and learning is described as increasingly troublesome in Sunniva's self narrative. Two possible explanations can be extracted from the empirical material: (1) The dominant trajectories of the diverse communities of practice she participates in and across become less permissive to deviations as a girl grows up – belonging becomes increasingly committed and deviations are sanctioned more strictly. (2) Historical and societal changes have resulted in an increased split across the diverse communities of practice she participates in and across. The former explanation finds support, for example, in the family's eagerness to safeguard their honour by trying to force Sunniva to pursue the marriage trajectory. The latter explanation finds support, for example, in Sunniva's descriptions of how the block of flats where the family has lived over the years has turned into a ghetto for ethnic migrants:

Sunniva: When we first moved to Aarhus not any of them lived here, that's us Arabs so to speak, not more than three families lived here, now about 100 live here.
Interviewer: Okay.
Sunniva: It's where we have lived all our lives, and that's where I grew up. To start with I grew up a lot with Danes in a way, so many lived here, but eventually they all moved away, so there are only Arabs in the flats. I would say that before I felt much better in a way, because I just had some Danish friends, my neighbours and so on, I played with, and I remember very well when I was little, I got upset when they moved. I was thinking now a new girl will move in but then it was Somalis who moved in or Arabs, and I didn't want to play with them, I had enough of them so to speak. I remember very well, I got so upset because I was thinking now they are all moving.

Sunniva experienced personally that the transformation from public utility accommodation to ethnic migrant ghetto, involved the loss of friendships with Danish girls. As a consequence of the Danish families moving out, Sunniva has fewer opportunities to establish contact and friendship with ethnic Danish children, something which may have contributed to her experiencing an increased split between the cultural communities of home and school. Within the broader historical and societal context, incidents such as 9/11 and the "Muhammad crisis" may have contributed to an increased split between the cultural communities of home and school. It seems obvious to argue that increased misbelief and hatred across cultural communities make it increasingly difficult to create a personal trajectory of identity and learning that transcends the division.

Concluding Remarks

In this chapter I have tried to demonstrate that a decentred social ontological analysis on learning as changing participation in and across communities of practice makes visible that changes in being mediate changes in learning – e.g. that desires for recognition and belonging in and across communities of practice mediate what learning is pursued and what learning is avoided. This dynamic also work in the opposite direction: fears of belonging and becoming mediate what learning is pursued and what is avoided – Sunniva's

paper I occasionally briefly refer to phenomena and findings from this research as particular instances of my general argument.

Learning as Mental and Individual or as Situated in Social Practice

In psychological research, learning is generally taken to be an individual,
mental process. This predominant framework has been subject to critique.
Thus, Lave called for a shift from studying "trees of knowledge into fields
for activity" (1988, chapter 6) in a pun paralleling the critique of cognitiv-
ism and the phylogenetic transition from primates living in trees to human
beings producing societies for their subsistence (Holzkamp, 1883; Schurig,
1976). She argued for conceiving of learning as situated and as occurring in
participation in social practice (Lave, 1993; Lave & Wenger, 1991). Likewise,
in a series of studies on apprenticeship learning, Kvale proposed to study
"landscapes of learning" (Nielsen & Kvale, 2003).

Movement as Trajectories in Social Practice

These arguments rest on coming to realize, once re-search for learning had
shifted from isolated individual heads into social practice, that learners are
not stationary. Being situated does not mean staying in the same place. Indeed, in social practice learners are moving, and these moves play a key role
in their accomplishment of learning. The very course of learning processes is
grounded in learners' movements in social practice. In that sense, I proposed
the study of learners' trajectories of learning in social practice (Dreier, 1999;
2003; 2008). This takes us beyond the assumption that learning simply follows standard procedures and obeys uniform mechanisms. It opens the doors
to finding learning as complex and varied processes, of varying duration and
composition, and even as proceeding by virtue of linking disparate occasions
and occurrences of learning. It also makes us realize that the continuation of
learning is mostly a discontinuous process. When a learning issue or assign-
ment emerges for the first time for a particular person or group of persons,
they encounter it in a situated way in a particular context. They address and
pursue it in a particular manner in that context depending on the particular
setup of materials, co-participants, and possibilities and on their particular

personal concerns in relation to that context. Often they distribute their engagement with the learning issue in a particular way among themselves, leaving particular parts to particular persons and all participants with a need to negotiate, coordinate, and combine, or fight over what they (want to) learn. All this is, thus, clearly the case when persons address learning issues emerging in therapy sessions.

But persons' pursuits of learning in relation to a particular learning issue are rarely finished in one learning situation and context. Their pursuits reach across diverse contexts with varying materials, co-participants, possibilities, and occasions for learning and with varying personal concerns for learning as well as for much else in these other contexts. In such complex learning trajectories, learners must therefore find appropriate ways to keep at their pursuits of learning. They need to find suitable ways of linking and combining their diverse activities of learning as well as the contents of what they learn in disparate times and places. Again, this is so when persons move from their therapy session into other contexts of their ordinary lives – such as their home, school, and workplace, and back again – and search for situated ways of continuing to learn about changing their troubles.

In pursuits of learning across places, the complex courses of learning that emerge incorporate many interruptions, and learners must find suitable times, places, and ways of picking up the pursuit of the learning issue anew. Indeed, they risk forgetting it in the intervals between learning episodes when it ceases to be on their mind while they are engaged in much else. This may not matter much to them as far as some learning issues are concerned, and that learning may then be abandoned. But discontinuing the pursuit of other learning issues may later turn into a problematic neglect. Persons must then find ways to come back to that learning issue again when, perhaps due to this neglect, it may have turned into a genuine problem which it is therefore more difficult to face and resolve. In this sense, they may learn the hard way not to neglect important learning issues and have to address these issues backwards, that is, to learn about them by unraveling them starting with the issue they have now turned into and reconsidering their emergence and course of change into that issue. The practice of therapeutically assisted change frequently contains such instances. As far as many learning issues are concerned, persons must, in other words, find ways to come back to them after an appropriate lapse of time. They must also find appropriate occasions for doing so and ways of picking an issue up again which their co-participants in the context and situation they are opting to use for picking it up again are willing to make room for and, perhaps, take part in. Identifying these occasions and ways may require various negotiations with various co-participants and may be hampered by various conflicts between them, including conflicts about when, how and whether to pick up the issue again and who is to play which part in doing so.

What is more, as learners move into different contexts from the context in which they first addressed a learning issue, the meaning of this issue for them may change, and other contexts may reveal other aspects of the learning issue and other opportunities for learning about it. This may provoke various processes of comparison, which may lead to a more complex understanding of the issue, like when a girl reconsiders the meaning and course of her bouts of anxiety in sessions, at home, in school, with friends and thereby reaches a more complex understanding of these troubles. It may also make learners reconsider the meaning of the learning issue and reevaluate their reliance on and use of their prior learning about it, like when parents at home realize that the topic in a prior session about their making demands on their children is really about the parents being unwilling to accept any longer that their children "are always cross". Indeed, persons often have various reservations about what they learn – even doubts or confusions about what they take it to mean and what they may want or not want to do with it. Persons must, therefore, make up their minds about what they learn, and this often requires reconsidering it across various relevant situations and contexts. In doing so, persons come to adopt particular personal stances on the learning issue, that is, to make up their minds about what they endorse and are against on the issue and its optional uses. In the course of reconsidering what they learned across various situations and contexts, and because other situations and contexts reveal other aspects of the learning issue, persons may even change their minds and adopt other stances, like when a father makes up his mind after six months of complex reconsiderations that the key problem behind many of his troubles is his not having been sufficiently able to act consistently across situations and contexts. Persons may even call themselves to account in relation to what they learned earlier, and change their minds quite markedly, like when a mother struggles with issues about the relations between love and self-sacrifice. In fact, some learning proceeds by first finding out what you do not want to believe, stand for, and do and take this as a starting point for complex searches for other understandings, stances, and ways of doing things, as was clearly the case in the last two instances mentioned.

It follows from the arguments above that much learning proceeds in an episodic manner, and that although deliberate plans may be made for complex learning trajectories, learning processes hold important emergent qualities. It also follows that much learning has no definite, immutable endpoint. What was once defined as an endpoint turns out to be just a point on the way in a complex learning trajectory, like when clients change their minds and ways of dealing with certain troubles away from what they had previously taken to be a complete and stable understanding. Much learning is, in other words, open-ended. This open-endedness makes it complicated for persons to define the status of their prior learning and their reliance on it.

Furthermore, in their ongoing social practice persons are engaged in much else than learning. This has two important implications for learning. First, much learning must be pursued as linked with varying other ongoing activities and concerns, and this affects the ways, processes, outcomes, meanings, and uses of learning. Second, much learning occurs as an emerging side effect of an activity with other primary purposes and concerns than learning. The predominant framework on learning plays down the significance of this kind of learning as revealed in the chosen term for it, "incidental learning". But such concomitant learning (Dreier, 2008), or as Holzkamp (1993) calls it "Mitlernen", may be very important even though it is difficult to preplan. Most learning in relation to therapy elsewhere outside sessions is thus pursued as being linked with varying other activities and concerns, and as concomitant learning alongside activities holding other main purposes.

Institutional Arrangements of Trajectories

In the previous section we saw that in social practice learning acquires eminently socio-practical dimensions and qualities as well as eminently personal dimensions and qualities. However, the above characterization of the social and personal dimensions and qualities of complex and varied trajectories of learning in social practice is abstract and oversimplified in one important respect: social practice is arranged. Learning issues always emerge, and persons experience, address, and pursue them within particular arrangements of social practice. In shaping and realizing their pursuits of various learning issues in social practice, persons must therefore take the arrangements of those practices into account. They must somehow manage to combine their personal pursuits with the setups and scopes of those arrangements. To succeed, they must at least partially understand those arrangements and gain such a good overview over them that they can direct their pursuits of learning in relation to them. Moreover, the forms and degrees of ordering of social arrangements vary. While some are detailed and strict, others are sketchy and loose. The usabilities of arrangements vary too. Finally, social arrangements specify particular sequences of activity which constitute particular socio-practical, institutional trajectories for participation.

Among these are particular institutional educational arrangements for trajectories of learning. We see them in the age grading of students' educational trajectories of learning, in the sequencing of educational trajectories into institutions of elementary, higher and specialized education with particular arrangements for advancement and transition, and in the sequencing and specification of tracks and curricula. We also see them in the arrangement of school years, terms, and timetables and the distribution of school subjects across them. The curricular planning of an educational sequence out of separate lessons for a particular school subject scattered across the timetable of weeks and school years is a further dimension of the institutional arrangement of trajectories of learning. This institutional arrangement is the basis for the assessment of student performances in a school subject across the school year as a cumulative effect of presumed immediate causal links between these separate lessons scattered across the timetable and school year and as being unaffected by whatever else the student is engaged in elsewhere in between. The institutional arrangement of the course of school days into lessons and breaks plus other regular and occasional activities affects the course and dynamics of learning about school subjects and about other issues involved in being a student and a growing person (Ingholt, 2007). The socio-material arrangements of ordinary classrooms affect the course and dynamics of learning processes in them, as is evident when comparing them to learning processes, say, in computer labs in schools (Sørensen, 2005). However, institutional arrangements for trajectories of learning also comprise the arrangement for addressing learning issues by reserving timeslots in secluded lessons for a concentrated engagement in an issue and nothing but that issue. This arrangement abstracts the issue from its ordinary contextual connections so that it appears as an entity in itself with essential properties of its own independently of its ordinary contextual connections. It constructs an isolated abstraction – or a set of isolated abstractions – and it conjures up a special way of engaging with these abstractions which we call "concentration", and which turns engaging in anything else, even in the various contextual connections of the learning issue, into disturbances of the learning process thus arranged.

On the basis of these arrangements of educational institutions, particular forms of learning and knowledge emerge which we can call "school learning" and "school knowledge" (Dreier, 1999). Because learning is mostly studied in relation to the practices of educational institutions and to teachers as experts in arranging and causing it, research on learning has generally taken school learning as the paradigm case of learning and conceptualized learning accordingly. The process of learning is then grasped as an isolated subject's secluded and parceled acquisition of a pre-given and secluded object of knowledge. Some educational researchers even argue that learning must take place at a distance from ordinary mundane practices in order to lead to knowledge at all as opposed to mere personal experience. The institutionally arranged forms of practice have thus led to the emergence of similar forms of thinking about the practice of learning couched in a positioned way from the position of expert teachers and researchers in relation to students. In fact, the institutional arrangements have infused the form of thinking so thoroughly that the significance of the practical arrangement for the process of learning is taken completely for granted and ignored. Few are concerned with what these arrangements were thought out for (Abbott, 2001), that is, with the history and ideas of learning and knowledge they represent, or with the work knowledge (Smith, 2005) it takes to be able to participate as a student in those institutional educational arrangements. Moreover, the personal pursuit of an educational trajectory of learning transcends these institutional arrangements and boundaries and incorporates other contexts, activities, and sources of learning (Nielsen, 1999). Education is, after all, instituted in order to make a difference in students' practices in their everyday lives outside those institutions. Whereas the dominating framework on learning assumes that all important learning takes place inside educational institutions and that when students move out into other practices they merely apply what they already learned in the institution, I argued that learning reaches beyond those institutional boundaries and is pursued further in many ways. Indeed, much learning takes places in other social practices, and is affected by the arrangements of those other social practices, so that we may find a variety of practices and trajectories of learning. Much learning is even pursued across social practices with diverse arrangements, and what is learned must be linked and combined across those diversities.

Similar Arrangements of Other Expert Practices

My analysis of personal trajectories and institutional arrangements has been inspired by discovering surprisingly similar arrangements and trajectories in various fields of social practice – even in practices normally believed to be quite distinct and different from each other. Let me briefly mention some striking similarities between the social practices of education, as sketched above, and therapy. The social practice of therapy is also generally arranged as a sequence of isolated sessions in a secluded room in which the troubles addressed in therapy are constructed as abstractions by means of a concentrated engagement with particular categories of problems/diseases so that clients in sessions deal with, experience, and come to understand their everyday troubles in special ways. Therapeutic experts are also seen as causes of the effects of therapy on their clients, and change is normally seen as a purely mental process. Research on therapy rests on all this as premises and, at the same time, it presumes that the very arrangement of therapy is of no significance for the dynamics of therapeutic change. In addition, although sessions are secluded from the everyday lives of clients, therapy is meant to work beyond their boundaries in the clients' everyday lives elsewhere. But no strict transfer of session insights, advice, and so forth is possible because in other places clients live their lives with other co-participants, other scopes of possibilities, and many other everyday engagements and concerns than those addressed in sessions. For those and other reasons, therapeutic change and learning are open-ended and must be pursued by clients in trajectories across diverse contextual practices. A further case in point is the field of practice of research, which is dominated by the "standard arrangement" (Holzkamp, 1996) of the experiment that deeply affects our basic conception of knowledge and learning and rests on a very similar social arrangement (Dreier, 2007; in press). These striking similarities made me reconsider my findings about therapy in the light of a more comprehensive and general approach. The sketched arrangements of practices of expertise have led to a hegemonial form of thinking about institutions and experts in relation to the everyday lives of just plain folks in which the former judge performances in the latter as mere applications of expert advice and knowledge. This amounts to an "institutional epistemology" (Rose, 1996) in which the idea of distance from the everyday as a condition of genuine knowledge overshadows the significances of the particular arrangements of these distant places. The concepts of trajectories of participation and learning replace this idea of distance. They let us study social practices as situated and arranged and persons as moving in and across diverse practices instead of as being immersed in their everyday lives or at the distance of a nowhere of privileged abstractions.

Structures of Social Practice in Social Practice

However, recent social theories, including social practice theories and their situated variants, pay scarce conceptual attention to structures of social practice and rather study processes in time. They are critical of some premises of traditional conceptions of social structure, but neglect to develop other conceptions of social structure instead. As a result, they tend not to pay systematic conceptual attention to the various arrangements of social practices and, even more so, to their interconnectedness in a nexus of social practices. One exception is Schatzki (2002), who distinguishes between three existing conceptions of social order as regularity, stability, and interdependence and proposes to integrate them in a fourth conception of social order as arrangement. In that sense, social structure is the ordering of manifold social practices in a nexus of social practice. Such a conception has the advantage of not separating structure from activity, and of seeing both as combined in structural arrangements in and for social practices. Structure is then seen as eminently practical by nature. Thus, the various ways of setting up and ordering practices in the shape of social contexts, and of separating and linking those social contexts and the social practices which take place within them and which reach across them, are structural arrangements of social practice. No context can then be grasped on its own, as an island, but must be analyzed as being involved somehow in structural arrangements of social practice.

In classic, mainstream social theories, social structure is the structure of a society seen as a bounded nation state. Such a conception is too abstract and insufficient for studying concrete local practices and the lives of particular persons in and across local social contexts. Adhering to it leads to an underdetermined, simplified, and functionalist view on concrete local practices and phenomena. It is simply not possible to determine the structural status of concrete, local situations and positions with sufficient precision from the point of view of such an overall, nation state-level social structure. In a reaction to futile attempts at deriving concrete phenomena from such a structure, many theorists turned to poststructuralist approaches in which the significance of structure is watered down or set aside altogether (e.g. Urry, 2000). For psychology, which studies concrete individuals in concrete situations, such a distant and abstract notion of structure is particularly problematic. As a result, psychologists taking the call to relate the study of psychological phenomena to social structures seriously face special difficulties. As a remedy, Holzkamp (1983) proposed to study how the functioning of concrete individuals in immediate situations is mediated by the overall social structure. The overall structure is seen as presenting itself in particular mediated ways in immediate situations, and thereby impacting the scope of possibilities and their meaning in those situations. Structure is then still believed to be located outside and above situations and to affect them from there. In the study of persons in concrete situations, there seems to be no structure in these situations because structure is merely captured as being of a mediated nature. So to persons in concrete situations, structure is seen as appearing as a particular meaning, or structure of meaning as Holzkamp puts it. As a result, it seems logical to search for the presence of structure in concrete situations as a phenomenon of language, thinking, and consciousness rather than as a particular practical arrangement. Furthermore, in such a theory, and in many others like it, the overall social structure is juxtaposed with an immediate life world. But because these theories neglect to work out the structural arrangements of ongoing social practices, they end up considering the life world as a homogenous space (Dreier, 2008), which is believed to call forth a homogeneous mode of individual functioning. However, social practice is not homogenous. It is divided into diverse local social contexts which are linked in a structure of ongoing social practice. These contexts are characterized by various arrangements for participation and for moving through them into various other contexts. In short, due to various structural arrangements, personal lives must unfold in movement through diverse contexts in the existing structure of social practice. Persons must shape their lives and pursue their concerns, including those for learning, by linking and separating their diverse participation in diverse contexts, and they must vary their modes of participating by taking the various arrangements of local contexts into account.

Challenges for Psychology: Persons in Structures of Social Practice

The theoretical arguments I have presented were triggered by studying persons in concrete social practices, especially persons somehow involved in expert psychological practices. Within the standard arrangement of psychological research, on the other hand, persons are studied in one isolated situation, as if that situation can be understood by itself and as if persons function in identical ways in all situations. It is done in this way regardless of the fact that persons do not live in one isolated situation. They conduct their lives in movement across a variety of diverse contexts in structures of social practice. This challenges the nature and scope of psychological theories. They must enable us to capture how persons move in structures of social practice, experience this and themselves in it, think and learn about it, and act in such ways in relation to those structures that they manage their lives, arrange themselves in these structures, and take part in their reproduction or change. They must also enable us to capture how persons come to conduct their lives by committing themselves to particular places, particular arrangements and rhythms of activities, particular social relations, and particular other persons (Dreier, 2008; Smith, 2005), as well as how this affects their psychological functioning. The learning of particular persons in social practice thus rests on and is affected by their particular commitments and conduct of life (Dreier, 2008). Until psychological theories consider all this, they will be affected by it blindly. Their conceptions turn into forms of thinking uncontrollably reflecting existing arrangements of social practice. They limit their capacities to think about and beyond the impacts of these forms of practice on the various dimensions and phenomena of being a person that psychology is meant to study. This is also the case in the study of learning which I have aimed to show, albeit briefly, in this paper. I have pointed to aspects of learning and of being a person which we cannot capture systematically without a conception of social structures of practice, and which would, therefore, also get lost in theories which merely take concepts of action, activity, relation, or conversation as their core concept about the relation between human beings and their social world.

Tone Saugstad
University of Copenhagen

ARISTOTLE IN THE 'KNOWLEDGE SOCIETY': BETWEEN SCHOLASTIC AND NON-SCHOLASTIC LEARNING

Introduction

In our contemporary 'knowledge society', changes in the field of practice as well as in the status of knowledge have led to a new educational awareness of learning *in* and *for* practice. The new awareness or what could be called the 'pragmatic turn in education' is noticeable in two different approaches. One approach operates inside school and is concerned with narrowing the methods and curriculum of schools to practical life. The other approach deals with adult learning in the workplace and is influenced by a mixture of learning theories such as organizational learning, situated learning, current ideals of lifelong learning as well as didactical theories. However, neither of the approaches seems to pay attention to the differences between learning in school and learning in practice. Instead of utilizing the advantages of each way of learning, the consequences is a neglect of both – a neglect that might result in accidental ad hoc learning both in school and in practice.

In this paper it is argued that the tendency to blend school learning and workplace learning stems from a poor understanding of the field of practice and a one-dimensional understanding of knowledge. Accordingly it is easy to ignore the fact that different knowledge forms are learnt in different ways. Aristotle's three categories of knowledge – the theoretical, the productive and the social-ethical can serve to expand modern comprehension of knowledge and learning[1]. One of Aristotle's points is that some forms of knowledge are best acquired in practical life, while others are best acquired in school. Keeping in mind the limitations which the historical distance and the many different receptions of the philosophy of Aristotle entail, his theories of knowledge and learning provide a weighty reminder that the differences between school learning and workplace learning entail more than different modes or methods of learning; they also entail paradigmatic differences. The differences can be mirrored in the two contemporary ways of understanding learning, the *scholastic* and *non-scholastic* paradigm of learning. The term *scholastic* refers to a didactical way of organizing the learning process. The term *non-scholastic* refers to workplace learning as a situated and apprenticeship-like way of organizing the learning process[2].

The "Pragmatic Turn" in Education

In order to fully understand 'the pragmatic turn' one has to consider the postmodern shift in the status of knowledge. According to the French philosopher Jean-Francois Lyotard, knowledge in the postmodern society is no longer produced for its truth value, but for its use value. In a flexible global knowledge economy, knowledge is transformed into a commodity and the educational ideal of cultivating 'Bildung' is replaced by the ideal of developing competences (Lyotard, 1984). The educational focus on competence indicates that goals for learning are directed towards practical life. The learning goals are to provide individuals with the competences to deal with unforeseen problems in new situations in a rapidly changing 'knowledge society'. According to 'The European Commission', traditional school knowledge can no longer meet the unpredicted demands of the 'knowledge society'. Learning in the 'knowledge society' has to take place in a life-wide and lifelong perspective both at the workplace, in daily life and in a flexible educational system. (The European Commission, 2000; 2001).

The 'pragmatic turn' in education is influenced both in school and in the field of practice by the new alliance between progressive educational ideas and management theory. For instance, the concept of competence has brought into the field of education from Human Management theory. Furthermore, John Dewey's progressive educational theories, directed towards school, have been brought into professional and organizational learning, partly via Argyris & Schön (1983 & 1996). Dewey claims that reflection and thinking takes its starting point in the meeting of a new situation/problem, which calls for reflection. This understanding fits well into today's understanding of competence as an ability to react to different (often new) practical situations through reflection (Dewey, 1991). The European Commission favors progressive educational ideas in the educational program of lifelong learning. The program recommends anti-authoritarian and self-directed methods of learning, and prefers project-oriented interdisciplinary teaching where teachers are transformed into coaches and classroom teaching into individualized mentoring (European Commission 2001).

As schools tend to monopolize all educational areas, including areas that are concerned with practical and professional education, scholastic scholars are inclined to overlook the fact that learning in practice differs radically from learning in school. Thus school tends to meet the new educational utility demands inside the logical framework of schools. The quality of the field of practice and practical learning is thus ignored. The following two strategies are seen most often in contemporary education:

1. *Longer and more academic school education, also in the field of professional education.* This strategy rests upon the assumption that general and de-contextual school knowledge can be readily transformed into practical knowledge in a practical situation. In this context school knowledge is understood as theoretical knowledge. Implicit in this understanding is that the term 'theory' attaches itself to scientific knowledge, and the term 'practice' attaches itself to individual actions. The knowledge acted on is thus understood as synonymous with applied scientific knowledge, and actions in practice are understood as rule-based, verbalized activities.

2. *To bring the school curriculum and school methods into harmony with practical life.* In this strategy the gap between school and life is regarded as a didactical and methodological problem. Attempts to narrow school and life have been inspired by the progressive educational ideas of John Dewey (Dewey, 1956) and others. According to John Dewey, a school's methods should be organized in consistence with 'methods of life' such as experience-based and inter-curricular learning methods, 'learning by doing', 'trial and error', and problem-based learning (Dewey, 1984). When learning in the classroom is believed to substitute for learning in practice, the particular qualities of the field of practice is ignored.

In contemporary workplace learning there is also a strong tendency to ignore the qualities of practical knowledge and learning in practice. Efforts to facilitate workplace learning in a lifelong and life-wide perspective tend

c) *Knowledge is categorized by its activity form, which is how knowledge is unfolded.*
Knowledge expressed on print detaches knowledge from person and situation so the relation between knowledge and how it is unfolded tends to be overlooked in a culture of literacy. However, when dealing with differences between areas of knowledge, Aristotle frequently states that the different categories of knowledge unfold in different ways that involve different activity forms. The activity form of theoretical knowledge, *theoria*, is to observe the world from God's angle without being involved in that which is being observed. Theoria is therefore a contemplative, analytical and understanding activity. The two practical activity forms are both participatory. According to Aristotle, participation takes place in two different ways. *Poiesis*, the activity form of techne, consists of producing and making. It is an instrumental activity because it aims at a product or a result outside the activity, *Praxis*, the activity form of phronesis, consists of good and just actions. It is a non-instrumental activity because its aim is the perfection of the action itself.

An overview of Aristotle's categorization of knowledge:

AREA	KNOWLEDGE	ACTIVITY FORM	PURPOSE
THEORETICAL	Episteme	Theoria: understand & contemplate	Insight into cosmos
PRACTICAL	Techne	Poiesis: produce & make	A better material life
	Phronesis	Praxis; good and just actions	A better social-ethical society

The paradigmatic differences between the theoretical and practical knowledge forms can be illustrated by replacing theoretical knowledge by the term *spectator knowledge* and practical knowledge by the term *participant knowledge*. The terms catch the quality, the purpose and the activity form of knowledge, and can thus illustrate how the different knowledge forms are learnt. By using the terms it becomes evident that we are concerned with two different forms of knowledge, which are not automatically interrelated and compatible.

The purpose of *spectator knowledge* is to see the world from outside without being involved. This knowledge is unfolded as a contemplative, cognitive and analytical activity that can neither guide action, nor be transferred directly into practice. The aim of spectator knowledge is to understand, illuminate, give reasons and explanations. The person dealing with spectator knowledge traces the general, the regular and the principal knowledge, and will only to a small degree capture the multiplicity, changeability and unpredictability of practice. *Participant knowledge* corresponds to the two practical knowledge forms, its purpose being to handle situations and problems in practical life. It is knowledge of how to participate in practical life according to practical life's shifting circumstances. It is unfolded as a 'coping skill' (techne) in relation to the practice one is undertaking and as an experience-based intuitive sense of occasion (phronesis). As participant knowledge deals with a field that could be otherwise, it can never become certain. It is a 'doxa' knowledge, which means that it is a casuistic, experience-based knowledge of the possible and the probable.

Aristotle on Learning

Aristotle understands learning as a situated activity in the sense that one learns by doing what one has to learn in the manner and the situation where the learning is to be used. This means that the different knowledge forms are learnt in different ways. For this reason it is crucial to find the optimal learning situation for each of the different categories of knowledge.

As spectator knowledge is de-contextual theoretical knowledge, so according to Aristotle it can be learned de-contextually. Consequently it is best learnt in school, which favors this kind of learning form. Aristotle states that achievement of insight into the theoretical area does not require life experience; accordingly, young people can learn it in the school's classroom. Young people can, for example, become good at mathematics; while a practical knowledge such as politics is unsuitable for young people without life experience (E.N. VI. Viii. p. 351).

School does not, however, develop professional identity and a sense of situation. It does not give pupils the necessary experience with practical situations, so they can judge when and how their school knowledge can be applied. Neither in law, medicine or other professions does one become an expert by studying textbooks unless one has gained practical experience.

Very possibly therefore, collections of laws and constitutions may be serviceable to students capable of studying them critically, and judging what measures are valuable or the reverse, and what kind of institutions are suited to what national characteristics. But those who pursue such compilations without possessing a trained faculty cannot be capable of judging them correctly. We do not see men become expert physicians from a study of medical handbooks. (N.E. X. ix. 20-21, pp. 641-643).

Participant knowledge is knowledge of how to participate in practical life, so it has to be learnt in practical life. In the *Nicomachean Ethics* Aristotle continuously states that aspects concerning practical life are best learnt in practical life. We learn best by doing what we are to learn in the situation where it is to be applied.

We learn an art or craft by doing the things that we shall have to do when we learn it, for instance men become builders by building houses, harpers by playing on the harp. Similarly we become just by doing just acts, temperate by doing temperate acts, brave by doing brave acts. (N.E. II. i. p.73).

Aristotle points out how important it is to have the right habitual attitude towards what one is learning. He talks about cultivating the right habits, or in Greek *hexis*. '*Again, theory and teaching are not, I fear, equally efficacious in all cases: the soil must have been previously tilled if it is to foster the seed, the mind of the pupil must have been prepared by cultivation of habits, so as to like and dislike aright.*' (N.E. X, ix, 6-7, p. 631). The fostering of the right attitude takes place by participation in real-life situations and is cultivated through fruitful experience and good role models. The habitual attitude goes beyond skill acquisition, as learning also involves socialization. And this takes time as one has to grow together with or absorb the knowledge one learns. ... *for knowledge has to become part of the tissue of the mind, and this takes time.* (N.E. VII, iii, 8, p. 391).

What we learn from Aristotle is that the school does not develop professional identity and a sense of situation. According to Aristotle, the practical field consists neither of isolated activities of the individual nor of the ritualized, bureaucratized and institutionalized activities based on general maxims and rules. Learning in practice is more than practical learning, such as learning with a practical element and/or learning in isolated practical situations inside or outside school. Learning in practice is also more than the so-called 'learning by doing', competence development or *ad hoc* learning at work in various teams or individually. Unless one has experience of particular situations, general school knowledge is of little use.

However, according to Aristotle experience is not identical with practical knowledge. What separates pure experience from practical knowledge is that an experienced person only has knowledge of particular conditions, but does not have knowledge of general laws and principle. Practical knowledge involves knowledge of both the general and the particular and knowledge about how to combine them. Therefore general knowledge, which is learned in school, is not irrelevant to the practical domain. But the changeability of practical life means that one can never foresee which general school knowledge should be implemented in a given practical situation. This has to be decided according to each situation on the basis of experience of similar situations.

The Scholastic Paradigm Seen through an Aristotelian Lens

When comparing the characteristics of spectator knowledge and school knowledge, attention is drawn to some striking similarities. The most important similarity is that both school knowledge and spectator knowledge are detached from the practical world, and thus neither is 'disturbed' by the necessities of practical life. This gives freedom to make speculative plans, formulate hypothesis, follow utopian ideas and imagine conditions differently – without being concerned by the utility use of the activities in practical life.

The freedom of schools is essential to understanding some main characteristics of the landscape of learning as constituted by school itself. The original meaning of *school*, in classical Greek, was actually 'leisure', 'free from work'. This indicates that one of the characteristics of a school, perceived as a general institution, is its 'freedom'. A school's freedom is seen in the fact that learning in school is not bound by the same conditions as learning in practical life. The written medium gives school its freedom to be located anywhere and to be open to anybody – because it is bound by neither time nor place. A school's 'freedom' is thus not only attached to the fact that it can constitute a work-free room; its 'freedom' also entails that it is not built upon a demand that what is learned has to be applied directly. A school can thus freely construct its own learning landscape, which I will henceforth refer to as a school's virtual landscape of learning.

Since a school's learning landscape is not determined by the 'necessity' of practice, it has, ideally, the freedom to determine the aims, content and form of learning, and to organize learning with regard to didactical principles. A school can choose methods of evaluation that suit the school's curriculum, and it can choose a curriculum that suits the school's aspirations for learning. In a school's virtual landscape of learning, pupils are shielded against the chaos and inflexible demands of 'reality'. In contrast to learning in practice, schools have the freedom to discard complex and confusing aspects and simplify a subject area by dividing it into topics and sub-topics. The didactical organization of the learning process typically moves from the simple to the complex, and from part to entirety. Because all of a school's learning takes place in a protected room, the pupils are given the opportunity of both practicing without practical consequences and also training themselves in isolated sub-elements whilst following a pedagogically planned progression.

A school is furthermore effective inasmuch as it can teach many pupils simultaneously by organizing teaching around classes with pupils of the same age who are ideally at the same stage with regard to both maturity and ability. Additionally, it can educate teachers and can develop a syllabus directed towards various target audiences, whilst still respecting the target audience's needs in relation to educational progression and learning tempo. With this, a school has the opportunity to standardize education by demanding the same from all learners in a particular field, and by shaping them in relation to the same didactical principles.

School's virtual learning landscape leads to a tendency for school to turn inwards upon itself. As there is no immediate demand that school knowledge has to be converted into practice, this invites the focus to be turned toward general forms of knowledge and toward planning the subject matter de-contextually. The forms of learning that are primarily applied in contemporary school also harmonize with literacy's conceptual thinking. Focus is put on the cognitive, verbal and textual forms of learning with particular emphasis on reflection and introspection. These are all forms of learning which are suited to the architecture of the classroom, and also to schools' de-contextual presentations of knowledge. Even when learning is connected to practical subjects or practical situations, forms of reflective and self-reflective learning often dominate. Moreover, such learning situations may be decomposed and reorganized in tune with the school's dominant rationality.

School's virtual landscape of learning is signified by a didactical rationality, such as:

- Full control of the learning process.
- Breaking up the learning process into small pieces.
- Learning in age-divided groups.
- Predominantly textually learning with opportunity for reflective distance.
- Aims of learning formulated in general preparations for the future.
- A protected learning room.
- A standardized, bureaucratically organized education.
- Evaluation according to the school's own standard.

The Non-scholastic Paradigm Seen through an Aristotelian Lens

According to Aristotle, practical knowledge is unfolded in practical life and is learnt by participation in practical life. The Aristotelian understanding of learning in the field of practice is largely in tune with non-scholastic understanding. The benchmark of non-scholastic learning theories is that professional learning should preferably take place in the same environment in which the learning is to be implemented. Non-scholastic learning is a situated and apprenticeship-like way of organizing and understanding the learning process in the field of practice or the practical landscape of learning (Nielsen & Kvale, 2006).

The term 'situated learning' indicates that learning is more than 'learning by doing' because 'learning is an integral and inseparable aspect of social practice' (Lave & Wenger, 1991, p. 31). According to Jean Lave, there is actually no such thing as de-contextual social practice, neither is learning an isolated and individualized activity (Chaiklin & Lave, 1993, p. 22). The community of practice is understood as a social unity with common goals. The learner goes from legitimate peripheral participation to full participation in the community of practice, and the participants are responsible for a joint aim or product (Lave & Wenger, 1997). Learning and activities in practice are closely connected, and learning is understood as changing positions in a changing social practice. Actually *'learning is a way of being in the social world, not a way of coming to know about it.'* (W. Hanks in foreword p. 24, Lave & Wenger, 1991).

Learning involves the whole person and consists of both a process of skill acquisition and socialization into a professional identity, as a doctor, teacher, carpenter etc. In accordance with Aristotle's understanding, advocates of situated learning hold that socialization also entails an active learning process. This understanding contrasts with scholastic learning theory, as scholastic educators often perceive learning and socialization as two different processes with socialization mostly being understood as forms of habitual, silent and bodily-anchored habits and dispositions. The process of socialization is generally perceived as an unconscious influence/imitation process (see e.g. Bourdieu's theories on *habitus*, 1977). According to situated learning theories, learning is understood as changing positions in a changing social practice.

It is important for non-scholastic scholars to emphasize that the learning landscape of practice contains some advantages, as compared to learning in school. In learning in practice the method and content of learning are mainly decided by context and subject matter. The coupling of learning and application causes learning to become more distinct and evident. Nielsen and Kvale point out that the learning landscape of practice facilitates learning by a variation of learning options, by continuous feedback, by imitation and corrections and by visible goals. Learning takes place in mixed age groups. Being in a community of practice gives the learners' continuous opportunities to evaluate the learning process and compare themselves with more experienced members of the community. Furthermore, the learning landscape of practice provides the opportunity for individual learning styles, as it allows room for experience, observation, learning by doing, caching, and for those reproductive learning elements like imitation and practicing that are overlooked and downgraded in contemporary pedagogy (Nielsen & Kvale, 1997; 1999).

The non-scholastic landscape of learning is signified by a 'practical rationality', such as:

- Authentic learning situations.
- Learning through a joint production in a community of practice.
- Coupling of learning and application.
- Coupling of skill learning and professional identity.
- Learning in mixed groups with many learning models.
- Learning in the individual's learning style and learning tempo.
- Distinct and evident aims of learning.
- Continuous evaluation.

Conclusion: Give to School What Belongs to School and to Practice What Belongs to Practice

In conclusion, it should be emphasized that with the Aristotelian understanding of the differences between theoretical knowledge and practical knowledge we are confronted with one of Aristotle's most important contributions to the educational field. The strength in Aristotle's position is that by linking knowledge and learning he creates a broader and subtler view of learning than both advocates of the scholastic paradigm and its non-scholastic counterpart represent. One of his points is precisely that some forms of knowledge are acquired in practical life, while other knowledge forms are acquired in school through the use of analytical and systematic principles of learning.

Efforts to narrow school and life too often neglect the fact that learning in school and learning in life are two different modes of learning. From an Aristotelian perspective it becomes clear that the school-life problem actually stems from the fact that school cannot encounter the learning forms of practical knowledge. With reference to school's virtual landscape of learning it is obvious that the gap between school and life cannot be overcome by more schooling, new methods, or by narrowing school's curriculum to practical life. What is open to criticism, therefore, is not that pupils learn general, decontextual school knowledge in the classroom, but the belief that this type of learning can replace learning in practice.

Furthermore, what we learn from Aristotle is that one should not expect the general, de-situated and de-contextual knowledge that is favored by schools to be of automatic and direct utility. This is because it is not always known beforehand which general knowledge would be useful in a particular practical situation. The sense of situation, which is inherent in the term *phronesis*, is precisely an ability to judge which general knowledge, which rules and methods have to be transferred into a particular practical situation. This ability is not learned in the classroom, but has to be learned through practical situations.

Learning *in* and *for* practice therefore requires experience of practical situations. So training does not merely concern itself with becoming better at *following* rules and principles, but concerns itself with becoming better at *finding* rules and principles and considering which are relevant in a specific situation. This is not learnt by reflection, as the Dewey-inspired scholastic ideas maintain, or by 'learning by doing' in the classroom, but by experiences of similar practical situations. Nor is it learnt in unstable, individualized ad hoc learning according to the shifting demands of the field of practice, but by cultivating the learning possibilities of the practical landscape of learning.

School knowledge is a spectator knowledge that does not accompany actions but, on the contrary, a knowledge which indicates the space and conditions of actions. One cannot be a spectator and a participant at the same time. The *theoretician's* spectator view has traces of regularity, the general and the principal. So it will capture the multiplicity, changeability and unpredictability of the field of practice to a small degree. The *practitioner's* participant view, on the other hand, seeks not the general and scientific regularity of the field of theory, but knowledge from which to act. Participant knowledge is useful in solving practical problems. Spectator knowledge is useful in anticipating and avoiding problems.

General school knowledge and practical knowledge are prerequisites for each other, insofar as the worthy practitioner must know the possibilities and limitations of action's parameters in order to be successful within them. If practical knowledge is not taken seriously as knowledge with its own qualities, then the learning and structuring of the practical-educational field will become either incidental as in competence-based learning, or inflexible as within scholastic structures. If school knowledge is not taken seriously, under the influence of the pragmatic turn we might enter the *knowledge society* risking leaving general theoretical knowledge behind. This is because knowledge is more than a commodity with utility in the form of competence.

The current demands that a school's task is to create a close connection between school and life may, in the name of progressive pedagogy, lead to a school relinquishing its most important sources of knowledge, namely the pedagogically trained teacher, the protected learning room and the pedagogically organized syllabus. The current ideals of organizational workplace learning may, on the other hand, lead to individual *ad hoc* learning without clear goals and community support. Therefore, I find it important to discuss how both theoretical knowledge and practical knowledge separately can be cultivated in educational life. Only by doing this can schools be given what belongs to schools and practice what belongs to practice.

Tone Saugstad, Department of Media, Cognition and Communication. Division of Education. University of Copenhagen, Njalsgade 80, DK-2399 Copenhagen (tsg@hum.ku.dk)

NOTES

1 In the following my references to Aristotle are primarily from *The Nicomachean Ethics (N.E.)*.

2 When I refer to non-scholastic scholars I primarily refer to the founders of the non-scholastic network, Jean Lave, Hubert Dreyfus, Steinar Kvale, Steen Wackerhausen, Ole Dreier and Klaus Nielsen. In spite of differences between their positions, they are all spokesmen of non-schlolastic learning in the form of apprenticeship and situated learning.

3 I have chosen to use the Greek terms because translation cannot successfully convey the correct meaning.

Hubert L. Dreyfus and Stuart E. Dreyfus

BEYOND EXPERTISE: SOME PRELIMINARY THOUGHTS ON MASTERY[1]

Mastery, the sixth stage in the acquisition of skill by means of instruction followed by experience, is achieved by only a small fraction of the thousands, or in certain domains millions, of individuals who are domain experts. To explain why, it is necessary first to review the five stages leading from novice to expert that we have previously identified. In doing this, we have introduced a subtle, but important, rethinking and rewording of what might be called one's "intuitive perspective" as it enters our account at stage four, proficiency. Mastery, it then turns out, is available only to strongly motivated experts who not only have exceptional natural talent but who are also willing and able continually to enlarge the number of intuitive perspectives and actions that, with experience, come naturally and effortlessly to them.

Stage 1: Novice

Normally, the instruction process begins with the instructor decomposing the task environment into context-free features that the beginner can recognize without the desired skill. The beginner is then given rules for determining actions on the basis of these features, like a computer following a program.

The student automobile driver learns to recognize such domain-independent features as speed (indicated by the speedometer), and is given rules such as shift to second when the speedometer needle points to ten. The novice chess player learns a numerical value for each type of piece regardless of its position, and the rule: "Always exchange if the total value of pieces captured exceeds the value of pieces lost." The player also learns to seek center control when no advantageous exchanges can be found, and is given a rule defining center squares and one for calculating extent of control.

But merely following rules will produce poor performance in the real world. A car stalls if one shifts too soon on a hill or when the car is heavily loaded; a chess player who always exchanges to gain points is sure to be the victim of a sacrifice by the opponent who gives up valuable pieces to gain a tactical advantage. The student needs not only the facts but also an understanding of the context in which that information makes sense.

Stage 2: Advanced Beginner

As the novice gains experience of actually coping with real situations and begins to develop an understanding of the relevant context, he or she begins to note, or an instructor points out, perspicuous examples of meaningful additional aspects of the situation or domain. After seeing a sufficient number of examples, the student learns to recognize these new aspects. Instructional *maxims* can then refer to these new situational *aspects*, recognized on the basis of experience, as well as to the objectively defined non-situational *features* recognizable by the novice.

The advanced beginner driver uses (situational) engine sounds as well as (non-situational) speed in deciding when to shift. He learns the maxim: Shift up when the motor sounds like it's racing and down when it sounds like it's straining. Engine sounds cannot be adequately captured by a list of features, so features cannot take the place of a few choice examples in learning the relevant distinctions.

With experience, the chess beginner learns to recognize overextended positions and how to avoid them. Similarly, she begins to recognize such situational aspects of positions as a weakened king's side or a strong pawn structure, despite the lack of precise and situation-free definitions. The player can then follow maxims such as: attack a weakened king's side. Unlike a rule, a maxim requires that one already has some understanding of the domain to which the maxim applies. Still, at this stage, learning can be carried on in a detached, analytic frame of mind, as the student follows instructions and is given examples.

Stage 3: Competence

With more experience, the number of potentially relevant elements and procedures that the learner is able to recognize and follow becomes overwhelming. At this point, since a sense of what is important in any particular situation is missing, performance becomes nerve-wracking and exhausting, and the student might well wonder how anybody ever masters the skill.

To cope with this overload and to achieve competence, people learn, through instruction or experience, to devise a plan, or choose a *perspective*, that then determines which elements of the situation or domain must be treated as important and which ones can be ignored. As students learn to restrict themselves to only a few of the vast number of possibly relevant features and aspects, understanding and decision making becomes easier.

Naturally, to avoid mistakes, the competent performer seeks rules and reasoning procedures to decide which plan or perspective to adopt. But such rules are not as easy to come by as are the rules and maxims given to beginners in manuals and lectures. Indeed, in any skill domain the performer encounters a vast number of situations differing from each other in subtle ways. There are, in fact, more situations than can be named or precisely defined, so no-one can prepare for the learner a list of types of possible situations and what to do or look for in each. Students, therefore, must decide for themselves in each situation what plan or perspective to adopt without being sure that it will turn out to be appropriate.

Given this uncertainty, coping becomes frightening rather than merely exhausting. Prior to this stage, if the rules don't work, the performer, rather than feeling remorse for his mistakes, can rationalize that he hadn't been given adequate rules. But since at this stage the result depends on the learner's choice of perspective, the learner feels responsible for his or her choice. Often, the choice leads to confusion and failure. But sometimes things work out well, and the competent student then experiences a kind of elation unknown to the beginner.

A competent driver, leaving the freeway on an off-ramp curve, learns to pay attention to the speed of the car, not whether to shift gears. After taking into account speed, surface condition, criticality of time, etc., he may decide he is going too fast. He then has to decide whether to let up on the accelerator, remove his foot altogether, or step on the brake, and precisely may simply lift off the accelerator and apply the appropriate pressure to the brake. What must be done, simply is done.

The chess grandmaster experiences a compelling intuitive perspective and a sense of the best move. Excellent chess players can play at the rate of 5 to 10 seconds a move and even faster without any serious decline in performance. At this speed they must depend almost entirely on intuition and hardly at all on analysis and comparison of alternatives. It has been estimated that an expert chess player can distinguish roughly 100,000 types of positions. For expert performance in other domains, the number of intuitive perspectives with associated actions, built up on the basis of experience, must be comparably large.

The skill model is summarized in the table below:

TABLE 1: FIVE STAGES OF SKILL ACQUISITION

SKILL LEVEL	COMPONENTS	PERSPECTIVE	ACTION	COMMITMENT
1. Novice	Context-free	None	Analytic	Detached
2. Advanced beginner	Context-free and situational	None	Analytic	Detached
3. Competent	Context-free and situational	Chosen	Analytic	Detached choice of saliences and of action. Involved in outcome
4. Proficient	Context-free and situational	Experienced	Analytic	Involved experience of saliences. Detached choice of action
5. Expert	Context-free and situational	Experienced	Intuitive	Involved

The expert generally acts in an environment requiring a sequence of actions, each one affecting the stimuli subsequently received from the environment by the body's sense organs. What constitutes an action in this context depends on the skill domain. Examples include an athlete's motor reactions, a writer's linguistic constructions, a chess player's move, and a craftsman's choice of material. The stimuli are directly experienced from a perspective, meaning the stimuli present themselves with various saliencies; some are crucial to action determination, some play a minor role, and others may be irrelevant. The current stimuli seen from a perspective, the past history of received stimuli as the sequential task is being performed, the influence of behaviors that have proven rewarding during past similar experiences, and the internal state of the organism's arousal and needs lead to an expert action.

The expert's brain has also learned under what circumstances during a sequence of actions to change perspective, and what the new saliencies should be. For example, an expert nurse will intuitively know if, or when, to reassess patient's situation during intensive care, and what to do if a reassessment presents new salient stimuli. For the expert athlete, chess player, musician, nurse, animal pursuing prey etc., after a great deal of learning all of this is accomplished in a way that usually leads to rewarding behavior without the need for any detached, effortful, time-consuming deliberation about perspective or action.

Obviously, an animal, incapable of deliberation, can, nevertheless, learn not only how to intercept a running prey, but also when to switch to the perspective required for blocking an escape route in circumstances when that is a better strategy. The animal does not "change its goal" since it is incapable of thinking "block its escape." It merely responds, on the basis of past experience, to new stimuli or saliencies which might include a tree that the prey might climb. It should come as no surprise that people can do likewise in their skill domain without deliberation and without thinking that they should change their goal. For example, if a fly ball is hit in his general direction, an expert baseball outfielder will initially see as salient the angle of ascent of the ball, perhaps the location of nearby fielders and maybe the location of the sun if he has learned to take account of this so as to move in a way that avoids looking directly at it. If the fly ball is well hit by a strong batter, the location of the ball as it goes over his head, the location of the likelihood that, when in a similar situation in the future, the newly established perspective and action will recur without conscious effort, and what might be called "enhanced expertise" results. The strongly motivated aspiring master will generally replay the memory of the rewarding experience many times and do so with the same emotional involvement as accompanied it in the first place. This will help solidify the perspective and behavior in the learner's repertoire.

A related alternative road to mastery presents itself to experts whose skill demands that they must sometimes respond to novel situations without time for deliberation. Such an expert, if motivated to excel, will not only assess the situation spontaneously and respond immediately, but also experience elation if the assessment and response is successful and dissatisfaction if it seems to him disappointing. But, unlike ordinary satisfied experts, if the developing master is dedicated to his profession and if time permits, he will recall and savor successes. Alternatively, in case of dissatisfaction there seem to be two possible ways to respond. He may *deliberate* about what should have been done and make a rule to do things a different way if a similar situation arises in the future. He then risks the temporary regression to competence that comes with resisting an intuitive response, but this new way of acting will, hopefully, become intuitive with more experience. Or, rather than analyzing what went wrong and making a rule for avoiding the mistake in the future, he may just dwell on the past events, feeling bad about what happened when things went wrong and feeling good when recalling the times they went well. Then simple pleasure and pain conditioning will rewire his neurons in a way that will lead him to repeat the successful types of performance and prevent him from acting in the unsatisfactory way in the future. In either case, the new behavior will become part of the master's ever-growing intuitive repertoire, activated immediately if a similar situation occurs in the future.

For example, a masterful professional basketball player known for his exceptional ability to pass the ball appropriately to a teammate in a better position to score will have undoubtedly done this many times during practice when honing this skill. He will be dedicated to his chosen sport, and will have savored successes during practice and played them over in his mind after the session. A dedicated musician, after acquiring expert technique, will often apprentice herself to a series of masters with their own differing styles, in the hope of developing, through imitation and advice, a style of her own that differs from that of any one teacher. This will establish her as a master in her own right. A dedicated craftsperson will try unusual combinations of materials, some of which will be successful and some not, in the process of learning just naturally to use the right materials to create masterpieces. An expert nurse, seeking to develop into a master because of her dedication to caregiving, cannot rely on improvement by trial and error but will notice situations in which she did the conventional thing and wished after an undesirable outcome that she had done things differently. By dwelling on that situation and imagining with emotional involvement what she might have noticed and then done and how it might have turned out better, she will respond differently and perhaps masterfully in similar situations in the future. Expert professors and lawyers, skilled in a profession that sometimes requires spontaneous responses, have available, if sufficiently dedicated, both the deliberative and the alternative, non-reflective road to mastery that can be used when time permits after the event.

To sum up, when an *expert* learns, she must either create a new perspective in a situation when a learned perspective has failed, or improve the action guided by a particular intuitive perspective when the intuitive action proves inadequate. A *master* will not only continue to do this, but will also, in situations where she is already capable of what is considered adequate expert performance, be open to a new intuitive perspective and accompanying action that will lead to performance that exceeds conventional expertise. Thus, the brain of the master doesn't use any different operational principles while performing at a higher level of skill than that of the expert. Rather, thanks to exceptional motivation due to their dedication to their chosen profession, the ability to savor and dwell on successes, and a willingness to persevere despite the risk of regression during learning, the master's brain comes to instantiate significantly more available perspectives with accompanying actions than the brain of an expert. Thanks to practice, these perspectives are invoked when they are appropriate, and the master's performance rises to a level above that of the ordinary expert.

NOTES

1   Stuart Dreyfus's contribution to the discussion of mastery resulted from the generous financial support provided by Statoil ASA, through its Project Academy and its Project Executive Program at the University of California, Berkeley, facilitated through the Institute of Industrial Relations. He also thanks Professor Liv Duesund for her support through the project

Kenneth and Mary Gergen

KNOWLEDGE AS RELATIONSHIP: EDUCATION IN A GLOBAL CONTEXT

The work of Steinar Kvale has long functioned as a provocative challenge to cozy conventions. Whether writing about methods of research, ideology, dialogue, phenomenology, or postmodernism, there is invariably an edge to Kvale's writing that slices through the barriers of common understanding and asks us to reconsider. In the present case we wish to extend the implications of but one of Kvale's catalytic proposals, namely that "the conversation may be conceived of as a *basic mode* of knowing." (Kvale, 1996) On this account, it is not the esteemed traditions of observation, reason, or systematic method that seem, on this account, to stimulate the flourishing of knowledge, but lowly conversation. Does this provocation not place in jeopardy the twin stars of the Enlightenment, both *knowledge* and *education?* As we are led to understand, by knowledge we are set free from religious dogmas to pursue a future of ever lasting progress, and by education we ensure the fruits of progress for future generations. As products of the Enlightenment, these particular concepts of knowledge and education are also wedded to the presumption of truth, not through conversation, but through observation and rational thinking. We are supplied with a vision of a discerning agent – possibly a Copernicus or a Newton – who observes and thinks about the world, who tests his thoughts against ever more careful observations, and ultimately approaches what we presume to be a state of objective knowledge. When others can assent to these proposals through their independent assays, we establish what we commonly take to be an approximation to universal and trans-historical truth. Education, on this account, should be devoted to implanting such grounded knowledge in the minds of the ignorant. With knowledge of the world now "in mind", the individual is equipped for more adaptive or effective action in the world.

Why should we attend, then, to mere conversation as a font of knowledge? We begin to sense the possibility in the fact that the separation of mind and world, invited by the Enlightenment tradition, has never rested easy within philosophical circles. Do the features of the world drive or determine states of mind, it is asked, or is it the reverse, or some combination of the two? How could we search for an answer without making one or another of these assumptions in order to place the search in motion? How can the material world have causal effects on the psychological world, or vice versa? How can a mental event, such as thought, affect a physical action? Despite the fact that such riddles have occupied philosophers for centuries, they remain unsolved. Many now hold that they are insoluble, primarily because of the very premises with which one begins. What, then, is a mind that it should reflect or register the world, and what is it to educate the mind? Let us bracket these philosophical conundrums, and challenge these assumptions in another way. We propose that these assumptions about knowledge and education contribute to division and conflict in the world today. The emphasis on conversation, or the collective generation of meaning, represents a significant and far-reaching alternative. In what follows we shall first sketch out our rationale for this critique of tradition. We shall then offer an alternative view of knowledge, closely allied with Kvale's provocative proposal. Finally, we shall consider several implications for educational policy and practice.

Conditions of Conflict

Conflict has always been a fixture in the landscape of human relationships. History books count the major conflicts of the past century in terms of what we call the World Wars. In the United States, we also have names for lesser wars, such as the Korean war, the Vietnam war, and the first and second Iraq wars. While highly destructive in their enactment and consequences, a certain simplicity prevailed in this catalogue of conflicts. In these cases we are able to identify when the conflicts began, what side we were on, and when they were terminated. But the landscape of human relationships and the potential for violence is quite something else, more complex, more universal, and more omnipresent than ever before. In the last two decades, especially, technologies have enabled millions of people to move rapidly from one locale to another, and to circulate statements of value and belief rapidly to all corners of the world; militant organizations spring quickly to life, and weapons can be secured with ease. And where conventional weapons of warfare cannot be obtained, there is no end to the creative ways in which destruction can be wrought across the land. In effect, lethal conflict is everywhere possible; every stranger is a potential enemy, and terrorism threatens to be a permanent fixture in human affairs.

What does all this have to do with education? Must we as educators do anything more than keep a watchful eye and continue teaching the verities? Or do we hope that lessons in geography, comparative religion, civic process and the like will somehow liberate our fledglings from the dogmas of the past, and enable them to deal more effectively with differences that seem so threatening? We don't wish to detract from watchful care or liberalizing curricula; these should surely remain in place. However, we confront perilous times, and whether our educational systems are adequate to them is a major question. To press the dialogue forward on these important matters, we wish to offer a radical proposal. We believe that in important respects the assumptions underlying the vast share of our educational practices contribute not to the diminution of conflict, but to its sustenance.

Why is this so? Much has been said about the way in which our curricula present a Euro-centered view of culture, geography, history, and religion. In such accounts non-Europeans are often constructed as exotic others, or as non-existent altogether. However, our concern here is not so much with the particular content of our courses. Rather, it is with the assumptions that we bring to our teaching – both in terms of content and practice – that we find unsettling. Consider some of the ideals that guide our enterprise: truth, objectivity, and rational thought. Do we not wish all our curricula to embody such ideals? And do we not generate pedagogical practices that attempt to install such ideals within the "minds and hearts" of our youth? We suspect that politically we also believe that should these ideals prevail, lethal conflict would slowly disappear. Objective truth would replace the interminable conflict of ideologies.

But let us consider the possibility that it is just such ideals – truth, objectivity, and reason – that stand as impediments to a more peaceful world. We say this largely because the way in which we have conceived of these ideals is

essentially culture free. We hold these ideals to be culturally transcendent –
to be embraced by all peoples. For example, we presume the importance of
"seeking the truth," and with careful empirical study "finding" "or "revealing" it. Truth precedes us; it precedes all cultures. The challenge is to discover
it. Thus, for example, we assume that guided by reason and observation, we
set out to learn the shape of the earth, and we found that it approximates a
sphere. We say that it is true that the earth is spherical, regardless of one's
culture or history. In the same way we hold that the truth is objective; if we
could all approach the earth without mental or ideological impediments, we
would all agree that it is round. This is an objective fact, and not a subjective
judgment. And too, we believe that there are logical truths, such as induction
and deduction – or the truths of mathematics – that transcend one's culture
and history. The theorems of geometry are true regardless of time or culture.
An effective education is one that will sustain these ideals against the tides
of fashion, collective stupidity, and totalitarianism.

But now consider: when we embrace these various ideals in our curricula
and pedagogical practices we begin to draw lines. These are lines that separate
the good from the bad. On the good side of the line fall truth, objectivity,
and reason; on the other side of the line dwells the darkness. We prepare
our curricula so that they celebrate what is on the side of the good. We do
not open discussion on the wrong side of the line, except to condemn it as
myth, bad thinking, or immorality. Should our students stray into the dark,
we are quick to correct them. If they cannot master what is on the side of the
good, we prevent their advancement in our systems of education. In effect,
the ideals that propel the engine of education are not ultimately liberating.
Rather, they sustain a particular way of life, and foster barriers of ignorance
and intolerance for that which is beyond.

Cultures of Verity

Terms such as "truth," "objectivity", and "rationality" are powerful rhetorical
devices. To make such claims about one's activities is to occupy the cultural
high ground. And it is on the basis of just such claims that many of the major
power struggles have taken place in Western culture. In their claims to truth,
objectivity, and rationality, the sciences have increasingly undermined the

authority of the church in societal affairs. And on just these grounds, public education in the United States is now largely secular as opposed to sacred in orientation. Religious institutions continue to occupy the high ground in terms of moral authority. However, as secularists have largely countered, morality has no rational foundations and is ultimately subjective.

For many readers the historical drift of the past several centuries may feel "just right." After all, we have observable facts to support claims to truth, objectivity and rationality. Statements about people's souls, or about what is just or morally right, have no basis in fact. They are mere opinions. Yet, for some readers, the matter becomes a little less clear when we turn to the struggles for power in our educational institutions. For here we find that certain fields of study are said to be less objective and rational than others. Physics, chemistry, and mathematics, for example, are given high marks, while the sciences of sociology, psychology, and education are often said to be "fuzzy," "empirically ungrounded," or "methodologically weak." Government grants, faculty positions and new buildings go to the natural sciences, while dwindling faculties in the classics, philosophy, and literature are often relegated to old and decrepit quarters. Truth again triumphs over subjectivism.

Within recent decades a slow but dramatic sea change has taken place in the academic world. An increasingly intense and sophisticated cadre of scholars has succeeded in placing truth in trouble. Perhaps the most important source of these catalytic dialogues can be found in the history of science. How, it was asked, can we account for advancements in knowledge over the centuries? Here Thomas Kuhn's famous book, *The Structure of Scientific Revolutions*, (1970) advanced an argument of reverberating significance. As he proposed, scientific knowledge does not accumulate in the way we have traditionally presumed. Increasing amounts of research do not lead us ever closer to the ultimate truth. The movement from Aristotelian physics, to Newtonian physics, to quantum mechanics is not a movement from poor to superior knowledge. Rather, such movements represent shifts in our way of viewing the world. We do not know more and more, but with each movement we know differently.

It was Kuhn's work that brought into common usage the term, "paradigm." A paradigm roughly consists of a set of interlocking assumptions, logics, values, research methods, and instruments of study. Thus, the assumptions, logics, and research instruments of the Newtonian physicist were not inherently inferior to those of the quantum physicist. They were simply different. They allowed a different set of questions to be asked, and had different spheres of application than those of the quantum physicist. Such arguments stimulated scores of sociologists and anthropologists to study social life in the scientific laboratory. To them it became increasingly apparent that the sciences are composed of various small communities, tribes, or cultures – people in conversation. Each of these communities can be identified by its own particular paradigm. In this sense, the cultures of science are not unlike the cultures and religions of the earth more generally. Each speaks its own language and favors its own ways of life.

It is one thing to realize that different fields of knowledge construct the world in very different ways – that there is no royal road to the "truly true." However, there is an additional issue that demands attention. We often look at fields of knowledge as non-partisan. That is, while various religious groups have value agendas, or ideologies, as we often say, fields of knowledge are value neutral. Mathematics, history, and biology, we say, have no politics.

Yet, as scores of post-Kuhnian scholars have made clear, all fields of knowledge contain implicit values and ideals. There is no value neutral perspective. For example, most subjects taught in public schools lay special stress on logic and evidence. We teach our students that these are the important ingredients of effective decision making. Yet, this emphasis implicitly degrades values, desires and passions as significant contributors to our decisions. The fact that one can develop a scientific model for steadily increasing industrial profits, and all the evidence supports such a logic, does not make the decision "good" in any moral sense. Yet, it is this "moral sense" that is largely marginalized by the curriculum. In similar fashion, we now gain consciousness of the politics of history, the Eurocentrism of traditional geography, the gender biases in biology, the individualist ideologies in psychology, and so on. Every knowledge community functions like a small religion; every curriculum expands the power of its implicit beliefs and values.

These searching dialogues on the social construction of knowledge have enormously important implications for education. In the present context, they are rich resources for deliberating on the contribution of education to the future of world peace. Specifically, it is when local claims to truth, objectivity, and reason begin to masquerade as universal that we enter the domain of danger. It is when we celebrate these virtues in our educational curricula and practices that dark regions of "ignorance" "backwardness," and "closed mindedness" become realities. We seem to know this very well in terms of our perceptions of other peoples. We say, "why can't *they* see that theirs is only one way of thinking among many," or "*they* should understand that others have as much right to their beliefs as they do?" What is more difficult is to appreciate the ways in which many of our ideas about knowledge and our goals for education are specific to *our* traditions. As a parallel in the international sphere, we in the West have no difficulty in seeing that monarchies, oligarchies, and rule by arms are products of specific cultures. And we are quick to criticize them for their weaknesses. It is when we begin to pursue democracy as a universal good that we lay the groundwork for anguished bloodshed.

Toward Relationally Conscious Education

In what follows we wish to explore some implications of these arguments for our curricula and our pedagogical practices. Again, we offer these proposals with certain humility. However, they do come reinforced by a total of eight decades of teaching experience between us, and by a wide range of important developments in educational practice. At a minimum, they should open important vistas of dialogue.

Curriculum and Conflict

First we take up implications of these proposals for curriculum design. How would our curricula more effectively contribute to a world climate in which dialogue might prevail over destruction? We offer three proposals.

RELATIVIZING REALITIES. When we ask our students to read novels or poems we do so in hopes that they will discover insights, wisdom, or beauty upon which they may draw in future years. We do not offer these materials as true or objective. Each author or poet may have a point of view to share, and we are enriched by the multitude of viewpoints. And so it is that we might approach all subject matters, from biology and geography to history and mathematics. It is when we teach that there is an ultimate and objective truth in such matters that we set the stage for division.

To illustrate the possibilities, consider our lessons in geography, and specifically the use of maps to reveal the truth about the shape of the world. A typical map of the local region will reveal it to be flat, and will furnish an excellent indicator of the relative distance between various cities and towns. However, a globe will reveal the earth to be round, and will tell us that the shortest distance between two points is not a direct line between them. Yet, neither map will reveal the mountains and valleys, nor the depth of the ocean floor. And still further maps might replace the lines that separate nations with indicators of ethnic population densities, crop distributions, air quality, temperatures variations, and so on. Each map will create a different sense of the world, each for different purposes. There is no one true map, only maps with different possibilities.

In our college courses we typically confront students with the multiple realities created by psychological science. Engaging dialogues follow on how to select among perspectives, and whether we should ever be committed to a single viewpoint. Our professional colleagues are not wholly pleased with this form of teaching. We are told that young people need to develop a committed belief of some kind. Later, perhaps in graduate school, they can come to see that theirs is but one belief among many. Our critics also point to research on college students showing that the ability to think in these relativistic ways does not generally emerge until late in one's university career. And yet, we scarcely find our young students suffer as a result of confronting multiple perspectives. On the contrary. If students do indeed feel they are lost without a "truly true" to which they can cling, then we may look to their educational experiences in which singular truth has been celebrated. The fact that students may not develop a healthy appreciation of multiplicity until late in their educational career says less about their innate capacities than it does about the assumptions typically informing our curricula until that point.

CONFRONTING VALUES. Where have all the values gone? As educational systems have become progressively secularized, and objectivity and reason increasingly embraced, values have largely been lost from the curriculum. In the late 19th century teachers could justifiably be concerned with the moral character of their students. They could enthusiastically build lessons on the moral good into the curriculum. Yet, because issues of value are "fuzzy," and "subjective," they have largely been abandoned. Worst still, should any teacher build a slate of moral values into a curriculum, he or she might well be branded an ideologue. As widely believed, public education should be politically and ideologically neutral; matters of moral value are personal, and moral training is not the responsibility of the educational system.

While there is a certain wisdom in this posture, it is also lacking in two important respects. First it fails to take account of the implicit values that we inevitably import into our curricula.

As proposed earlier, all cultures of verity support certain ways of life and their attendant values. Thus, to teach about the evolution of the species is already to discard divine creation; to make simple distinctions between two genders is to set the stage for homophobia, and to teach about the nature of our government is to presume that the institution is normal and right. In spite of our denials, we inevitably teach values. This bears on the second shortcoming of our current curricula: the failure to recognize and to deliberate on our values. Full dialogues on what is good, worthwhile, and significant in life are left languishing.

We are not at all arguing for a return to religious or moral education. Rather, what we do see as important is a confrontation with values within our curricula. It is not enough, for example, to teach about how to maintain healthy bodies. We must also confront the hard questions of value, indeed the questions that thrust societies into conflict. For example, when does human life begin, is human life sacred, do embryos created in a petri dish constitute human life? To be sure, there may be no logically and empirically justified answers to such questions. Yet, facts and logic only contribute to a decision when values are already in place. An education that does not foster deep deliberation on values leaves its students fundamentally incapacitated. They enter the global scene of deep value conflicts without any resources for understanding, for flexible negotiation, and amalgamation – all ingredients for transcending conflict.

CULTIVATING AMBIGUITY. This quest for a single correct answer also furnishes one reason for the greater honor typically granted to the natural sciences over such subjects as literature, philosophy, or sociology. In the former, there are clear and singular answers to many questions, while the latter raise questions that yield no clear and compelling solutions. Yet, it is precisely this quest for clarity that must be softened in education for peace. It is often said that people have an innate need for clear and simple answers to their questions. We doubt this very much. Children do not demand such answers; most would be content to learn that different people have different ideas about an issue. It is our educational systems that are largely responsible for teaching the logic of the "single best," or "correct" answer to various questions. We should not be closing down options, stunting the creative impulse, and discouraging dialogue through our curricula and our forms of evaluating students, but the reverse.

This is not to say that clarity and precision have no place in the curriculum. Within a circumscribed logic (such as algebra), only certain solutions may be permitted. However, what we consider a "correct" answer is most usefully tied to practical consequences. We typically grade our students, for example, on whether they can master the rules of grammar and spelling. We do not entertain discussion of right and wrong in such instances. The rules are typically very clear. And yet, for substantial numbers of students such rules are not only alien to their sub-culture, but to fashion their speech according to these rules would destroy their social efficacy. In the same way, we often fear that the sophisticated writing of the scholarly community is unreadable by the vast majority of the population. In our smug contentment with our superior mastery of the language, we lose the capacity to engage in the kinds of public dialogue that shape the future of society.

Pedagogical Practice as Prophetic

In terms of sharing knowledge, the major priority is typically the content. Yet, one must ask, how much do students retain in the way of content? Most research on this subject suggests that students scarcely retain as much as 30 % of the content of a course even a few months after its completion. At the same time, while content may recede from one's grasp, one's capacity for action – writing, engaging in critical analysis, scanning books or the web for resources, forming essays or websites, and the like – may remain as significant resources. One might say that it is pedagogical practice, and not content, that is the chief outcome of the educational process. Or to draw on a longstanding distinction: *knowing how* may be more important as an outcome than *knowing that*.

More boldly speaking, our pedagogical practices are prophetic. They contain important ingredients for what we can later become as people. In this light, what can our practices contribute to a more promising global future? We touch here on three important possibilities:

Collaboration

When we are certain of what is true, rational and right, we know with certainty what actions must be taken. We need not ask others' opinions. In effect, certainty on such matters lends itself to autonomous action. At the same time, to act autonomously is also to divide the world into those who are with you as opposed to those who are either in the way or against. There is a close relationship, then, between autonomy and conflict. However, when we understand the possibility of multiple realities and their associated ways of life, we open the door to collaborative action. We understand that multiple values are at stake, and that ambiguity surrounds all decisions. And we appreciate that success in our projects depends on bringing people together, exchanging opinions and values, and joining forces to produce the best possible outcomes for all.

In terms of classroom practice, then, preparation for peace calls us to think in terms of collaborative student projects. Over the past decade, the movement toward collaborative practices in education has been lively and productive. The typical role of the teacher as an organizer and conveyer of knowledge is abandoned in favor of a role as a facilitator and model. Students are often assigned specific challenges by the teacher, but the way in which they organize themselves, explore the relevant issues, present their results or opinions, and evaluate their work is typically under their control. Not only do students learn the arts of productive collaboration by this means, but they also learn from others in the group how to approach various problems. Further, by placing trust in the students, the teacher demonstrates respect for them, an element that is central to the current proposals.

And yet, in this shift toward collaborative practice we must also think beyond the classroom. It is now very clear that the walls of the school are misleading. The walls suggest that the school is separated from its surrounds; that its success depends on what takes place within. At the same time, it has become increasingly apparent over recent decades that what takes place in the classroom can never be separated from the family life of the students, local politics, the economy, and so on. At the same time, while most of us are fully aware of these interdependencies, the response is too often a shrug of the shoulders: "what can I do about that?"

Collaboratively oriented education is a call to action. It is an invitation to bring school systems into active participation with the surrounding community. In one impressive example of collaborative education, Barbara Rogoff and her colleagues (2001) developed a program which brought students, teachers, and adults from the community together. Their shared belief was that learning occurs most effectively through interested participation with other learners. In effect, education issues from active relationships. Thus, drawing from their respective interests, teachers joined together with parents and students to develop the curriculum and classroom activities. Even the youngest students were brought into the planning. Parents also came to school to serve as co-teachers. At times, students from different grades were brought together to co-learn. The result was the successful creation of a broad community of learners, each drawing from each other and from the adventure in collaboration.

Dialogue

Critical to all successful collaboration is the capacity to carry out effective dialogue. Traditional educational practices do not serve us well in this respect. On the one hand students are most typically prepared to "reach their own conclusions," and to articulate their ideas in their own exams and papers. In effect, they become skilled in monologue. Further, when dialogue is invited, it is typically introduced as debate: one side vs. the other. In the context of truth through reason, the assumption is typically that debate will ultimately place us on the side of the right. Yet, in this context, how often do we find our students congratulating each other on making a good point, or adding their insights to ideas offered by others? At the same time, it is precisely these kinds of entries into conversation that lend themselves to effective collaboration.

It is not the expansion of one's individual vocabulary that will ultimately yield benefits for society and the world. As every scholar knows, a highly enriched vocabulary is the route to incomprehensibility. You may dazzle, but you will scarcely be understood. More vital is a vocabulary of dialogic actions, that is, a set of resources for moving effectively in conversation with people from differing backgrounds. For example, affirming and building on others' ideas, expressing curiosity, admitting doubts in one's own offerings, asking about what others might feel about an issue, and indulging in humor are all essential to such a vocabulary. There are only beginnings.

In our own efforts, we have experienced especially good outcomes through the use of dialogue as an evaluation device. Rather than subjecting individual students to the piercing light of assessment, one of us (KJG) arranges for small groups of students to work together on a given problem. They will not be evaluated as individuals, they are told, but on the quality of the dialogue among them. Prior to the event, the students work together to generate what they feel are the criteria of good dialogue. Here it is interesting to note that these criteria are quite different from those we value in the monologic essay. Where the good essay, for example, is one that is logically coherent and leads to a single best conclusion, the effective dialogue is one that entertains multiple ideas and does not close down voices of possibility. As the students also opine, in a good dialogue the participants care for each other. In contrast, the individual essay is typically built around a logic of self-protection and self enhancement. The final dialogue is typically carried out over electronic mail. This allows a recording to be made of the entire conversation as it unfolds. Typically, most students are fully engaged in these dialogues, and are enthusiastic about this practice as a learning experience.

Ecologically Embedded Education

In recent years we have seen a growing emphasis on "learning in context." Rather than mastering abstract concepts in an isolated classroom, the attempt is to link the abstract ideas to specific practices. This shift toward an ecologically based education is salutary on many counts. However, it gains an additional dimension in the light of our present concerns. First, we begin to teach that ideas are important primarily because of their practical consequences. We move, then, toward an understanding of truth as contextual as opposed to universal. Second, when we are working within practical domains questions of value are more easily introduced. Students might be asked, for example, to plan a new road that would help the poor of a city find new jobs. However, in doing so they would face problems of what the new road would destroy in the way of farmland and neighborhoods. Finally, when students are confronted with challenges of practical significance, they are more likely to seek out dialogue and to realize the value of ambiguity. A student who must offer a plan for neighborhood re-cycling, will certainly wish to speak with his or her neighbors about the matter.

At the same time, when learning is moved from the classroom into the surrounds, we also begin to cross lines that otherwise separate and isolate. For one, traditional education rewards students for "doing well in school." It is their own state of excellence that is important. Self and community concerns are separated. Yet, by moving educational experiences into the surrounding world, increasing importance is placed in the good of the community. The value of one's projects can be judged in terms of what they can contribute to the world as opposed to the self.

We are also concerned with the divisions existing among various cultures of veritas. We treat the separation among subject matters such as biology, history, and literature as natural, as if they reflected divisions in the natural order of things. Yet, such distinctions are lodged in specific periods of history, and their increasing independence reflects academic politics and economics as opposed to intrinsic difference. The result is an archipelago of isolated islands of intellect, separated by a gulf of mutual ignorance and antipathy. However, when we shift our concerns to practical problems of society – problems of environment, crime, technology, peace, terrorism, and the like – the traditional divisions begin to recede. Collaborative dialogue is required across the spectrum of scholarship. For us, collaborative dialogue is another name for conversation, as Steiner Kvale envisioned it.

In Conclusion

Traditionally we have viewed education as a means of enhancing individual competence. We educate individuals so they may lead successful lives. Indirectly we hope that education will enable students to contribute to our larger institutions – economic, legal, medical, and the like. We now enter a new era in history in which we must think beyond the borders of our own society. It is neither the individual mind nor the local order upon which our future well-being depends, but the global. We must begin to think seriously about whether our current educational efforts lend themselves to a global future of peace as opposed to ever increasing fear and mutual extermination. In our view the hope for global peace is ill served by our traditional emphases on truth, objectivity, and rationality. Rather, as we have proposed, if our educational programs are to make a positive contribution to the future we must develop curricula that recognize multiple constructions of the world, that confront important conflicts in value, and that cultivate appreciation for ambiguity over certainty. Further, we must develop pedagogical practices that are increasingly collaborative, that develop skills in effective dialogue, and that link scholarly understanding to broader contexts of practice. We are scarcely optimistic enough to suggest that such alterations are sufficient for securing a better world. Ultimately we must look to collaborations of mammoth proportion. In our view, collaboratively conscious education can facilitate just such efforts.

Lene Tanggaard

LOOPING-EFFECTS OF THEORIES OF LEARNING

"The technological ideology in current educational practice is pervasive. The theories of learning are not only scientific ones; they are also propagated through popular psychological literature, and may contribute ideologically to shaping the self-understanding of modern man" (Kvale, 1976, p. 108)

Introduction

In the present paper, I am inspired by Kvale's idea of the ideological function of learning theories. Kvale's viewpoint is that "theories of learning have the ideological function of rendering a technological approach to learning self-evident and dominating" (Op. cit. p. 106). Ideology is defined by Kvale as a system of ideas which mystify a subject matter with oppressive and restrictive consequences. In the present context, I argue more specifically that learning theories are part of the looping effects of human beings and their behavior. The concept of looping effects has been described by Ian Hacking (1995), and it indicates that concepts and theories in the social- and human sciences reflect and are shaped by current societal conditions, and that they also impact on human self-understanding: "People classified in a certain way tend to conform to or grow into the ways they are described: but they also evolve in their own ways, so that the classifications and descriptions have to be constantly revised" (Hacking, 1995, p. 21). In particular, I will pay attention to the looping effects of the post-modern and very popular notion or concept of lifelong learning. However, before considering these issues, a more detailed description of the concept of looping effects will be presented.

The Looping-Effects of Learning Theories

If it is valid to assume that learning theories generate looping effects on the self-understanding of human beings, it will mean that our lives and self-understanding are influenced by the newspapers, journal articles and books we read. For example, when reading about ourselves as responsible for our own learning, we may begin to think about ourselves as such. It may influence the way we educate our children and what we take upon ourselves as life goals. While, for example, the grass outside my window does not care how I describe it, human beings are different (Hacking, 1995). In other words, theories of learning do not reside innocently in the minds, books or publications of researchers. They act as intellectual and political technologies in current human life. For example, if we learn that self-reflection is the most valued endpoint of learning, we may encourage ourselves to become more self-reflective, and this ideology may influence our ideas about not only effective and valuable learning, but also about what constitutes a good life. However, it is important to bear in mind that looping effects do not work mechanically, proceeding from theory to human acts. Looping-effects occur when people actively take upon themselves the ideologies implied in what they read or hear. This means that learning theories and, not least, their popular versions presented in newspapers and in popular magazines are enormously powerful human technologies.

From Modernity to Post-Modernity – a Change in Concepts of Learning

In order to analyze the exemplars of the looping effects of learning, I distinguish analytically between learning theories in modernity and in post-modernity. While it may seem problematic to choose the adjective *post-modernistic* (there can be no movement away from modernity, modernity can be only reformulated Lyotard (2001)), a dramatic change in our ideas about learning has taken place from 1920 to the present. One major change is that the goal of learning seems to have been transformed from cultivating rationality and acquiring knowledge (in modernity), to cultivating a desire for lifelong learning (in *post*-modernity). An outline of this dramatic change in the image of the learner will be presented in the following, so as to lay the ground for a more specific analysis of the looping effects involved in this educational paradigm shift.

Put very briefly, in the learning theories of the 20th century, the ideal goal of learning processes, as described in learning theories, is for individuals to become rational, considerate and independent (masculine) beings. As evident in the following table, the task of teachers is considered to be the development of the self-regulated individual:

TABLE 1:

THEME	BEHAVIORISM (1920-1930)	COGNITIVE PSYCHOLOGY (1950- 1960)	SOCIAL-COGNITIVE THEORY (1970-1980)
Learning defined as	Behavioral change	An internal mental phenomenon potentially reflected in behavior	An internal mental phenomenon potentially reflected in behavior
Focus of scientific investigation	Observation of stimuli and response sequences,	Cognitive processes	Change of behavior and cognitive processes
Principles of learning	Behavior is changed according to stimulus-response sequences	Learning occurs when people process information and construct knowledge through experience	People's observations of others will influence their behavior and cognitive processes
Consequences of action	Must be experienced directly if they are to influence learning	Not considered	Can be experienced directly or through others
Learning and behavior is controlled	Primarily by circumstances in particular situations	Primarily by cognitive processes within the individual	Both by cognitive processes and by environment (people tend to become more self-regulated)
Educational focus on how to help pupils and students	The goal is to ensure appropriate behaviour in the classroom	The goal is to process information effectively and to construct precise and complete information about topics in the classroom	The goal is to learn effectively by observing others

The table is based directly on Ormrod's model (Ormrod, 2003, p. 364)

According to the behaviorist perspective, learning is defined as a change of behavior, whereas social cognitive theory defines learning as an internal mental process – influenced, however, by imitating or modelling others. The centre of attention is individual learning, and these theories often lead to a focus on how pupils and students can learn more effectively. Learning is framed as a change in behavior or as the mental processing of knowledge by individuals situated in educational institutions. The most important problem associated with these approaches is how pupils and students can be assisted so that they are learning more effectively or more (quantitatively) through the interventions of the teacher. Either way, the task is to establish conditions for productive behavior in the classroom or, as in cognitive psychology, to process information effectively – much in the manner of a computer. It is the rational, comprehensive and precise processing of information or a strongly regulated change of behavior which is conceived as the essential process of learning. In some of the later theories, such as social-cognitive theories of learning, the end goal of learning is for the learner to become a self-regulated individual who is able to set goals, to control his or her attention, and to choose among various learning or self-monitoring strategies and self-assessment (Ormrod, 2003, p. 355). The learning subject is described as the rational, calculative human being optimizing his or her achievement in the classroom by learning to be a self-regulating individual. This image of the learner may reflect the dominant modernist faith in human rationality and the modernist belief in education as the vehicle of a progressive development of a better society. But now, what kinds of change occur in *post*-modernity?

In post-modern theories of learning, the goal of learning is no longer considered to be only the development of the rational and independent individual. Learning subjects are now described as constantly changing, situated beings. As argued by Steinar Kvale (2004), the educational system in post-modernity can be said to prepare its pupils and students for change and so that they can "learn to learn". According to Usher & Edwards (1994, p. 11), in post-modernity, sensibilities are attuned to the pleasure of constant and new experiences, a desire which is an end in itself. In educational terms, one could say that the tasks of teachers have increasingly become the cultivation of *desire* rather than the cultivation of *rationality*. This may have to do with a general decentering of the subject, influenced in particular by the poststructuralist thinking of, among others, Foucault (1982). This thinking implies a critique of the central premise of modernity that individuals are the central agents initiating human change and learning. In contrast to the idea of learning as initiated from within the individual, in post-modernity it is recognized that the learning subject comes of age while learning.

In the post-modern rewriting of modernity, resulting from a number of factors, including human looping effects, a change in the educational orientation of teachers and researchers can be said to occur. That is, from focusing on education, to centering on cultivating the desire of pupils and students to learn on a lifelong basis. While education and learning has historically been related to schooling, as the most important and common frame for the formation of conscientious and productive citizens of western societies, in post-modernity, lifelong learning has become progressively more the life project of the individual and, as such, spread diffusely across both school, working life and spare time. Implicitly, this shift questions the existence of authoritative centers of knowledge and the idea that any knowledge can be conceived as canonical. As argued by Usher & Edwards (1994; 2001), the guiding assumption is that there is a diversity of ways, centers and sources of learning and for the production of knowledge.

The learning theories of post-modernity can be said to suspend the notion that rationality and certain kinds of knowledge are the ultimate objective of learning, and that, by definition, learning takes place in the classroom. Theories of learning now concern ideas about workplace learning (Elkjær, 1999; Bottrup, 1999), the learning organization (Senge, 1990), and responsibility for one's own learning (Bjørgen, 1999). This modern form of "apprenticeship" has, as argued by Elmholdt & Brinkmann (2006), a focus on learning as ongoing, mobile and flexible. However, the general discourse of lifelong learning represents the most striking example of a post-modern idea of learning (see Fejes, 2006). An important aspect of the discourse of lifelong learning in post-modernity is that the process of learning is seen, in principle, as independent of formal education. The close modernistic relationship between education, teaching, and learning is questioned.

The Looping Effects of Rewriting Modernity

What looping effects does the shift in educational orientation, from modernity to post-modernity, imply – if such a shift can indeed be said to have occurred? Kvale (1976) argues that the learning theories of modernity were influenced by the logic of industrial society and the intention to render effective, optimize and standardize the production of factories. The goal of learning in school became, as evident in the table above, identical. Learning processes were meant to optimize the productivity of classrooms, training pupils to act rationally both within the classroom and beyond in later life.

While the teacher in the classroom was a central agent of learning in modernity, in the post-modern moment, the teacher may not be seen as such an agent or controller of learning, because learning is not seen as restricted to a classroom. Elmholdt & Brinkmann (2006) argue that new discourses of lifelong learning have become part of installing and constituting the reflective and flexible learner in current workplaces and beyond. One could argue that the presently dominant discourse of lifelong learning, rather than being a description of the "true" nature of learning, reflects the current ideas of the ideal worker. A lifelong learner (worker) does not stop learning (working) when formal education has come to an end. One example of the "inflation" of the lifelong learning discourse is that it now figures in political documents in the EU as an important task for adults: "The Communication notes that, although lifelong learning is gaining ground in Europe, TOO FEW ADULTS ARE PARTICIPATING IN LIFELONG LEARNING and national strategies should urgently be implemented in all countries." (http://europa.eu/rapid/pressReleasesAction.do?reference=IP/05/1405&format=HTML&aged=0&language=EN&guiLanguage=en) (Retrieved from the internet, August 31st, 2007).

Could the looping effects of seeing learning as a lifelong endeavor be that we learn to regulate ourselves rather than being regulated by others, to discipline ourselves rather than being disciplined by others, and to be monitored by ourselves rather than by others? We may learn to see ourselves as not restricted by teachers or by the educational system in itself, because learning is now said to be a process happening everywhere or at least as being a process beyond the teachers' control. As argued by Usher & Edwards (1994, 2001) and Popkewitz & Brennan (1998), an earlier focus on formation, education and didactics has now been replaced by notions or visions of learning as independent of formal education and teacher control.

However, there are, of course, substantial differences between theories and discourses of learning in post-modernity. They do not all endorse an isolated view on learning as a vehicle of economic growth. While situated learning, as expressed initially by Lave & Wenger (1991), does question the implicit modernist idea of a close connection between learning and the classroom, they do not deny that learning is regulated by others and in part controlled by the values and standards of communities of practice. Their philosophy is certainly not to see learning as only cultivating the desire (to learn). One can also question the idea of an analytic distinction between modernity and post-modernity, because many of the concepts of learning developed in post-modernity are still very modernist and because the idea of categories of time is also a modernistic construction. Nonetheless, new looping effects seem to have occurred with the new discourse of lifelong learning.

Kvale (2004) argues that a central pillar of the educational system in post-modernity is the free choice of educational entities, tasks and learning content. The looping effects of this may be that the value of knowing particular things is questioned, because the ability to learn to learn or to let the pupils decide themselves what they would like to learn has become a guiding ideal. Kvale argues that the authority of the teacher thereby risks being reduced to a therapeutic role-model for the self-development of pupils.

In a likewise critical perspective, Kraft (1997) makes the point that the educational system in post-modernity is reduced to being first and foremost a contributor of the most popular forms of education to students who have learned to see themselves as customers, and to the business world seeing itself as the market for the educational system. Old-fashioned ideas of education as the forming of citizens and for the acquisition of knowledge are fading away. One interpretation of this situation is that the concept of learning has been set free from the restricted institutional frame of the modern school, only to be caught up again in the net of the market.

Lifelong Learning as the Regulating Principle of Post-Modernity

Have pupils of the post-modern school learned to see themselves as able to control their own learning processes by being invited to pursue their own interests and life-worlds? Taking a critical perspective, it can be argued that the power relations in the educational system are now more *in*visible than ever before. But are the regulation and distribution of power removed from this system? Surely not! When learning about ourselves in post-modernity through conversations with our coaches or advisors (which is conceived as the central way for learning to occur), we learn about our own weaknesses and strengths. We are meant to discover and develop ourselves (or invent ourselves), but this may mean that this self becomes an entity that can easily be regulated and controlled by others. We have learned that education and learning concern not only acquiring new knowledge and skills, but also increasingly the development of individuals desiring new experiences.

Biesta (2005) recently argued that lifelong learning is now a potent way of regulating politics and social practices globally and individuals locally. The rhetoric of lifelong learning has become part of a broader shift, in which governments are trying to increase the ability of their citizens to take responsibility for their own lives. As forecasted by Lyotard (1996), institutional education no longer has a monopoly on the production of knowledge. Its authority and power are discussed both in the media and by researchers and teachers themselves. Given that learning is now recognized in many and varied social practices, more and more activities are said to involve learning and education. Lifelong education has become a metaphor bringing the boundlessness of learning into focus, because it is seen today as a process which cannot be reserved for particular moments and which cannot be determined by particular goals, formal institutions and epistemological control (Usher & Edwards, 2001).

Is it true that individuals and organisations are now expected to be engaged in constant and reflective learning, to seek new challenges, and to act positively towards all kinds of changes? Lifelong learning has certainly become an important productive power and a self-technology, but ironically, it has the power to produce the very insecurity that it is meant to eradiate. Lifelong learning enables the adult worker to take on new and more challenging jobs, but the rhetoric may also teach us that our existing skills and self (selves) are not good enough. We may never be sure or secure about the market value of our skills, knowledge and self. There is now an increased focus on what Lyotard (1996) terms *performativity* – learning is meant to increase the effectiveness of economic and social systems. To ensure this, lifelong learning has become part of post-modern business life. The responsibility for facilitating and taking care of learning is no longer the exclusive domain of the teacher – so-called informal communities of practice among colleagues and peers are also seen as valuable learning contexts. It is something of a paradox that an earlier emphasis on knowledge and substantive education at schools and in universities is minimized, while the political emphasis on these same institutions is increased as part of a new economic logic of the knowledge society in which learning, innovation and creativity are seen as an important factor in international economic competition. As argued by Usher & Edwards (2001), lifelong learning has become part of a constant apprenticeship, in which the master himself needs to conform to the pressure of constant learning and flexibility.

The Cultivation of Lifelong Consumers

Is the looping effect of the post-modern discourse of lifelong learners that we now see ourselves as lifelong consumers of learning? Steinar Kvale (2004, p. 36) argues that from 1970 onwards, the dominant reform pedagogies, the critical experienced-based learning theories of Rogers (1961) and in Denmark of Illeris, (1981, 2005) unintentionally became part of converting pupils into consumers. Kvale identifies how the post-modern society's center of gravity has been removed from the factory of industrial production to the market and from industrial production to the consumption of entities, from the savings account to the credit card. Loyal and obedient industrial workers cannot function as a productive force in the economic growth of society, because creativity, independence and innovation have become the buzz-words of post-modernity. The marketplace is in need of customers who are willing to buy, believing enough in their credit cards to ensure the increase of private consumption and the expansion of economic growth. Pupils, students and employees in public and private companies have learned, it would seem, through the looping effects of discourses of lifelong learning, to see themselves as customers who are free and have a right to choose between the various products on offer in the educational market. The task of educators may rapidly become to cultivate a customer or to teach pupils to customize themselves to ensure the growth of the market – the all-embracing sign and symbol of human success in post-modernity. The looping effects of this process may be that the goals of educators change from delivering knowledge (as a possession) towards developing effective performers.

Free from Educational Constraints?

If it is a sound assumption that the educational system in post-modernity does not have a monopoly on defining what counts as learning, one conclusion could be that it sets free enormous potential for social mobility. Recognizing all kinds of learning as valid learning processes may enable people, who were formerly prevented from being recognized as learners to see themselves as such in this role. Workplace learning and all kinds of free-market courses seem to be exploding. However it is often only people in solid and well-paid forms of employment who are allowed to monitor their growing competence. While the formal educational system is characterized by certain mechanisms of in- and exclusion relating to the selection of students, grades and examination (Popkewitz & Brennan, 1998), these in- or excluding processes do not disappear merely because the concept of learning has been "set free". Instead, they change their form and content. People who are prevented from the constant monitoring of their own competences may be excluded from the labour market, while good grades may not necessarily count in the market for competence.

Growing numbers of researchers have begun to investigate critically what I have here chosen to call the looping effects of the current learning discourse. Biesta (2005) is critical of the change from talking in terms of education to talking in terms of learning. He argues that we need to reinvent a language for education because learning is increasingly referred to in economic terms. Through this critical analysis, he identifies four different criteria within the discourse of lifelong learning which do contain their own looping effects:

1) New theories of learning. New constructivist or social-constructivist theories emphasize that learning has nothing to do with the passive absorption of new information. In these theories, learning is seen as actively constructed by the learner and as possibly without formal education.

2) Post-modernity. Education is a modernistic project related to the notion of the enlightenment of people. In post-modernity, both the value of education and its liberating perspective have been questioned, including its potential for increasing social mobility. One conclusion that can be drawn from the diminution of the legitimacy of education is that what is left is only learning.

3) The 'silent' explosion. In recent years, the market for informal kinds of learning practices in fitness clubs, through self-help manuals and e-learning has been growing. The form and content of adult and further education has changed, because many adults today, primarily fight with themselves to change themselves, their bodies and their identities. The individual character of these activities makes learning a suitable term for them.

4) The demolishment of the welfare state. Through the political reduction of the welfare state, the relationship between the state and its citizens has changed from being essentially one of duties, to becoming one of consumption or rights. Value for money has become the most important principle of transactions between the state and the individual, and this logic has moved into the educational system as well. One example of this is evident from a recent investigation at Linköping University in Sweden, which demonstrated that university students have become progressively more oriented towards consumption in their choice of education (Eva Bergstedt. LiU-nytt, 2005, no. 6, p. 6/7).

According to Biesta (2005), one important problem involved in understanding education only in terms of economic transactions is that it is difficult to know what may be useful or valuable for one to learn. One of the difficulties may be to find out what one needs to learn. The consumerism of post-modern education implies that the content and goals are defined more by the market and less by experts in particular fields of expertise. One consequence is that it becomes more difficult for the experts to deliver such education, and secondly

CRITIQUING THEORY

Amedeo Giorgi
Saybrook Graduate School

THE MINIMALIZATION OF SUBJECTIVITY IN MAINSTREAM PSYCHOLOGICAL RESEARCH

Introduction

For centuries, psychology's subject matter consisted of the mind of individuals or the mental processes that took place within the awareness of human beings. Scholars interested in psychological subject matter were interested in such subjective processes as perceiving, remembering, imagining, willing, speaking and so on. When psychology changed from a philosophical style of scholarship and began to function as an experimental science in the 19th Century, such processes were still being investigated initially even though the attempt was made to tie the processes to standard physical conditions (Wundt, 1883).

Then with the behaviorist revolution in the early 20th Century, the perspective shifted from that of the experiencing subject to that of the experimental observer. In the name of objectivity, only that which was manifest to the consciousness of the researcher was allowed to be called "data". Actually, less than what was perceived was defined as "data", since one spontaneously perceives the expressions that an individual has as he or she is acting, but since the perception of expressions could be in error, only that which was relatively certain was acceptable and so the "data" became behavior or performance. What the individual was actually experiencing or living through while performing was deemed irrelevant. The behaviorist believed that a full human psychology could be constructed based upon behavioral data alone in interaction with the geographic environment. Of course, the behaviorists did admit linguistic use under the rubric of "verbal behavior"(Watson, 1919; Skinner, 1957). However, since so many behaviorists worked with animals rather than humans, that fact did not modify their procedures too much.

"Verbal behavior", after all, was still looking at the use of language from the experimenter's perspective. Only that which was publicly uttered and potentially reifiable could be used as data.

This state of affairs lasted for some time, but eventually a few psychologists began to notice what was happening and began to write articles protesting the objectivistic trend and wondering why experiential data were being excluded.

Some Reactions to the Established Objective Procedures

Once the objectifying, external perspective initiated by behaviorism took hold, it achieved a dominance that has not yet been fully relinquished. But some psychologists began questioning the logic behind the procedure, and in an article of this size, only a few questioners can be covered. Perhaps the most important is Sigmund Koch's (1959) concerns about the lack of experiential categories in the studies he surveyed. Koch (1959, p. 764) noticed that there was a trend toward increasing interest in perception and central processes, and this led him to investigate a certain turning towards "experiential analysis". Consequently, he (Koch, 1959) investigated this trend and came up with three types of experiential analyses in the studies. The first he labeled "presystematic analysis of experience", a second, "transactional cases", and the third, "systematic phenomenology (Koch, 1959, p. 767). Koch wrote that presystematic experiential analysis was "a necessary condition to the psychological enterprise", and he found that it was spoken about "in a more direct and less apologetic sense than has been usual". The transitional cases that Koch found were those that included experiential analyses that were between presystematic and systematic use. He notes that the most instructive example was Tolman and Koch (1959, p. 767) writes that Tolman "expresses the dependence of his theorizing on his own phenomenology in a way which makes the objectivist nuances of his theory language broadly metaphorical". Koch (1959, p. 767) also referred to certain psychologists who study "the person and the social setting and whose tendency to hold on to the language of 'behavior' and associated imagery is rendered obsolete by the nature of their problems ..." Finally, Koch (1959, p. 768) cites authors such as Gibson, Asch, Murray and Rogers as holding the view that "variables having direct experiential reference as legitimate elements of systematic analysis". These trends were all reactions to the exclusive use of behavioral data.

However, ultimately, Koch (1959) was not optimistic about the turn to experiential categories. He was aware that the overturning of the dominant trend would be difficult because he (Koch, 1959, p. 766) wrote: "But no one can deny that for more than forty years behaviorist epistemology has had the *pragmatic effect* of fostering a set of attitudes which tend to either devalue or divert attention from most problems which, by virtue of historical or extra-scientific associations, have an 'experiential odor' – quite independently of whether the investigation believes the problem compatible, in principle, with behavioristic methods" (italics in original). This pragmatic impact has been so strong that, after looking at the three classes of experiential efforts, Koch (1959, p. 768) was forced to write:

In general though, it can be said that whatever the attitude taken towards experiential analysis, there has been no marked tendency among authors in the present study (with the single exception of Henry Murray) to join in any explicit way the many methodological and empirical questions that might be asked concerning fruitful and rigorous utilization of experiential data ... Yet, issues concerning optimal techniques for experiential observation, the formulation of adequate dependent variable categories, the integration of behavioral and experiential data, the construction of theoretical concepts from experiential data, etc., have been addressed by indirection, if at all.

However, the question of the relevance of experiential categories was addressed prior to Koch's publication by Paul Bakan (1956), and again by Richardson (1965), a few years after Koch's study appeared. Bakan (1956) had 100 participants memorize a list of 20 nonsense syllables, but then included a seventy-five item post-experimental questionnaire that the participants had to answer immediately after the experiment. Among the findings that the experiential data provided was the fact that the participants who agreed with certain subjective statements recalled significantly more nonsense syllables than the others. It was clear that tapping into the experiential, subjective aspects of the experimental situation helped to clarify the meaning of the performance data. This was true even though Bakan (1956) collected experiential data in an objective fashion. He presented the participants with statements to which they had to answer "Yes or No". But among the sources for the statements was the experimenter's analysis of the experimental situation (i.e., his own awareness of what might be important) and the retrospective accounts given by participants in a pilot study. Either Bakan was still under the influence of the objectivistic trend, or else he devised objective statements in order to meet the criteria of those he wanted to influence, but the basic source of the objective statements were experiential reports.

The chief conclusion that Bakan (1956, p. 378) arrived at regarding his study was that it was important to obtain the description of an experimental situation on the part of participants because it helped clarify the meaning of the results. In addition, he (Bakan, 1956, p. 378) stated that experiential data helped to discover what the significant variables were as well as to make possible the study of the relationship between objective and subjective variables. The latter task is not possible if no effort is made to discover what the subjective variables are.

Subsequently, Richardson (1965) tried to assess the value of subjective experience for experimental research. Richardson's specific purpose was to attempt to distinguish the concept of behavior from the concept of experience in order to see if there was any value in trying to keep the two concepts distinct. Richardson (1965) first presents the behaviorist argument claiming that experiential categories are not necessary. A summary of the behaviorist argument is that if experience referred to a conscious event that is essentially private and incommunicable, then such an event has no place in a science of psychology. On the other hand, if "experience refers to a class of conscious events that can be communicated in a written, spoken or key-pressing form, then it has become just like all other observable behavior so that the continued use of the term 'experience" is simply redundant" (Richardson, 1965, p. 224).

But Richardson points out the fallacy in this argument. He (1965, p. 224) notes that the argument uses the term "behavior" in two different senses. In the first sense, it is used as

the antithesis of experience, (and) it refers to all forms of overt action that are of interest in their own right. Secondly, it refers to a tangible, observable set of dial readings, pen-recorder tracings, check marks or questionnaires, tape recordings or whatever, that serve as indices of some process or state which may be either behavioral or experiential.

In the latter case, it is not the motor behavior as such that the researcher is interested in, but the subjective experience it refers to. Richardson (1965) then goes on to list about a dozen phenomena (e.g. daydreaming) that absolutely would require the input of subjective experiences even if additional behavioral data is collected. Richardson (1965) concludes that psychology would benefit greatly if experiential categories were included in all research.

Finally, I (Giorgi, 1967) was also interested in seeing whether experiential reports would make a difference in understanding psychological phenomena, and so I conducted a classic nonsense syllable versus words learning experiment. After the experimental session was over, when no interference with the classic experiment was possible, I asked the participants about their experience. The performance data for learning words or syllables was not statistically significantly different. However, when I analyzed the experiential data, I understood better what the lack of statistical significance meant. It did not mean that there was no difference in learning words as opposed to syllables, but that there were just as many "words easier" learners as there were "syllables easier" learners. But individuals did experience learning words or syllables as different. Moreover, the experiential reports showed that whether one found words or syllables easier depended upon the strategy adopted by the participant, and the meanings associated with the words were either a help or a hindrance depending upon the strategy adopted. Finally, I discovered that the meaning in the psychological sense that was an aid to learning was not the dictionary meaning associated with the word, but the way that the participant could construe the item to be learned within the strategy he or she adopted.

It seems to me that all four sources just covered give powerful reasons for including experiential reports in research studies. In the research that I have just reviewed, I checked to see how prevalent the use of experiential reports was, and I (Giorgi, 1967, p. 112) noted that in reviewing the first volume of the relatively new *Journal of Verbal Learning and Behavior* (1962) only 6 research reports out of 50 (12 %) included anything like post-experimental verbal reports or questionnaires. I wondered whether the trend had changed at all, so I went to the library and researched the issue once again.

Experiential Categories in Contemporary Research: I decided to investigate the *Journal of Experimental Psychology* because it was precisely the work of mainstream psychology that I wanted to cover because until all of psychology can appreciate the value of experiential data I believe that psychology's contributions will be muted and less comprehensive than they can be. I chose one of the two volumes from the year 1974 (Volume 103) because it was the last year that the journal remained single. The following year the journal broke up into four independent and distributed sections, and it differentiated even further later on. In addition, 1974 is some ten to fifteen years after the publications we reviewed above appeared, and if there was going to be some impact of the publications arguing for experiential categories, they should have taken effect by 1974. I went through the entire bound Volume 103, reading the methodology section of each article, looking for the inclusion of experiential data. What I found was that there were 193 articles that used human subjects (those conducting research on animals were obviously excluded) reporting on 283 experiments. The number of experiments exceeds the number of articles because many articles included multiple experiments. Out of the 283 experiments only 16 (6 %) made any kind of reference to what the participants experienced, and of these 16 only 3 (18 %) really asked about the participants' experiences in an open-ended way. The best example of using experiential categories well was by Shanteau (1974) who asked his participants to explain in their own words what their task was in order to be sure that they understood the task well. Read, Read and Excell (1974) questioned their participants about their general awareness of the experiment, as did Hellige and Grant (1974). Read, Read and Excell (1974) found that the feedback helped their interpretation of the findings. That was not the case with Hellige and Grant. Davis and Lamberth (1974) stated that their participants were debriefed, but no mention was made of how the information that was obtained was used. Four of the experiments used post-experimental questionnaires, sometimes simply to check on an aspect of the experiment. Two other experiments required the participants to estimate time or the success of their own work. Five experiments asked the participants to rate some aspect of their performance in an objective way.

Light and Berger (1974) stated that they obtained confidence ratings from their participants, but then they neither analyzed nor discussed them in the article. Consequently, of all those that made some effort to obtain some kind of experiential data I would consider only the first three (1 %) to have done it in such a way that some genuine additional information was gained. But then only two of the three reported on the findings of the debriefings. Hellige and Grant (1974) basically found no effects on performance of the specific question asked of the participants.

I also decided to check on the research articles for the year 2004, since the response to the recommendations may have been a delayed one. Surely, if there was to be a permanent impact of the desire for experiential data, it would have shown up almost a half-century later than the appearance of the original recommendations. So I selected the bound Volume 30, July-November publications of the *Journal of Experimental Psychology: Learning, Memory and Cognition*. There were 43 articles in that volume reporting 135 experiments, and only three (2 %) had any reference whatsoever to the experiential data that participants could have provided. None of the three were anything like what one would have hoped for if the experiential recommendations were to be heeded. Clare and Lewandowsky (2004) tried to determine the difficulties participants may have had in verbalizing what they had to do, but they tested for that fact statistically. Smith and Bayen (2004) stated that all participants had to complete a post-test questionnaire, but no more was said about those findings. Finally, McKenzie, Wixted and Noelle (2004) stated that when their participants were asked about the confidence they had in the research, they were also asked if they believed the instructions they were given. These researchers did tally the results of the post experimental findings, and were able to discriminate what they called "believers and skeptics" for the instructed and uninstructed groups (McKenzie et al., 2004, p. 953).

Thus, overall, in 1974, only 5.6 % of experiments had any reference to the experiences of the participants and of those, according to our criterion, only 1 % had consulted the experiences in a preferred way. In 2004 only 2 % of the experiments made reference to the experiences of the participants, but none of them did it in a preferred way. The preferred way is an interview in which one simply asks participants what they experienced, with follow-up questions when interesting answers come forth. McKenzie et al. (2004) used

Ian Parker

REMEMBERING MAO

What connection in the discipline of psychology might be made between qualitative research and psychoanalysis? The provocative answer Steinar Kvale provides in his 1975 paper is Chairman Mao (Kvale, 1975). The occasion for addressing the connection between two very marginal approaches in the discipline was a consideration of the orthodox methodological tradition of work on the cognitive processes that are supposed to underpin memory. The ostensible focus of his critique is the experimental study of nonsense syllables carried out by Ebbinghaus (1964) at the dawn of the twentieth century. Kvale characterizes this empiricist tradition as 'metaphysical', and already by the second page of his article we are arriving at a much more profound question about epistemological assumptions in psychology: The techniques empiricists employ in psychological research entail:

(1) *tailoring* the stimulus material to fit the metaphysical philosophy, (2) *indoctrinating* the subjects with the metaphysical way of thinking, (3) *manipulating* the experimental situation such that the subjects cannot avoid thinking metaphysically and (4) *quantifying* the data such that they are forced into the world of metaphysics. (Kvale, 1975, p. 206).

These assumptions are then teased out in the course of the paper, and it is in that narrative that we meet debates about qualitative research and psychoanalysis, the deeper concerns that are reflected in Kvale's later work and for which he is best known in the English-speaking world.

I recall this classic paper in the history of what we have nowadays come to term 'critical psychology' with fondness, and have often wondered why it is of psychology, and Marxist critiques that value psychoanalysis, come to that (Giorgi, 1994).

It is possible to see this aspect of Giorgi's interest in radical alternatives to mainstream psychology in his championing (actually a rather too-phenomenological reframing in my opinion, but that is another story) of the work of Georges Politzer (1994). Here, if we are mindful of Mao's (1968) argument that we should study a thing internally and in its relation to other things, we can see something of what Kvale is concerned with as a writer intervening in psychology and what his relation to other critical writers might indicate to us about the political valence of his interventions.

The political stakes in the conceptual battles over methodology in psychology are all the more clear when we take the first mistake Ebbinghaus and his followers make in the context of the other mistakes that Kvale draws attention to. Let us turn to these now. The second mistake is that the traditional and still dominant research tradition must recruit its subjects as willing participants, but this does not at all mean that they are fully aware of what it is they are participating in – and so Kvale refers to the second technique as that of 'indoctrinating' them. We have to recall that the history of experimental psychological research from the beginning required that the subject who engaged in introspection had to be a skilled observer of what they imagined to be their own mental processes.

In the early days of psychology at the end of the nineteenth century the 'experimenter' might change places with the 'subject', and this gave to the participants some illusion of the situation being an equal relationship, an illusion that required that the existence of other unskilled 'non-psychologists' should be kept well out of the laboratory. As the laboratory-experimental paradigm in psychology shifted its geographical centre of gravity from Europe to the United States, this democratic illusion gave way to a more explicit division between the psychologists who conducted the research and those who were subject to it, who played the role of subjects within it. However, when 'introspection' was employed as a technique in these new conditions, it now necessitated a deeper implantation of 'psychology' inside each individual subject; this in the sense that each individual would imagine that what went on inside them was a cognitive mental process.

As Politzer (1994, p. 53) puts it, the 'introspective' psychologist 'expects from his subject a study that is already psychological, and he must always assume the presence of a psychologist in his subject'. There is thus an insidious process by which the technique of 'indoctrinating' the subject requires the third Ebbinghaus mistake Kvale outlines, in which some good deal of effort has to be put into making sure that the subject will not be able to find any meaning in the stimulus materials; this state of affairs is brought about 'by manipulating the experimental situation, so that the subject is forced to behave in accordance with the metaphysical theories of memory' (Kvale, 1975, p. 207).

So, the 'tailoring', 'indoctrinating' and 'manipulating' – the first three mistakes of the Ebbinghaus tradition of research – are material practices by which the subjects are manoeuvred and coerced into a position whereby they can do nothing other than confirm the presuppositions of the experimental psychologist. Then it is quite logical – in this world of metaphysical rather than dialectical logic – that the data must be 'quantified', and so we arrive at the fourth mistake by which the elements of nonsense are rearranged by the psychologist. This process ensures that contradiction is wiped out of the equation and the meaningful existence of the subject is by necessity also wiped out; and so, 'the more nonsensical things are, the less likely they are related to other events in the subject's life' (Kvale, 1975, p. 210). As he then points out:

By analyzing only that which reveals a quantitative increase or decrease in memory, one is further safeguarded against discovering qualitative leaps in memory. In a dialectical approach, a stringently conducted qualitative analysis does not necessarily have to be quantified in order to gain scientific respectability. (Kvale, 1975, p. 210).

Here is a theme that will echo throughout Kvale's writing on qualitative research in the next three decades. Qualitative research is treated by mainstream psychologists as a poor cousin of quantitative research, which is assumed to be the only source of rich and reliable enough 'data' to build a genuinely scientific psychology. This treatment is part of a series of rhetorical moves by a discipline that imagines that it is scientific, but which a detailed study of the Ebbinghaus tradition of research shows to be itself totally without foundation. If we go to the heart of mainstream psychology – and the studies of cognition and memory are often treated as the pure gold of psychology that must surely withstand the encroaching critiques of the humanists and phenomenologists – we can see, and Kvale shows us, that this supposedly scientific methodology is actually not much more than a metaphysical worldview. And then, he makes clear in a number of interventions in methodological debates in the discipline, it can be shown that good qualitative research will take questions of validity – the very 'validity' that is fetishised by mainstream psychology – seriously, and demystify it so that it then "comes to depend on the quality of craftsmanship during investigation, continually checking, questioning, and theoretically interpreting the findings" (Kvale, 1996, p. 241).

A Contradiction in Terms

It is here in these later texts that other theoretical resources are employed, and it is now, it seems, postmodernism rather than dialectical materialism that is able to reframe the theoretical interpretation of methodology and also key in more effectively to the debates already occurring among those who are concerned about the mistakes psychology made and who are trying to find a way out. So, he argues that a concept of validity as a quality of craftsmanship 'becomes pivotal with a postmodern dismissal of an objective reality against which knowledge is to be measured' (Kvale, 1996, p. 241). This argument about validity is in the context of an exploration and outline of new ways forward for conducting interviews, and the connection between that aspect of qualitative research and postmodernism is made very clearly elsewhere, when he argues that in several respects, "the knowledge produced in an interview comes close to postmodern conceptions of knowledge as conversational, narrative, linguistic, contextual and interrelational" (Kvale, 1992, p. 51).

It should be noted that the tactical role of 'postmodernism' in his argument for interviewing, particularly when reframed by a theoretically-informed reworking of notions of validity which challenges fake-scientific psychology, is perhaps more evident than is the role of Mao in his argument against the Ebbinghaus tradition. His enthusiasm for postmodernism was, even at its most urgent and even in the context of an edited collection devoted to bringing these ideas to a wider audience in the discipline, still muted by the acknowledgement that if we were to see postmodernism as 'the ideology of a consumer society', then it is quite possible that "postmodern discourse, including the few attempts towards a postmodern psychology, merely mirrors consumerism" (Kvale, 1992, p. 55).

It could be argued that epistemological doubt is the order of the day in postmodern discourse, and that it would be bad form to nail one's colors too firmly to the mast even when, or because one is, surrounded by enthusiasts for the approach. But even so, his acknowledgement of the ideological dangers of postmodernism still jars with postmodern discourse, on two counts. First, the real paid up postmodernists are happy to ditch any old-fashioned reference to 'ideology', and they see such references as harboring the belief that there is one view of the world that is more false – in this case, the ideology of postmodernism – than another, here the reality of present-day consumer society. Second, the postmodernists who go all the way with relativist conceptions of truth that dissolves it into a flux of language games would be very suspicious – and they always seem to reserve their suspicion for some ideas more than others – of such a reference to 'consumer society' in the first place. Does Kvale, they would ask, really still believe that he knows how to characterize a society, as if he has a better theoretical and political vantage point from which to understand it?

I think the answer – and we can treat this answer as derived from a textual interpretation of Kvale's writing very much in line with Freud's (1901) interpretation of slips of the pen – is that he does really believe that. And this belief is manifested in the particular kinds of doubts he voices about postmodernism and, significantly and dialectically interrelated with those doubts, in the absence of any such doubts over his use of dialectical materialism, let alone agonized liberal worries about whether it is a good idea to quote Mao as part of a critical assault on mainstream psychology.

Free Association

Phenomenological reference points are prominent in *InterViews* (Kvale, 1996), but while Giorgi is the most-cited author in the book (if one simply goes by the number of page references in the author index), the second most-cited is Freud. Even if we temper this observation with the fact that Freud ranks second jointly with Socrates, we still find that the key discussion of

Socratic dialogue is where Socrates interprets Agathon's views on Eros. It is the famous dialogue which ends up in what amounts to one of the earliest interpretations of transference when Socrates draws attention to Alcibiades' displaced desire for Agathon (Plato, 1997), and so psychoanalysis reappears on the stage of qualitative research.

In Kvale's contrast between Ebbinghaus and Mao, Freud is one of the figures who is aligned close to Mao as a starting point for a 'dialectical ma-terialist psychology (Kvale, 1975, p. 214), and it is the method of 'free as-sociation' that opens the promise not only of a better methodology but of a process of change that will anticipate the world that we may prefer, if we had real choice, as an alternative to capitalism (see also Kvale, 2003).

As was pointed out by Marxist critics many decades ago, this associative and interpretative approach – an interpretation that changes the world in the very process of interpreting it – in psychoanalysis is very different from 'introspection'; 'Freud does not use introspection but rather a method that we can only call introspective as a last resort and which, according to him, is just a variant of the method of deciphering' (Politzer, 1994, p. 50). If it is true that there is, 'in *free associations*, neither associations, nor freedom' (Politzer, 1994, p. 67), then psychoanalysis itself needs to be handled dialecti-cally as a resource. It highlights the lack of freedom and the constraints that pertain to association precisely so we can better understand – potentially we can better understand if we link psychoanalysis to other radical political resources – power, and as we interpret that power we reposition ourselves so that life conditions change, the condition for struggling against oppression changes.

Notice again how the hesitations and doubts in Kvale's discussion of quali-tative research function to draw attention to the political stakes of research methodologies. In a detailed review of how psychoanalytic approaches to interviewing have been marginalized, forgotten by mainstream psychology, he points out that while qualitative interviews are often viewed as progres-sive alternatives to behaviorism – and he is presenting them as such alterna-tives – we should not forget that 'a large part of psychological qualitative interviewing takes place in the interest of management control of workers and in particular by the manipulation of consumer behavior' (Kvale, 2003, p. 294). Against this control and manipulation, psychoanalysis is represented as providing a reflexive liberating practice by which the conditions that require repression at the level of the individual are also unmasked.

So, while Mao may connect qualitative research and psychoanalysis, a dialectical materialist view of things will also unravel the ways in which ostensibly progressive frameworks that have been developed in the context of bourgeois society also serve to cover over their own contradictions and implication in power. As Kvale points out,

While sensitive to the forms of neurotic suffering in a capitalist society, psychoanalysis has tended to consider the effects of capitalist forms of oppression as universal laws of behavior, neglecting their specific social and historical character. The tendency of psychoanalysis to individualize behavioral problems, or restricting them to family influences in childhood, may have diverted from the conflict producing structure of this society. (Kvale, 1975, p. 215).

This is why it is necessary to keep a politically-astute analysis of the conditions in which every form of psychology emerges to the fore. It is only then that the radical impulse of psychoanalysis can be released from its conservative shell. Then it would make sense to say that psychoanalysis situates 'individual mystification and repression' in the context of economic exploitation of workers under capitalism (Kvale, 1975, p. 215). Psychology is then seen as just one expression of the reified consciousness that capitalism calls upon and requires in order to keep political resistance and a world of genuinely free associations between human beings at bay.

This is why Mao, for Kvale, provides the connection between qualitative research and psychoanalysis, for his dialectical materialist conception of contradiction and change can energize and politicize both domains at the very moment that it shows how and why they must confront a common enemy, psychology, in which:

The lived and meaningful world of the subject is split up into isolated fragments; he is denied the possibility of creating meaning; he is indoctrinated to behave as a mechanical robot; he is manipulated through the repetitions and the time pressure of the memory drum; and the individual products of his behavior are mystified by a quantifying statistical analysis. (Kvale, 1975, p. 218)

The true significance of great writing in psychology – and we are concerned here with writing in and against psychology – is that present-day texts are dialectically interrelated, defined by the texts that have been produced at other historical moments in the context of other political debates. Kvale's little text on traditional empiricist memory research serves to remind us of the importance of dialectical materialism, here specifically Mao, to genuinely radical psychology. This text repays a close re-reading, and it can then have a retroactive effect so that we may interpret and change the false psychology that is still dominant, increasingly triumphant across the world. Kvale's interventions have functioned as an energizing force in challenging received wisdom in psychology, and this is why I have tried to show that this particular text provides one such challenge, why it is such a valuable present from the past.

Svend Brinkmann

COMTE AND HOUELLEBECQ: TOWARDS A RADICAL PHENOMENOLOGY OF BEHAVIOR

We are the true positivists.

EDMUND HUSSERL

Exactly forty years ago, in 1967, Steinar Kvale published the article "Skinner and Sartre: Towards a radical phenomenology of behavior" together with Carl Erik Grenness (Kvale & Grenness, 1967). The article stands out as an ambitious and surprising attempt to combine Skinnerian behaviorism and Sartrean phenomenology as the basis for a psychology which eschews the illusions of "the double world" and "the inner man". The rise of cognitive science in psychology within the last forty years is proof that a critique of atomistic, representationalist psychology is more needed than ever. As a tribute to Steinar Kvale and his work, in this paper I shall attempt to take up the thread of the 1967 article, and show the relevance of its arguments to a radical phenomenological understanding of human life in the postmodern condition.

Instead of Skinner, however, my main scientific protagonist will be the founder of positivism and sociology, Auguste Comte (1798-1857), who formulated a program for social science not unlike Skinner's, although Comte (like Marx) was much more sensitive to the historical situatedness of human behavior. And instead of Sartre, at once a philosopher and writer of fiction, the postmodern literary voice in this paper will be represented by the French writer, Michel Houellebecq (born 1958). I shall argue that some of the most compelling qualitative descriptions of postmodern life are found in what could be called Houellebecq's "literary sociology", and I shall provide quite a few examples of his diagnoses of human conduct in an age dominated by consumer capitalism. Houellebecq considers himself an heir to Comte's philosophy (he frequently refers to Comte in his novels, and he has prefaced a recent French book on Comte), and, in line with Comte's classical positivist approach, Houellebecq's style of writing is objectivist, sociological, behaviorist, and starkly anti-psychological.

Comte's Classical Positivism

A distinctive feature of Steinar's impressive career has been a unique and almost heretic ability to employ unlikely authors and perspectives in eye-opening and thought-provoking interpretations of significant societal and psychological processes. Throughout the years, to give just a few examples, Steinar has provided us with a reading of B.F. Skinner as a radical phenomenologist (Kvale & Grenness, 1967), a critique of mechanistic memory research based on Mao Tse-Tung (Kvale, 1975), deconstructions of the critical potentials of critical pedagogies (Kvale, 2004) as well as of the emancipatory potentials of 'dialogical interviewing' (Kvale, 2006), which is unusual for a best-selling author on qualitative interviewing (Kvale, 1996). Recently, and perhaps most surprisingly, in the coming revised edition of *InterViews*, Steinar has begun to rehabilitate positivism; not, however, in its methodological form, developed by members of the Vienna circle in the 1920s such as Schlick, Carnap, and Neurath, but in its classical form, inaugurated by Comte.

Is it not a mystery how a leading exponent of qualitative inquiry can turn to positivism? The answer depends on what we mean by 'positivism', and it may be illuminating to draw a distinction between classical (Comte), methodological (e.g. Schlick), and radical (e.g. Houellebecq?) positivism, paralleling the better known distinction between classical, methodological, and radical behaviorism. In the article by Kvale & Grenness (1967), it is Skinner's *radical* behaviorism that is emphasized. That is, his radical anti-mentalistic repudiations of psychology's illusions of "the inner man" and "the double world". But behaviorism also comes in a *classical* form (represented by J.B. Watson) and a *methodological* form, the latter being a quantitative study of third person behavior, which has drifted into contemporary psychology in general, and mainstream cognitive psychology in particular. With these distinctions in mind, we can say that when Steinar seeks a rehabilitation of positivism, it is not in its methodological form, but in its classical and – as I wish to add here – *radical* forms, represented by Comte and Houellebecq, as we shall see below.

Many self-proclaimed progressive social scientists today reject positivism out of hand and in all its forms. 'Positivism' has simply become a term of abuse, especially in texts on qualitative inquiry. Few, however, seem to be familiar with the work of Comte (1830), although his classical positivism deserves merit in moving social science forward by reacting against religious dogma and metaphysical speculation. Comte advocated a return to what is positively observable – the *phenomena* – and he famously argued that human knowledge passes through three different states: The theological, the metaphysical, and the scientific or positive states (p. 1). In the first theological state, "the human mind directs its researches mainly toward the inner nature of beings" (p. 2) rather than "abstract forces" (the metaphysical state) or "the connection established between different particular phenomena and some general facts" (the positive state) (p. 2).

One reason why few psychologists have taken an interest in Comte could be that he rejected the possibility that psychology was a science. In his view, psychology was merely "the last transformation of theology" (Comte, 1830, p. 20), belonging to the first state of human knowledge that explains the observable by recourse to mysterious and unobservable (mental) mechanisms and entities. Comte presaged Skinner in his view that "direct contemplation of the mind by itself is a pure illusion" (p. 20) – "the human mind can observe all phenomena directly, except its own" (p. 21). This was later echoed in Skinner's repudiation of representationalist epistemology and the doubling of the world. According to Comte, as well as Skinner, Sartre, and Merleau-Ponty (cf. Kvale & Grenness, 1967), we perceive things directly, rather than mediated by mental mechanisms.

Unlike later methodological positivists, but in line with Skinner's "descriptive behaviorism" (Kvale & Grenness, 1967), Comte argued that the study of social phenomena should not necessarily involve quantification, but rather careful qualitative descriptions. Positivist philosophy is often given the responsibility for the quantitative rule in the social sciences, but this is unfair given Comte's belief that social phenomena were too complex to be subjected to mathematical analysis:

our business is to study phenomena, in the characters and relations in which they present themselves to us, abstaining from introducing considerations of quantities, and mathematical laws, which is beyond our power to apply (Comte quoted from Michell, 2003, p. 13).

According to Steinar's recent depiction of classical positivism (in the second edition of *InterViews*), Comte's positivism also had an extended influence on the arts of the 19th century, inspiring a move from mythological and aristocratic themes to a new realism, depicting the lives of ordinary men and women. The opera Carmen, the realistic descriptions by Zola and Flaubert, and also impressionist paintings, sticking to the immediate sense impressions, can be mentioned as pieces of art inspired by classical positivism. The early positivism was also a political inspiration for feminism, and it was the feminist Harriet Martineau who translated Comte's *Positive Philosophy* into English. In philosophy, the founder of phenomenological philosophy, Edmund Husserl, stated that if positivism means being faithful to the phenomena, then we, the phenomenologists, are the true positivists. The insistence in Comte's positivism to stay close to observed phenomena rather than engaging in metaphysical speculation about theoretical entities in fact comes close to a postmodern emphasis on the importance of staying close to surface phenomena rather than deep structures.

Comte was deeply interested in politics and morality, and, like Skinner in his utopian novel *Walden Two*, Comte advocated the use of social engineering on a scientific basis to establish social order under the anomic conditions of modernity. Comte began, but never finished, a grand work on the science of *la morale*, but it was not psychology that was to serve as the backbone of a moral science. It was Comte's general conviction that there are two classes of phenomena of interest to human scientists: biological/organic on the one hand, and societal/collective on the other. The first class of phenomena was to be dealt with by biology, while the second class was the province of "social physics" or "sociology" (the word itself was Comte's invention) – and this left nothing for psychology to study (see Cahan & White, 1992). There is, according to Comte, no ontological realm of individual mental phenomena to be studied by psychology between the biological and the sociological sciences.

Comte never wrote his treatise on the science of *la morale*, but we know that he called this science-to-be "a sacred science" (Samelson, 1974, p. 221), and found that "*science* proper is as preliminary as are theology or metaphysics, and must finally be eliminated by the universal religion" (Comte quoted in Samelson, 1974, p. 222). The science of *la morale* was to culminate in a form of communitarian, human religion, emphasizing "the dependence of man on society (humanity in its historical totality), [and it] considered the isolated individual a false abstraction" (p. 222). It is quite clear that Comte's *morale*, like his positivism in general, contained much more than pure methodology, and he did not take the stance of a value-free or politically neutral scientist, but rather resembled Marx in his insistence on the importance of the historical situatedness of human behavior.

Houellebecq: Towards a Radical Postmodern Positivism

As we have seen, there are a number of similarities between Skinner and Comte. Likewise, I believe that there are many points of convergence between Sartre and Houellebecq: Both are philosophically inclined, literary artists of an existential bent, but whereas Sartre remained with the humanist dichotomy of *l'être en soi* and *l'être pour soi*, as the basis of human dignity, Houellebecq is a radical, naturalistic posthumanist, who envisages a near future of human cloning. The behaviors of Houellebecq's characters in the postmodern "sex-and-shopping society" are not explained with reference to inner, psychological mechanisms, but with reference to the market relations in which they take part. Like Comte, who limited the study of human beings to physiology and sociology, we shall see below how Houllebecq explains human behavior with exclusive references to bodily factors on the one hand, notably hedonist sexuality, and sociological factors in consumer capitalism on the other. I believe we can say that he represents a radical postmodern positivism.

Houellebecq plays with, and implicitly deconstructs, the modernist distinction between art and science. His books are filled with references to social science, especially sociology, and also to natural sciences such as physics, chemistry, and biology, and, in some of the novels (*Atomized*, *The Possibility of an Island*), Houellebecq presents a technological "solution" to the problems of the painful human existence in the hedonistic, postmodern world. In a near future, human beings are replaced by posthuman individuals (through cloning and other forms of biotechnology) that are unable to desire, suffer, and love, but instead live eternal lives in a condition of indifference, which evokes images of Nirvana in Buddhism.

The main theme in Houellebecq is the total marketization of human relations in consumer society. Relationships are described as an exchange of goods, where good relationships are those that maximize individuals' capacities to have pleasant and intense experiences, particularly concerning sex. Tellingly, the narrator in *Whatever* argues that "in societies like ours sex truly represents a second system of differentiation, completely independent of money; and as a system of differentiation it functions quite as mercilessly." (Houellebecq, 1999, p. 99). The losers in the novels are the unattractive people that have little to offer on the sexual marketplace, and prostitution comes to play a significant role, especially in *Platform*, and is described in positive terms as the possibility for unappealing people to buy access to the market for sexual experience. Family life and love become reduced to pure sexual relationships: "the couple and the family were to be the last bastion of primitive communism in liberal society. The sexual revolution was to destroy the last unit separating the individual from the market." (Houellebecq, 2001, p. 136). Although all Houellebecq's characters long for love, the marketized society in which they live makes this an impossible dream.

In *Atomized* (which has also been published under the title *The Elementary Particles*), we follow half-brothers Michel and Bruno, who act as lay sociologists throughout the book and analyze the contemporary consumer society – or "the sex-and-shopping society", as Michel calls it (Houellebecq, 2001, p. 192) – "where desire is marshalled and organized and blown up out of all proportion. For society to function, for competition to continue, people have to want more and more until it fills their lives and finally devours them." (p. 192). Bruno tells us of his life and his relationship with his son:

I work for someone else, I rent my apartment from someone else, there's nothing for my son to inherit. I have no craft to teach him, I haven't a clue what he might do when he's older. By the time he grows up, the rules I lived by will be meaningless – the world will be completely different. If a man accepts the fact that everything must change, then his life is reduced to nothing more than the sum of his own experience – past and future generations mean nothing to him. That's how we live now. (Houellebecq, 2001, p. 201).

As Bruno is aware, consumer society is an experience society (and tourism plays a significant role in Houellebecq's books, most directly in *Platform* and *Lanzarote*), where a person's life is reduced to the sum of his or her experiences. The New Age and hippie movements of the sixties are described as leading ideologies of experience-seeking consumers. Houellebecq's moral verdict against these emancipatory movements is harsh; they are seen as "libertines forever in search of new and more violent sensations." (Houellebecq, 2001, p. 252):

Having exhausted the possibilities of sexual pleasure, it was reasonable that individuals, liberated from the constraints of ordinary morality, should turn their attentions to the wider pleasures of cruelty. Two hundred years earlier, de Sade had done precisely the same thing. In a sense, the serial killers of the 1990s were the spiritual children of the hippies of the Sixties. (Houellebecq, 2001, p. 252).

People in the sex-and-shopping society consider life as worth living only if it provides them, continuously, with chances to have intense sensations and experiences, and, as their bodies inevitably grow older and gradually decay, these chances are diminished:

More than at any time or in any other civilisation, human beings are obsessed with ageing. Each individual has a simple view of the future: a time will come when the sum of pleasures that life has to offer is outweighed by the sum of pain [...]. This weighing up of pleasure and pain which, sooner or later, everyone is forced to make, leads logically, at a certain age, to suicide. (Houllebecq, 2001, p. 297).

The body plays a special role in the lives of Houellebecqian characters. Their identities are defined in bodily rather than psychological terms, it is how their bodies look, move, dress, and suffer that define them as persons. The body is all that belong to individuals qua individuals, according to Houellebecq; the rest is suprapersonal history and sociology, as we see in the following passage, where Michel considers the life of his half-brother:

Was it possible to think of Bruno as an individual? The decay of his organs was particular to him, and he would suffer his decline and death as an individual. On these dimensions of our lives. Perhaps such forms of psychology should be based on a radical phenomenology of behavior – perhaps it should build on a radical postmodern positivism?

CHALLENGING QUALITATIVE RESEARCH

Donald E. Polkinghorne
University of Southern California

QUALITATIVE INTERVIEWING AS A MORAL ENTERPRISE

Abstract

Kvale portrays the qualitative interview as a conversation. As a conversation the ethical issues of an interview extend beyond that described in research codes. Kvale offers interviewers three major ethical systems as frames of reference for thinking about the extended ethical dimensions. These frames of reference have been criticized by postmodern philosophers and held to be inadequate as sources for ethics. Levinas' thought is presented as an alternative frame of reference for ethical thinking in qualitative interviewing. Levinas holds that the place of the ethical is located in the face-to-face encounter with another person. His ideas of the Face, the Said and Saying, and Desire are explored. The chapter concludes with a discussion of the implications of Levinas' ethics for qualitative interviewers.

Throughout his distinguished academic career, Kvale has been a leading proponent of the use of qualitative interviews in the development of knowledge about persons. His celebrated and often referenced book *InterViews* (Kvale, 1996) has served many students and teachers as the primary source for understanding and conducting research interviews. He has framed the interview as a conversational interaction between persons rather than simply an operation in which information is extracted from another.

His publications have not only instructed his readers on how to conduct effective interviews through the use of main questions, follow-up questions, and probes, but they also call readers' attention to the moral responsibilities involved in engaging another person in the interview process. Kvale has been concerned about the ethical dimension of qualitative interviewing in his writings and in several unpublished convention presentations. His chapter six in *InterViews*, "Ethical Issues in Interview Inquiries," opens with the sentence "An interview inquiry is a moral enterprise" (1996, p. 109). Qualitative interviews differ from other data gathering practices in the social sciences. Unlike the generation of scores and information through test instruments and survey questionnaires, qualitative interviews primarily take place as extended face-to-face dialogue with a research participant. Although short-answer survey interviews include brief face-to-face researcher-participant interactions, they do not involve participants in a temporally extended encounter. Nor do survey interviews seek to lead interviewees into an in-depth discussion of their experiences and understandings. To achieve its purpose the qualitative interview needs to allow the interviewer-interviewee "interaction to get beyond merely a polite conversation or exchange of ideas" (Kvale, 1996, p. 125). The generation of rich and vibrant data is dependent on the willingness of the interviewee to share openly his or her views and remembrances.

As with other researchers, qualitative interviewers operate under the same important legal and institutional ethical demands – such as lack of deception, lack of co-optation, informed consent, protection of confidentiality, and doing no harm. The roles of interviewer and interviewee are socially defined in such a way that places the interviewer in the position of power; the interviewer "defines the situation, introduces the topics of the conversation, and... steers the course of the interview" (Rubin & Rubin, 2005, p. 34). Because of this asymmetry of power, the ethical responsibility for the interviewee lies heavily on the researcher. The asymmetry in the interviewer-interviewee relationship means that qualitative interviewers need to approach with care the use of empathy to establish rapport with an interviewee. The interviewee can be drawn into revealing thoughts and experiences that she would prefer not to share. In addition to the asymmetry of power there is an asymmetry in the benefits gained from a qualitative interview. The benefits that accrue to the interviewer can include graduation or promotion and the recognition that comes from publication. The benefit the interviewee gains is the experience of having someone thoughtfully and carefully listen to what they have to say. It is an ethical concern if being listened to in his way serves to balance the time and sharing that the interviewee gives. Should participants receive more than the simple appreciation of the interviewers?

Knowledge of the full range of ethical issues that arise in the face-to-face interactions of qualitative interviewing extends beyond knowledge of codes and rules. It entails sensitivity to the needs and concerns of the participant not covered in the codes and rules of Institutional Review Boards. Kvale writes, "Moral research behavior is more than ethical knowledge and cognitive choices," (1996, p. 117), and continues with a quote from Eisner and Peshkin: "They [researchers] need two attributes: the sensitivity to identify an ethical issue and the responsibility to feel committed to acting appropriately in regard to such issues" (Kvale, 1996, p. 117). To assist researchers engaged in qualitative interviewing in recognizing the extended ethical issues that arise in a qualitative interview, Kvale says that they should be aware of the "three major philosophical ethical positions" (p. 121) – Kantian duty-based ethics, utilitarian ethics of consequences, and Aristotle's virtue ethics. Kvale presents these three philosophical positions as "frames of reference for thinking about specific ethical issues in research" (Kvale, 1996, p. 121).

Kvale also notes that "to understand human activity it is necessary to know the culture, the social and historical situation, in which the activity takes place" (Kvale, 1992, p. 31), and he identifies the current age as the postmodern age. In chapter three (pp. 38-58) he presents a discussion of postmodernist thought as it pertains to the contemporary issues in the construction of knowledge. This chapter is an extension of his discussion of postmodernism into the area of ethics. Postmodern philosophy has called into question the legitimacy of the three major philosophical positions he describes (pp. 121-123) as frames for thinking about ethical issues. The culture in which current qualitative interviewing is undertaken is one that has been penetrated with postmodern ideas; thus, a frame of reference that takes into account postmodern critiques of the three major ethical systems is needed.

Morality and Postmodern Philosophy

Postmodern philosophy questioned the premises that underlay the development of Western ontology from the sixth century B.C. with the pre-Socratic Greek philosophers, through to the early twentieth century A.D. Ontology had assumed that behind the flux of everyday experience and underneath the apparent differences in historical epochs and cultural beliefs there existed a permanent and universal order. Because of their capacity to think and reason, humans are able to gain access to this order and thereby know and describe it. The domain of thought, that is, consciousness, was the essence of humanness and was considered to be separate and somewhat independent of the material realm. Philosophy was carried out as an activity of consciousness which searched for the unities and kinds of things of which individual items and surface phenomena were instances. It was in the realm of these unities (ideas or concepts) that the order was located. The unities were mapped on a set of words which represented their presence. The comprehension of this order of the "What Is" was the focus of the philosophical conversation.

The conversations of philosophers were about what Is the nature of this order and about the kind of thought necessary to know it. Did it consist of a pre-Socratic physical substrate, a hierarchy of Platonic forms, a mind-like Being of the idealists, matter in motion of the materialists, or something else? Does the order disclose itself in our clear and distinct ideas, or does access come through the use of the rationality of deductive logic? What characterizes the order? Does it have the precise structure of geometry, mathematics, or logic? Within these discussions, knowledge of what humans ought to do was to be based on the answers to these questions about the underlying order.

The conversations took a decided shift in the eighteenth century, when they took on a critical stance about human access to the underlying order. Hume and Kant proposed that what appeared in human understanding did not reflect the actual order, but was itself a simulated order constructed by the operations of the human mind. The stability that appeared was the effect of the same mental operations that structured all human thought. Philosophical thought refocused on consciousness and how phenomena made their appearance in awareness.

The challenge of postmodern philosophy (or non-philosophy) to prior philosophical thought focused on the understanding of the words used in the conversations. The conversations had assumed that words (such as *substance* and *attribute*, and *form* and *matter*) had a stable reference over time to the concepts or ideas mapped on them. Instead, postmodern philosophy held that the meaning of words (that is, the concepts they referred to) changed over time and varied according to the context in which they were expressed. They also held that the meanings or concepts themselves referred to by words were not stable. The ideas used by thought to comprehend order were fluid and detached from specific references. Words become meaningful not by bringing to presence something outside language but only by their differences from other words in a language system. The meanings of words were a consequence of social convention varying from site to site and era to era. Linguistic meaning was fundamentally indeterminate because the contexts which fix meaning are never stable. Words did not reflect the divisions and organization within the order of what Is; rather, the divisions they do reflect are impositions of various language communities.

Postmodern philosophy understood that thought was enclosed in language and consisted of the manipulating and connecting of words. And because words signify only in relation to other words, thought itself cannot break out of language to become present to what Is. There is no access to a point of reference outside the field of discourse. Derrida wrote:

[The] structural possibility of being weaned from the referent or from the signified... seems to me to make every mark, including those which are oral, a grapheme in general; which is to say, as we have seen, the non-present remainder of a differential mark cut off from its putative "production" or origin. And I shall even extend this law to all "experience" in general if it is conceded that there is no experience consisting of pure presence but only of chains of differential marks. (Derrida, 1988, p. 10).

Without the re-presentation of what Is in language, philosophical discourse was no longer understood to be able to directly address ontological questions. What is left for philosophers is to engage in "non-philosophical" discourse (Silverman, 1988, p. 4). Such a discourse is cautious about its language and aware of the sedimentations of meanings in words retained from the notion that words re-present the real.

Within non-philosophical conversations, the topic of ethics is no longer about deriving universal commandments or rules grounded on knowledge of the nature of the ultimate. Instead of looking to the what Is for ethical instruction, non-philosophy turns toward the context of personal experience. Emmanuel Levinas is the most prominent philosopher with sensitivity to the postmodern approach to language to address its neglected topic of ethics. In Levinas' work, the meaning of the word *ethics* is deepened from its traditional focus on people's actions to the place in which ethics happen. For Levinas, *ethics* signifies the fact of the face-to-face encounter with another particular person. Thus, because the qualitative interview is one of the occasions in which individual persons meet, it itself is a domain of the ethical.

Levinas

The postmodern critique of the search for universal norms of ethics appeared to give credence to the idea that the notions for guiding human behavior were relativistic and merely a means for a society's powerful to control the less powerful (Foucault, 1975/1979). By relocating the ethical underneath the "what is" as it is referenced in language, Levinas reintroduces the dimension of the ethical into postmodern thought (Bauman, 1993; Critchley, 1992).

The Self and Other

The ethical domain is the actual relationship of the self and a particular Other[1]. In *Totality and Infinity* (Levinas, 1961/1991), Levinas describes the discovery of the priority of the ethical as the self's move from interiority to exteriority; that is, from a solipsistic or separated self to a self that realizes that it depends on a prior Other. The self of interiority is one of appetitive enjoyment; the self of exteriority is one of solicitous desire.

The idea of the self had been de-centered in postmodern philosophy (Schrag, 1997). Previously Marxism and structuralism had dissolved the self into historical forces or underlying structural systems. Postmodern thought presented the concept of self as an artifact of grammar. Human practices are not the result of personal will and choice; rather, they are simply enactments of culturally developed scripts. Levinas, however, presents a defense of the subject.

This book then does present itself as a defense of the subjectivity, but it will apprehend the subjectivity not at the level of its purely egoist protestation against totality, nor in its anguish before death, but as founded in the idea of infinity [the Other]. (Levinas, 1961/1991, p. 26).

Levinas approaches the self not as a disembodied consciousness, but as the presence of the I to itself. There is no division between the soul and body; we are flesh and blood. Peperzak writes: "Perhaps Levinas is the first philosopher who gave a phenomenology of the living being – the animal or *zooion* – that we all, without exception and still uniquely and originally, are" (Peperzak, 1993, p. 154). The self is localized; it is a particular body in a particular space. Thus, a person cannot be understood simply as an instance of a species; rather each person is unique and the actor of his or her own life drama.

The interiorized self is at home in the world. It has a zest for life and enjoys its existence. "Life is *love of* life, a relation with contents that are not my being but more dear than my being: thinking, eating, sleeping, reading, working, warming oneself in the sun.... The reality of life is already on the level of happiness,... Happiness is not an accident of being, since being is risked for happiness" (Levinas, 1961/1991, p. 112). To live is not to anxiously await death, but is itself pleasurable. In enjoying the world the body feels itself acting on and being acted on by the world. One interacts and appropriates the objects of the world to satisfy one's needs. Worldly goods appear as things to be stalked and taken in, not as a spectacle to be observed (Moyn, 2005). The selfhood of interiority, which Levinas calls the *same*, is pragmatic rather than theoretical.

As it satisfies its needs by consuming objects of the world, it experiences pleasure. It takes in food and drink not merely to relieve hunger or quench thirst, but also for the satisfaction involved in fulfilling a need. Levinas explains:

Nourishment, as a means of invigoration, is the transmutation of the other into the same, which is in the essence of enjoyment: an energy that is other, recognized as other, recognized, we will see, as sustaining the very act that is directed upon it, becomes, in enjoyment, my own energy, my strength, me. All enjoyment is in the sense alimentation. (Levinas, 1961/1991, p. 111).

Pleasure is experienced not only in meeting biological needs, but also in transforming worldly things into houses and shelters, producing art and music, and, perhaps, completion of a research project. But the life of enjoyment is a solitary one; the felt pleasures are only experiences within the interiority of the self.

The life of the interiorized self is one devoted to its self-maintenance, and is where the things of the world are cared about only in so far as they can be grasped to satisfy my needs. It is egoistic and hedonistic with its focus on its own happiness. Although Levinas presents the interiorized life as a limited way of living, his descriptions of it are not entirely negative; instead, his accounts are meant to restore some dignity to the life of enjoyment and pleasure. He holds that the self-centered life is a necessary stage in human existence in which a separate ego acquires its substantiality and autonomy. These attributes are the precondition for a self's encounter with the Other. Unlike the other objects in the world, the Other cannot be incorporated into the self. The encounter with a wholly Other interrupts the interiorized way of being and calls the ego to put limits on its right to satisfy itself and to re-direct itself to respond to the needs of the Other.

The Other, the person before me, differs from all other beings in the world.[2] Levinas, who introduced Husserl's phenomenology to France in the 1930s (Levinas, 1930/1973), holds that the Other does not show itself to the self in the manner of other objects. They do not appear as phenomena which are brought to comprehension as a kind of thing through the correlation between noesis and noema. Husserl's notion of intentionality has an optical bias which proposes that it is the light of one's consciousness that brings the world to appearance for the self.

Qua phenomenology [phenomenological description] remains within the world of light, the world of the solitary ego which has no relationship with the Other qua Other for whom the Other is another me, an *alter ego* known by sympathy, that is, by a return to oneself. (Levinas, 1947/1988, p. 85).

For Husserl, what appears in my consciousness is merely the material form of other persons, not persons themselves. I assume the other's personhood exists through sympathetic analogy whereby because my consciousness resides in a material form similar to the material form of others, there must reside in the other's human form a consciousness like mine.

For Levinas the personhood of the other is not a conjecture, but is that which directly and bodily encounters me. The Other who is met presents a surplus of meaning which is beyond the capacity of my consciousness to comprehend. The relationship with the Other is more fundamental than knowledge. He or she cannot be tamed by the conceptualizating or thematizing operations of consciousness. Levinas says the Other is experienced as an enigma that is more than I can think. He uses various terms to describe the Other: "Infinity, transcendence, exteriority, alternity. The infinite is the Other; its alternity is also transcendence and exteriority because it is outside, above and beyond the powers of the subject" (Davis, 1996, p. 40).

The Other remains external and separate from me; and yet in relationship with me. Encountering the Other awakens me from the interiority of myself in which what is, is what can be known by my consciousness. The self cannot control or master the subject. But neither is the self absorbed or merged into the Other; in the encounter the self remains independent and self-sufficient. Although the resistance of the Other cannot be subdued by bringing it to the subject's interiority, the Other does not overcome the subject, but leaves the subject with its freedom to choose and act. In the presence of the separate Other, the subject is aware of a desire to respond. The desire is not something that is derived from rational thought as in Kant; it is feeling that arises in the encounter with an Other. The desire is a primal experience[3], different from the ordinary worldly experiences. The subject cannot avoid hearing the call from the Other to respond, but it remains free to not heed the call.

The encounter with the Other is a peaceful, rather than hostile meeting. It does not take place as a Hobbesian struggle by equal wills for dominance, nor as a contract to limit each other's aggressiveness. Although the Other offers resistance to being taken in by an interiorized self, unlike the things of the world, its resistance does not have the power to make the other self respond "There is here a relation not with a very great resistance, but with something absolutely *other;* the resistance of what has no resistance – the ethical resistance" (Levinas, 1961/1991, p. 199). It is resistance that cannot be observed, but is heard as a call out of weakness and unprotected nakedness of the Other.

Levinas employs three connected ideas – *the Face, the Saying and the Said,* and *Desire* – to clarify the ethical space that opens up in the meeting of a self and the enigmatic Other.

The Face

The discussion of the face is one of the most well recognized parts of Levinas' philosophy. As Levinas uses the term *face*, it does not refer to the part of the physical head where the eyes, nose, and mouth are located. The face is not a perceptual object. The *face* refers to the presence of the personhood of an Other that occurs in a meeting.

The way in which the Other presents himself, exceeding the *idea of the Other in me*, we here name face. This mode does not consist in figuring as a theme under my gaze, in spreading itself forth as a set of qualities forming an image. The face of the Other at each moment destroys and overflows the plastic image it leaves me. (Levinas, 1961/1991, pp. 50-51).

Through the face, the Other is experienced as a distinct, individual person-hood, not an impersonal and anonymous other. The face is "the channel through which alterity presents itself to me, and as such it lies outside and beyond what can be seen or experienced" (Davis, 1996, p. 135).

The face is not a symbol pointing to the Other or mask behind which the Other dwells. Thus, the Other is not uncovered by interpretation of the face or by recovery of something hidden behind the surface. The face undercuts the approach to the other as an instance of a role or some type of person. In the face, the Other is immediately present to the subject and makes a claim on the subject to whom it "appears."

The face is a reminder that the Other is not some spirit or soul attached to a body, but is a flesh and blood Other in front of me. Levinas' philosophy recognizes that a human being is a corporal being. "The otherness does not lie behind the surface of somebody we see, hear, touch and violate. It is just his or her otherness. It is the other as such and not some aspect of him or her that is condensed in the face" (Waldenfels, 2002, p. 65). The face-to-face encounter is a meeting of two real embodied persons.

Discourse – Saying and the Said

The words of language point to the concepts and ideas by which thinking identifies the world's objects as specific kinds of things. Language implies the existence of a stable, comprehensible reality. Ontological discourse is made up of statements and propositions about the characteristics and attributes of the world, reality, personal identity, and truth. It consists of assertions whose truth or falsity can be argued. Levinas identifies this kind of discourse as the Said. When he engages in philosophy, he necessarily speaks in the language of the Said.

In an encounter I am positioned proximately with the Other. In this proximity I receive an address from the Other to respond to his or her needs. The address asks that I do no violence and that I respond by offering up the "bread" I had intended to use for my own enjoyment. The address takes place underneath the words that are spoken. It occurs through the gestures and sounds that are exchanged. Levinas uses the word *saying* to designate this call to respond within an encounter.

The Saying that occurs in an encounter does not translate well into the themes of the Said which are used in philosophical discourse. Thus to communicate philosophically what he understands about the call to respond in an encounter, Levinas resorts to writing in fragments, aphorisms, and hyperbole in his 1978 book, *Otherwise than Being or Beyond Essence*, (Levinas, 1978/1991). He places knots or hints in the string of the text in which the traces of the experience of meeting an Other show up. The knots interrupt the rationally presented Said about the Saying of relationship. The problem Levinas addressed is that language is inadequate to express the encounter with an Other (the Saying); yet, he needs to employ language (the Said) to express his ideas about the ethical domain.

Desire

The practices of the life of interiority are dominated by the motivation to satisfy needs. When needs are appeased, they lose their motivational force. The structure of interiority is one of privation followed by the pleasure of satisfaction; it is an economy of neediness and satiation. "The acute experiences of the human in the twentieth century teach that the thoughts of men are borne by needs which explain society and history, that hunger and fear can prevail over every human resistance and every freedom" (Levinas, 1961/1991, p. 35). In the encounter with the Other, a different structure prevails. The subject's responsiveness to the other is governed by desire rather than need; it is without limit and does not end with the satisfaction of completion. "The metaphysical[4] desire... desires beyond everything that can simply complete it. It is like goodness – the Desired does not fulfill it, but deepens it" (Levinas, 1961/1991, p. 34). The desire to respond to the Other grows the more the subject tries to satisfy it. Subjects never reach the point where they have done all that must be done for the Other; there is always more to do.

For Levinas, the experience of the encounter with the other does not consist of feeling that the Other owes me a similar responsiveness. Performances within the ethical relationship do not depend on the expectation that the subject will get something in return, not even the satisfaction of the need to feel that in responding one is being a moral person. Davis notes: "One of the most distinctive aspects of his [Levinas'] ethics is his insistence of the asymmetrical nature of the ethical relationship" (Davis, 1996, p. 51). For Levinas, priority, which had been assigned to the self in modern ethics, is accorded to the Other.

The knot of subjectivity consists in going to the other [Other] without concerning oneself with his movement toward me. Or, more exactly, it consists in approaching in such a way that, over and beyond all the reciprocal relations that do not fail to get set up between me and the neighbor, I have always taken one step more toward him.... Without asking myself: What then is it to me? Where does he get his right to command? What have I done to be from the start in debt? (Levinas, 1982/1985, p. 100-101).

The response to the Other is unconditional. It is not something earned by the Other, nor does it depend on the merits of the Other. The obligation to respond is not a matter of fulfilling the conditions of a contract with the other. The subject is obligated because of the presence of the Other; it is not something he or she decides to take on. What is to be decided is whether or not I will respond to the already present felt obligation. I am the one who is in the presence of the Other, and I cannot assign someone else to take on my obligation.

Levinas' work is focused on the recovery of an ethical realm after the dismantling by postmodern philosophy of the previous sites that had been proposed by traditional philosophy. After the rejection of external sources of universal obligations, such as the divine and disembodied reason, the sources of obligation were relocated and placed by recent philosophy in the demands of social groups or in the self's needs for survival and/or pleasure. For Levinas, the source of obligation is the face of the Other who is before us. The Other is the source of our felt desire to interrupt our life of enjoyment and turn our concern toward service of the Who is other than me.

Levinas does not offer a set of rules or a decision matrix for deciding on what to do in responding to the Other. The Other is always a particular person, not an instance of humankind. The Other is flesh located in the encounter that takes place at a particular time and in a particular space. Judgments about which responses fit the situation take into account the distinctiveness of the event of encounter and the particularity of the Other. In his virtue ethics, Aristotle calls this kind of judgment *phronesis* (Polkinghorne, 2004). However, for Aristotle the source of these actions is my own virtue not the obligation to the Other. Actions for the other are in the service of my need to live a fulfilled life. For Levinas these actions are for the Other without benefit to me.[5]

Conclusion

The qualitative interview places the interviewer directly in the domain of the ethical. By placing oneself face-to-face with an Other, the interviewer's obligations are extended beyond what is asked for in research codes and rules. The face of the interviewee calls for a response to his or her needs. The interviewer feels the call as a primal desire to respond. However, interviewers can muffle the call by focusing their attention on satisfying their own needs to extract data from the Other. When the call is muffled, the interviewee is attended to only as another resource for the interviewer's use. The identity of the Other as a particular person is transformed into something that satisfies the criteria of a purposeful sample. The worth and usefulness of the Other is judged by the quality of data that they can give. The technique of building rapport is engaged in to make the interviewee more pliable and forthcoming.

Levinas' philosophy refashions the site of the ethical in qualitative interviewing. It provides a frame of reference which sensitizes the interviewer to the obligation to respond and serve the interviewee as a unique person. Violence in Levinas' frame occurs when the interviewee is approached as simply an object to be used to meet the interiorized needs of the self. The interviewer retains the freedom to not listen to the call of the Other and to act as if they are under no obligation to respond to the call.

NOTES

1 The *Other* (capitalized) is contrasted with *other* (not capitalized) in the convention used in the translation of Levinas' publications. *Other* (capitalized) refers to the particular person who is before me in a face-to-face encounter (*l'autrui*); *other* (not capitalized) refers to the objects in the world.

2 Critchley (1992) proposes that Levinas' ethics is not limited to encounters with human beings. "If the condition of possibility for ethical obligation is sensibility toward the face of the Other, then the purview of the *Autrui* [Other] can be extended to all sentient beings.... The question with regard to human obligations toward animals is not 'Can they reason? or Can they talk? But, *Can they suffer?*'"

3 In writings about Levinas, the word *experience* carries two meanings. In one usage *experience* retains its ordinary meaning and refers to the appearances that occur in a person's awareness including perceptions of worldly objects as well as memories and imaginations. This is the realm of knowledge in which something appears *as* something having been co-constituted by conscious intentionality and sense matter. In the other usage, *experience* refers to a primal level of recognition that does not appear in awareness as something; and, it thus, does not become an object of comprehension. The experience of the Other and his or her call to responsiveness occurs at this second "level" of experience.

4 Levinas uses the term *metaphysical* to describe the realm other than the worldy objects of comprehension; that is, the realm of the encounter.

5 I have not discussed Levinas' social ethics and justice, in which he posits a commonality among equals. He approaches the topic from the perspective of the third party or humanity as a whole (see Critchley, 1992, pp. 225-236).

Julianne Cheek,
University of Oslo and University of South Australia

BEYOND THE 'HOW TO': THE IMPORTANCE OF THINKING ABOUT, NOT SIMPLY DOING, QUALITATIVE RESEARCH

This chapter focuses on two interrelated aspects of Steinar Kvale's work that have impacted on the development of qualitative research generally, and also on me personally as a qualitative researcher. The first aspect is the serious and sustained contribution that his work has made to our understandings of the interview. The second is his incisive, challenging and often witty analysis and critique of the wider political context in which qualitative research is conducted and in which we, as qualitative researchers, find ourselves working and researching. It is Kvale's ability to connect the development and employment of methods such as the interview with the wider macro contexts in which such methods and their deployment are situated that makes his work so innovative, insightful, and increasingly important in the contemporary context in which many qualitative researchers find themselves working. In order to establish the parameters for the discussion to follow, it is important to take a brief look at what that contemporary context is with respect to the development of qualitative methods and qualitative enquiry.

The opening decade of the twenty-first century has seen the continued growth and development of qualitative research, a development that has consistently extended and challenged both methodological and substantive research boundaries within qualitative research itself, as well as in research more generally. Accompanying such growth and development has been a rapid proliferation of texts, articles and courses about qualitative research, mostly focusing on how to do qualitative enquiry and usually written with the needs of students in mind. As Denzin, Lincoln and Giardina (2006, p. 778) point out, there are more students than ever learning about and embracing these approaches and, as inquirers-in-training, they want "to know all they can about how to practice such arts and sciences".

Somewhat paradoxically however, the same decade has seen the emergence of a sustained and serious threat to the credibility and future of qualitative research. Much of this has stemmed from the quest for certainty about, and concomitant narrowing conceptions of, what constitutes research and research evidence. Drawing on notions of research that are influenced by neo-positivism, certain understandings of what constitutes evidence have achieved truth status in much of the writing and thinking about research and evidence: this has occurred especially in fields such as medicine, health, psychology, and education. Such understandings are part of a politics of evidence in which one type of research evidence is privileged over another. Holmes et al. (2006, p. 181) state that health care evidence-based discourse "is outrageously exclusionary and dangerously normative with regard to scientific knowledge".

Such a politics and its outworking impacts on researchers daily. It shapes and permeates all aspects of the research endeavor – the type of methods used, the theoretical orientations and epistemological assumptions underpinning the research in the first place, the type and nature of analyses done or even possible, and, very significantly, the value assigned, or credibility given, to the findings of the research. One outworking of this politics and its quest for certainty has been an increased interference in research activity by governments under the guise of ensuring quality outputs and value for money (see Cheek, 2006; Denzin & Giardina, 2006; Denzin & Lincoln, 2005; Torrance, 2006). Such interference is premised on neo-liberal understandings in which the principles of the marketplace, competition and enterprise are paramount.

In this chapter, I want to focus on what I see as a significant point of collision in such a context. While qualitative research approaches become seemingly more mainstream and sought after by students and others, resulting in the desire for more guidance in these approaches by inquirers-in-training; there is also a growing contemporary obsession and fetishism in the desire for certainty. Stemming from this desire for certainty are disturbingly limited notions of evidence and research both from without the ranks of qualitative research *but importantly, also potentially from within*. It is about this point of collision, and the concomitant tensions both precipitating and emanating from such a collision, that Kvale has something very important to say.

Whilst being cognisant of and stressing the importance of acknowledging the theoretical parameters that underpin any research endeavor, at the same time he provides invaluable practical and useful insights and considerations for students and teachers, novice and experienced proponents of qualitative research alike, as they attempt to navigate this contested and increasingly fraught research terrain.

This ability to make the theoretical and often seemingly more obtuse aspects of the qualitative research endeavor relevant to, and able to meld with, the realm of the practical, by speaking to the messy realities of the worlds in which qualitative researchers live and research, is a somewhat unique and very powerful aspect of Kvale's work. To use his own words, qualitative research and the associated development and nurturing of qualitative researchers must be as much about 'how to think about' a method or approach as it is about 'how to do' that method or approach (Kvale, 1996, p. xv). This is a key point requiring further exploration. I attempt to do this in what follows, using Kvale's writing about the interview as both the impetus and the vehicle for discussion.

Beyond The "How To Do": Guarding Against a Form of Qualitative Positivism

One danger of the seeming success of qualitative research in terms of its increased popularity and the subsequent need for 'training' in this type of research, is that 'how to do' research can be prioritized over the thinking that underpins the methods to be used, that is, 'how to think about' research. Qualitative research can become reduced to a series of steps to be undertaken: worse, it can become reduced to a series of steps that *must* be undertaken in order to produce a predetermined form of research report or finding. The effect of this is to introduce rigidity and a type of codification into the way qualitative research is thought about and enacted. Some of Kvale's more recent work (e.g. Kvale, 2006, May) saliently points out that such a trend may be the outworking of a new form of qualitative positivism. Another way of putting this is that it is a form of 'methodolatry' (Chamberlain, 2000) potentially emanating from within qualitative research itself. Such methodolatry, with an overemphasis on locating the "correct" or "proper" methods, reifies methods, with a resultant "privileging of methodological concerns over other considerations in qualitative health research" (Chamberlain, 2000, p. 285). Chamberlain has suggested strategies to avoid, or at least, stem, the potential rise of methodolatry in the qualitative research arena. These include the promotion of discussion and debate about such matters, different emphases and foci in research training and associated activities, and providing more guidance and support for researchers who are entering and engaging with the field of qualitative research (Chamberlain, 2000, p. 294).

Kvale's work contributes to, and is in keeping with, such strategies. One of his most simple yet most telling insights is to remind us that all aspects of qualitative research design have embedded in them three interdependent and related dimensions, namely, the theoretical, methodological and ethical. This insight is one that is often overlooked in the scramble for the 'how to do' at the expense of the 'how to think about'. It is to forget that what otherwise might be considered as no more than techniques to be used in an overall research design, for example the interview or the observation, are themselves constructed by theoretical, methodological and/or ethical considerations. Put another way, there is a tendency for discussions about the interview or the observation to focus on how to use them (the doing) rather than also considering what they are and what assumptions have shaped them in the first place (the thinking about).

"Doing" an interview or using interviews in a research design, far from being a neutral tool or something able to be simply selected and inserted into a piece of research, *itself* involves theoretical, methodological and ethical considerations and choices on the part of the researcher. Too often, methods are written about as a given, as sets of instructions or rules of procedure: studies become little more than the employment of a set of data-collection techniques. As Janesick (2000, p. 387) points out, "merely employing a qualitative technique here and there does not make a study qualitative". If the recipe or steps to be followed become thought of as synonymous with method or, in practice, with what method is reduced or stripped to, then the emphasis will be placed on establishing and following rules rather than developing an understanding of the principles that shape the way a particular method is thought about, the effect this might have on the research, and the purpose for which a method might be used.

The type of reflection on method advocated by Kvale and arising from a consideration of his arguments is particularly relevant to, indeed crucial in, a context that has seen an explosion of so-called "methods" courses and texts. Not surprisingly, their focus is on getting the research done, given the demands of course requirements for many students, which are often time delimited. In addition, completion by the student within a set period of time is actually used as a measure of quality for both student and research supervisor. In such a context there are calls for quick and easy guides and checklists to understand and evaluate qualitative research (see Barbour, 2001). Accompanying such calls is the creation of a market for more prescriptive, detailed and unambiguous step-by-step descriptions of how to undertake particular qualitative methods.

Even a brief glance at the outline statements of many method courses, and/or the contents pages of many texts on research methods, highlights their clear focus on the provision of techniques or steps to follow. Texts that are more 'how to' manuals than discussions of thinking about methods serve to create a sense of reassurance and security for students and teachers alike, with respect to following set procedures and training pathways in the tenets of qualitative research. However, this may well be a false security (Chamberlain, 2000), anchored as it is in positivistic assumptions. Positivistic thinking has the effect of reducing successful research training to following a series of steps or procedures. The sum of these is assumed to add up to the entity we call a method, such as an interview or observation, *and in turn* the sum of the methods is assumed to add up to, and produce, an entity called qualitative research.

There is a danger that such market forces, premised on certain understandings of methods and research training, will shape the very concept of qualitative research itself. This is a danger that Kvale (2003, p. 596) has pointed to with respect to the discipline of psychology when he asserts that under the contemporary reign of the market, issues "such as whether psychology is a natural science or a human science – in earlier periods the topic of heated theoretical controversies – are today simply left to the market". He gives the example of the editors of an influential handbook on psychology endorsing psychology as natural science, at least partly, because if psychology is classified as a natural science then funding is usually more adequate. Ironically, Kvale

(2003, p. 597) suggests, "where there is funding there is also psychology in the postmodern age". This sounds a warning and cautionary note to us when looking at the increased production of, and funding for, qualitative method texts. There is the potential for the skewing of texts on research methods in response to such market-derived and market-driven demands. Is it a case of where there is a market then there can be qualitative method texts?

There is a dynamic at play here: the production of such texts is fuelled by understandings of what it is to do qualitative research; in turn, such texts serve to feed into and perpetuate those understandings. If volume of sales is a determinant of what can be published on a commercial basis, then it may well be that this will perpetuate the dominance, mainframing and mainstreaming of the 'how to' type of text designed to be a set textbook or required reading in a numerically large cohort of students. The proliferation of this type of text and writing about qualitative research is an outworking of the reductionist trend in much contemporary thinking about the scholarship of research itself and, concomitantly, about research training.

This is not to argue against the need for or potential contribution of texts that clearly explain qualitative research and give ideas and strategies for how it might be approached and conducted. Rather, it is to argue against the trend to produce only one type of text that is narrow and limited with respect to both the concept of qualitative research, and research methods. Other types of possible research texts, and/or views about how research might be thought about and subsequently taught, could instead be relegated to, and remain on, the margins. As Kvale points out, this potentially would be at the expense of theoretical understandings of the research. This would limit us to the 'how to', and a limited 'how to' at that – not pushing into the 'how to think about'.

Beyond The 'How To': Implications For, and From, The Inter View
Kvale asserts that there is often an overemphasis on context-free rules of procedure with respect to method. Consequently, in his work on the interview he argues for a consideration of interviewing as a craft with concomitant de-emphasizing of interviewing as a method (Kvale, 1996; 2006, May). Whilst it is not the purpose of this chapter to explore in any depth the notion of interviewing as craft or researcher as craftsperson, the notion of the craft is a

useful tool or metaphor to drive what is the focus of the discussion – namely Kvale's contribution to highlighting the need to *think about*, not just 'how to', with respect to qualitative research. This is in keeping with his central and important contribution – thinking about the interview as an *inter view* rather than *an interview*. Reference to an inter view situates the act of interviewing in a wider context and de-emphasizes delimited notions of the interview as simply the exchange of a series of questions enacted in a particular way, or a schedule of probes to be followed. Rather, the inter view comprises a "situation of knowledge production in which knowledge is created between the views of the two partners in the conversation" (Kvale, 1996, p. 296). Such knowledge is produced as much from the initial impetus for the research, the formation of questions for the interview, the interpretation of data gained, the way the data is subsequently thought about and spoken about, and to whom, as it is from the actual interaction between interviewer and interviewee in their exchange of dialogue and words.

Drawing on the notion of interviewing as a craft, Kvale argues that as with learning any craft, to become a craftsperson with respect to interviewing takes time, training and much practice, explicitly involving a degree of personal insight before, during and after the interview. In his conception of a craft-like approach to the interview, the focus is on undertaking a multidimensional and multifaceted process, as opposed to operationalizing methods *per se*. Kvale uses a metaphor of the researcher as traveler to capture this idea: "The interviewer-traveler wanders through the landscape and enters into conversations with the people encountered. The traveler explores the many domains of the country, as unknown territory or with maps, roaming freely around the territory" (1996, p. 4). This is to highlight that the researcher makes judgments and decisions about the interview throughout the entire research process, and in so doing, Kvale argues for the insertion and recognition of the *person of the researcher* as research instrument in the conduct and concept of the interview. Kvale (1996, p. 88) explores this in the reflexive analysis and critique of his own postulation of seven stages in a research interview. He uses Bourdieu's (1999) work, which he describes as a "more craftsman-like approach to interviewing" to reflexively re-explore, critique and extend these seven stages, particularly with respect to the analysis of the interview.

It is Kvale's reflexivity, re-exploration and critique that, for the purposes of this discussion, is the focus rather than an in-depth exploration and critique of his notion of craftsmanship per se. Such reflexivity is an example of the outworking of the thinking *about* methods and qualitative research, and demonstrates cogently the possibilities opened up by thinking beyond the 'how to'. For example, it highlights that Kvale's idea of seven stages in an interview investigation are open to critique as well as to ongoing development and debate. This is crucial as, read acritically, and taken out of context on their own without the discussion that surrounds their development, his seven stages could be read as prescriptive and rigid – the 'how to'. Such a reading is not in keeping with premises that Kvale puts forward in the rest of his book and in his more recent work. However, the production of a list of seven stages that forms the organizing construct for much of his writing about the interview in his 1996 text does open him to the possibility of criticism, or even to the charge of a form of reductionist and methodologically prescriptive thinking with respect to the design and conduct of interviews. In later work Kvale (2006, May) acknowledges that his presentation of the seven stages of an interview (and perhaps the use of the word 'the' with respect to these stages is unfortunate as it does have the connotation of a set series of steps) is more formalistic and prescriptive than what he terms Bourdieu's more craftsman-like approach.

If we accept, or at least work with, Kvale's notion of 'thinking about' rather than just thinking about the "how to do" with respect to qualitative research more generally, and particular methods more specifically, then this has implications for the way we teach what we commonly term qualitative methods – interviews, observations and the like. Any inclination towards following standardized guidelines or training in techniques is de-emphasized in order to focus on the thinking and understandings that underpin these techniques, which is to view them as research processes and as socially situated. This involves long periods of reflection and training in these techniques, which constitutes a point of collision and tension for many students who find themselves having to conduct research in relatively, and increasingly, short delimited time frames that do not allow for this type of development. Yet, given the contemporary context in which students, teachers and practitioners of research alike find themselves, such considerations are more crucial than ever. At the very least they enable a type of thinking about what is happening, and what is being done in such a context, that offers the possibility for opening up to scrutiny, otherwise assumed, to be given with respect to the conduct and teaching of research generally, and qualitative research specifically.

Beyond The How To: Where To From Here?

Qualitative research continues to grow and flourish. This is despite incessant pressure and demands on both qualitative researchers and qualitative research itself, emanating from a politics of evidence that is shaping much of the contemporary research landscape. Kvale's work on the inter view, in concert with his more recent commentary on the potential effects of the outworking of a politics of evidence both from without, but crucially also *within* qualitative research, provides a serious and important contribution to understanding, and thereby navigating, such a contested and troubled research terrain. One of the dangers he has pointed out and stridently critiqued is a tendency to reduce the understanding and practice of qualitative research to prescriptive methods – the 'how to do'. The challenge for those who practice and teach qualitative research is how to retain the integrity of qualitative approaches in such an environment. In fact, perhaps even more important is how to understand and then make explicit what retaining that integrity might mean. Exploring what the outworking of an emphasis on what Kvale has termed the 'how to think about' rather than simply the 'how to do' might mean, provides an accessible and useful entry point to such considerations.

The notion of both inter view and inter viewing as craft highlights the need to consider the inter-connectedness of, and relationship between, the broader social context in which the inter view is both conducted and constructed. Such a consideration is to recognize both "power dynamics within a research interview and also the immersion of interviews in the societal exertion of power" (Kvale, 2006, p. 496). This is to challenge notions of the interview as a conflict- and power-free zone, and so brings in the idea of the interview as a dialogue under scrutiny. Kvale (2006) points out that qualitative interviews have often been regarded as a progressive form of social research – sometimes referred to as a dialogue between interviewer and interviewee. Dialogue, he notes, may be thought of as a conversation between egalitarian partners where such a dialogue is a joint endeavor related to mutual interests. However, in the interview it is the researcher's search for knowledge that initiates and shapes the process, and ultimately the interpretation of it. If the interview is thought of as necessarily synonymous with a dialogue between interviewer and interviewee, or, put another way, researcher and researched, then it is possible that the asymmetry of the power relations built into the interview will remain hidden and therefore unexamined. Kvale points out that to ignore this contributes to the perpetuation of a qualitative progressivity myth, where caring dialogical interviews in themselves come to be regarded as good and emancipating (Brinkmann & Kvale, 2005).

Whether or not one agrees with this, it is important that the point Kvale raises be considered and given more thought and discussion, both in the research literature itself and in learning programs designed for the development of qualitative researchers. This is particularly so, given a trend in some writing about interviews, and about qualitative research more generally, that suggests an unproblematic equal partnership, giving both power and voice to participants during and through the research process (e.g. Mischler, 1986; Rappaport, 1990, 1995; Lykes, 1997). Of course, this may not be a case of all or nothing: in many instances qualitative research and interviews may well assist in giving presence to groups that otherwise are ignored, disenfranchised and invisible. But the mere fact of conducting an interview or employing a qualitative research approach does not in itself eliminate differential power relations and positions in the research. This does not mean that interviews are not 'good' or that power being present is necessarily 'bad', but *overlooking the possibility of such power relations is*. Kvale is right to remind us of the need for caution with regard to conceiving the qualitative interview as some type of unique, democratic and even authentic dialogue. Such caution, and the hesitation it calls for when thinking about and conducting inter views, emphasizes the importance of 'how to think about' such interviews rather than just 'how to do' them.

Emphasizing the 'how to think about' resonates with contemporary challenges for qualitative research at a number of points, including, as we have explored in this chapter, the interconnectedness of theory and method; implications for students of qualitative enquiry and their training/development; the inter view as metaphor for the relationship between research context and research method/design; and the relationship between the researcher and the researched. This type of deep and sustained thinking creates possibilities for resisting prescribed notions of the interview, qualitative research and research more generally. In promoting the need for thinking about theory and context, in conjunction with, and indeed as inseparable from, discussions of methods and research design, Kvale eloquently and powerfully speaks to the issues that continue to mutate and arise in the wake of the politics of evidence. In many ways his work can be read as a plea for us to hesitate before acting, and to think deeply about what we are doing. It is less a conclusion and "more a comment within an ongoing discussion" (Maxey, 1999, p. 206). This is because engaged critical reflexivity such as that employed by Kvale enables us to be able to "celebrate the value of our contingent, flawed efforts" thereby being "far freer to add our next contribution to the conversation" (Maxey, 1999, p. 206).

Further, the idea of 'thinking about' rather than simply 'how to do' can be equally useful to a consideration of the broader field and idea of qualitative research more generally as qualitative researchers attempt to articulate and define just what it is they mean by this term (see Schwandt, 2006). The very notion of just what qualitative enquiry is or is not requires much thinking about, particularly in the light of contemporary contexts replete with market-driven interference in research in new and mutated ways. This is what makes Kvale's work so powerful and so relevant. He highlights the levels of complexity in the interaction between context, researcher, research and research methods. He has been able to apply his analysis of how understandings of psychology are reflective of, and impacted by, the wider culture and context to qualitative research. His assertion that "psychology is a cultural and historical activity" (Kvale, 2003, p. 579) is one that we would do well to keep at the forefront of our thinking about qualitative research. His call to psychology as needing to reconsider its own practice and view its own activity critically is just as relevant to, and important for, qualitative research.

Imitating Kvale's own style, in which he often (and sometimes in a very witty fashion) uses the fairy tale, the mythical, or lessons from literature or history to ground and make his point, I wish to conclude with the opening words from Charles Dickens's classic work, *A Tale of Two Cities*. This quote captures the idea of a contested reality, replete with paradoxes and concomitant choices and consequences. It reflects the messy realities of the worlds that we, as qualitative researchers, live and research in, and that Kvale's work speaks to us from and about.

It was the best of times, it was the worst of times, it was the age of wisdom, it was the age of foolishness, it was the epoch of belief, it was the epoch of incredulity, it was the season of Light, it was the season of Darkness, it was the spring of hope, it was the winter of despair, we had everything before us, we had nothing before us, we were all going direct to Heaven, we were all going direct the other way. (Charles Dickens, *A Tale of Two Cities*, 1859).

Norman K. Denzin
University of Illinois at Urbana-Champaign

ETHICS, ETHICISM AND CRITICAL INDIGENOUS INQUIRY[1]

Drawing on the critical insights of Kvale (2008, 2003), and Brinkmann and Kvale (2008, 2005), I want to read the current controversies and scandals surrounding Institutional Review Boards (IRBs) and qualitative inquiry within a critical pedagogical discourse. With Kvale and Brinkman, I understand that indigenous, radical democratic and social justice-based studies are under threat from several sides. First, and externally, "there are federal government demands for evidence-based practice, where experimental and quantified knowledge becomes the privileged form of scientific evidence" (Kvale, 2008, p. 1; Timmermans & Berg, 2003, p. 7). Further, within the North American and European academy, the bureaucracies of Institutional Review Boards threaten to stifle what little qualitative human subject research does get done (Christians, 2005).

Indeed, at the local departmental level, IRBs micro-manage qualitative research, thereby shaping its impact, relevance and use at the macro-community or market level (Gunsalus et al., 2007; Dash, 2007; Cannella & Lincoln, 2007; Lincoln, 1995; Christians, 2007a, b). This has the effect of interfering with academic freedom. IRB panels not only regulate who gives informed consent, but they also make stipulations concerning research design, and researcher-subject relationships (Tierney & Corwin, 2007). This creates a moral dilemma. There is a blurring of the "hard boundaries between quality, rigor and ethics .... emerging standards for quality ... are also standards for ethics" (Lincoln, 1995, p. 287). But whose ethics, whose standards? Researchers cannot be constituted as ethical selves antecedently, outside a dialogical space (Christians, 2007, p. 443).

A second threat arises from within the qualitative research community itself. There is, as Kvale (2008) and Brinkmann and Kvale (2005) observe, a tendency to "portray qualitative inquiry as inherently ethical, or at least more ethical than quantitative research" (2008, p. 10; Brinkmann & Kvale, 2005, p. 162). They call this qualitative ethicism; that is the inclination to see research within ethical terms, with the belief that qualitative research uniquely embodies these goals. The dangers with qualitative ethicism are two-fold. It can lead to an uncritical romanticizing of qualitative research. At the same time, it can direct attention away from the ways in which qualitative inquiry in the form of focus groups, open-ended interviewing, and ethnography is used to sell products in the consumer marketplace (Kvale, 2008, p. 16).

Qualitative researchers cannot claim a mantel of ethical superiority. They must also be vigilant in terms of how their methodologies are used in the consumer marketplace. The rush to embrace the interpretive turn in consumer research is a mixed ethical blessing.

***

I want to move in several directions at the same time. Extending Kvale and Brinkmann, I view ethics as pedagogies of practice. Multiple ethical theories, ranging from duty, to consequence, virtue, and care circulate in these spaces (Brinkman & Kvale, 2008, p. 261). IRBs are institutional apparatuses that regulate at the micro and macro levels a particular form of ethical conduct, a form that is no longer workable in a trans-disciplinary, global and postcolonial world. Smith (1999) reminds us that in many parts of the world research has become a dirty word. Further, for the world's indigenous peoples the ethical directives of IRBs are no longer regarded as sacrosanct. Foucault (1980, p. 267) and Lather (2007, p. 162) tell us that our ethical choices are always moral and political. We are responsible for the political consequences of our inquiry practices.

I seek a progressive performative cultural politics that enacts a performance ethics based on feminist, communitarian assumptions. I will attempt to align these assumptions with the call by First and Fourth World scholars for an indigenous research ethic (Smith, 1999; Bishop, 1998; Rains, Archibald & Deyhle, 2000). This call is consistent with Brinkmann and Kvale's

(2008) communitarian argument that grounding qualitative inquiry "in a research community where ethical and scientific values are integrated into daily practices may foster an integrated ethical qualitative behaviour" (p. 278).

This move allows me to criticize the dominant bio-medical ethical model that operates in many North American and European universities today.

I then turn to the preliminary outline of an indigenous, feminist, communitarian research ethic. This ethic has four implications. It would replace the current utilitarian ethical model that IRBs utilize. It would call for a two-track, or three-track IRB model within university settings. It would create communities of practice based on shared goals and values. It would facilitate dialogue and discussions about ethics, inquiry, and social justice.

Building on Kvale (2008) and Brinkmann and Kvale (2008), I move to a discussion of an indigenous ethical system developed by the Mi'kmaq Nation and the Mi'kmaw Ethics Watch (Ethics Eskinuapimk). This system is intended to protect indigenous knowledge (Battiste, 2008; Battiste & Youngblood, 2000).

CULTURAL POLITICS AND AN INDIGENOUS RESEARCH ETHICS

Maori scholars Linda Tuhiwai Smith (1999) and Russell Bishop (1998) are committed to a set of moral and pedagogical imperatives and "to acts of reclaiming, reformulating, and reconstituting indigenous cultures and languages ... to the struggle to become self-determining" (Smith, p. 142). A specific participatory, collaborative approach to inquiry is required. Dialogue is critical. The Maori moral position privileges storytelling, listening, and personal performance narratives (see also Collins, 1991, pp. 208-12). This moral pedagogy rests on an ethic of care and love and personal accountability that honors individual uniqueness and emotional meaning (Collins, 1991, pp. 215-17). This is an ethic grounded in the ritual, sacred spaces of family, community and everyday moral life (Bishop, 1998, p. 203). It is not imposed by some external, bureaucratic agency.

The Performative as a Site of Resistance

Because it expresses and embodies moral ties to the community, the performative view of meaning serves to legitimate indigenous worldviews. Meaning and resistance are embodied in the act of performance itself. The performative is political, the site of resistance. The performative is where the soul of the culture resides. In attacking the performative, the critics attack the culture.[2] Smith states the issue clearly, "The struggle for the validity of indigenous knowledges may no longer be over the RECOGNITION that indigenous people have ways of knowing the world which are unique, but over proving the authenticity of, and control over, our own forms of knowledge" (p. 104, italics in original).[3]

More is involved at this level, for the grand battle may not be between traditional science and communitarian values.[4] The professional work of educators and those in the human services is often driven by practical constraints, by humanistic concerns tempered by utilitarianism. In such spaces, as Bishop (2005, p. 110) notes, the practical constraints of doing empowering education under a colonial regime may be impossible, or difficult at best. Communitarian scholars who collaborate with persons at the front lines are under two injunctions. First, they must work to insure that their research does not advance the benefits, interests, and concerns of the larger neocolonial society. Second, they must insure that their work does more than just serve the lofty ideals of communitarianism (Bishop, 2005, p. 131).

A Moral Code

A set of moral and ethical research protocols is required. Fitted to the indigenous (and non-indigenous) perspective, these are moral matters. They are shaped by the feminist, communitarian principles of sharing, reciprocity, relationality, community and neighborliness discussed in previous chapters (Lincoln, 1995, p. 287). They embody a dialogic ethic of love and faith grounded in compassion (Bracci & Christians, 2002, p. 13; West, 1993). Accordingly, the purpose of research is not the production of new knowledge, per se. Rather, the purposes are pedagogical, political, moral, and ethical, involving the enhancement of moral agency, the production of moral discernment, a commitment to praxis, justice, an ethic of resistance, a performative pedagogy that resists oppression (Christians, 2002, p. 409).

Unlike the North American Belmont Code (see below), which is not content driven, this feminist, indigenous moral code is anchored in a culture and its way of life. Unlike the Belmont Code, it connects its moral model to a set of political and ethical actions which will increase well-being in Maori culture. The code refuses to turn indigenous peoples into subjects who have been turned into the natural objects of white inquiry (Smith, 1999, p. 118). These principles argue that Western legal definitions of ethical codes privilege the utilitarian model of the individual as someone who has rights distinct from the rights of the larger group, "for example the right of an individual to give his or her own knowledge, or the right to give informed consent ... community and indigenous rights or views in this area are generally not ... respected" (p. 118).

Bishop's (1998) and Smith's (1999, pp. 116-119) ethical and moral models call into question the more generic, utilitarian, bio-medical, Western model of ethical inquiry (see Christians, 1997; 1998; 1995; 2000; 2005; 2007). A brief review of the bio-medical model, also known as the Belmont Principles, will serve to clarify the power of the indigenous position.

THE BIO-MEDICAL MODEL OF ETHICS AND THE BELMONT PRINCIPLES

As Gunsalus (2002, p. B-24) observes, the rules governing human subject research in the United States are rooted in scandal: the Tuskegee Syphilis Study (AAUP, 1981, p. 358), the Willowbrook Hepatitis Experiment, Project Camelot in the 1960s, and a series of events in the 1970s, including Milgram's deceptions of experimental subjects, Laud Humphrey's covert research on homosexuals, and the complicity of social scientists with military initiatives in Vietnam (Christians, 2002, p. 141). Concern for research ethics during the 1980s and 1990, support from foundations, the development of professional codes of ethics, and extensions of the IRB apparatus "are credited by their advocates with curbing outrageous abuses" (Christians, 2002, p. 141). However, these efforts were framed, from the 1960s forward, in terms of a bio-medical model of research. As implemented, this model involves institutional review boards, informed consent forms, value-neutral conceptions of the human subject, and utilitarian theories of risk and benefits.[5]

Today, the institutional protection of human subjects has expanded far beyond these original impulses, leading many to fear that there may be a growing "harm to academic freedom and scholars' First Amendment rights if the authority of IRBs is interpreted too broadly or becomes too intrusive" (Gunsalus, 2002, p. B-24). Puglisi (2001) demurs, arguing that these regulations "are extremely flexible and should present no impediment to well-designed behavioral and social science research" (p. 1). This, however, is not the case.

The Professional Associations and Societies

In 1998 numerous professional associations in the United States, including the American Historical Association, the Oral History Association, the Organization of American Historians, and the American Anthropological Association started communicating with one another and with over 700 Institutional Review Boards (IRBs) to encourage them to take account of the standards of practice relevant to the research in their specific disciplines (AAUP, 2001, p. 56).

Concern within the professional societies involved the bio-medical definition of research, and the corresponding definitions of harm, beneficence, respect, justice, and informed consent. The problems start with how the regulations define research. Research is defined as:

any activity designed to test an hypothesis, permit conclusions to be drawn, and thereby to develop or contribute to generalizable knowledge expressed in theories, principles, and statements of relationships. Research is described in a formal protocol that sets forth an objective and a set of procedures designed to reach that objective.

This definition turns human beings into research subjects who may be exposed to harm because of the protocols that implement the research design.

The model works outward from the Belmont Report and its ethical principles (see Christians, 2000; Lincoln & Tierney, 2002; Lincoln & Cannella, 2002; Pritchard, 2002: AAUP, 2001; 2002). The current version of these rules, the 1991 regulations, and their revisions, are also known as the "Common Rule" (AAUP, 2001, p. 55; 2002). The Common Rule describes the procedures of review that are used by more than 17 different federal agencies. It is presumed that this single regulatory framework will fit all styles and forms of research, but as Pritchard notes (see below) this is not always the case (2002, p. 8). In principle, the Common Rule is implemented through informed consent.

The Belmont Report sets forth three basic ethical principles: respect for persons, beneficence, and justice. The three principles of respect, beneficence, and justice are implemented through a set of procedures, administered by IRBs who follow the Common Rule. RESPECT is implemented through voluntarily granted INFORMED CONSENT (passive, versus active, third-party), although deception may be allowed.[6] BENEFICENCE is determined through a complex set of procedures that assess RISKS (HARM) and BENEFITS. Risk must be minimal, if warranted, and balanced by a surplus of benefits (Pritchard, 2002, p. 8). Risks at the individual level may be justified, if the benefits serve a larger cause.

The principle of JUSTICE is expressed in the assurance that there be fair procedures and outcomes in the SELECTION of research subjects. Special populations should not be unduly burdened by being required to participate in research projects. The benefits of research should not be unfairly distributed throughout a subject population, nor made available only to those who can afford them.

Criticisms of the Model

This regulatory model, with the apparatus of the Institutional Review Board, and the Common Rule, has been subjected to considerable criticism. Criticisms center on the meanings brought to the terms human subject, scientific research, harm, benefits, respect, and ethical conduct. Recent summaries by the AAUP (2001; 2002; 2006) center on controversies surrounding these terms. These reservations include the following:

Research, and Human Subjects:
** a failure by IRBs to be aware of new interpretive and qualitative developments in the social sciences, including participant observation, ethnography, autoethnography, and oral history research;

** the application of a concept of research and science that privileges the biomedical model of science and not the model of trust, negotiation and respect that must be established in ethnographic or historical inquiry, where research is not ON, but is rather WITH other human beings;
** an event-based and not a process-based conception of research and the consent process;

Ethics:
** a failure to see human beings as social creatures located in complex historical, political and cultural spaces;
** infringements on academic freedom, by not allowing certain types of inquiry to go forward;
** inappropriate applications of the "Common Rule" in assessing potential harm;
** overly restrictive applications of the informed consent rule;

IRBs as Institutional Structures:
** a failure to have an adequate appeal system in place;
** the need to insure that IRBs have members from the newer interpretive paradigms;

Academic Freedom:
** First Amendment and academic freedom infringements;
** policing of inquiry in the humanities, including oral history research;
** policing and obstructing research seminars and dissertation projects;
** constraints on critical inquiry, including historical or journalistic work that contributes to the public knowledge of the past, while incriminating, or passing negative judgment on persons and institutions;
** a failure to consider or incorporate existing forms of regulation into the Common Rule, including laws of libel, of copyright, of intellectual property right;
** the general extension of IRB powers across disciplines, creating a negative effect on what will, or will not be studied;
** vastly different applications of the Common Rule across campus communities;

Important Topics Not Regulated:

** the conduct of research with indigenous peoples (see below);

** the regulation of unorthodox, or problematic conduct in the field, e.g. sexual relations;

** relations between IRBs, and ethical codes involving universal human rights;

** disciplinary codes of ethics and IRBs, and new codes of ethics and moral perspectives coming from feminist, queer and racialized standpoint epistemologies;

** appeal mechanisms for human subjects who need to grieve and who seek some form of restorative justice as a result of harm experienced as a research subject;

** Fourth world discourses and alternative views of research, science and human beings.

Disciplining and Constraining Ethical Conduct

The consequence of these restrictions, as Christians (2007), Shopes (2000), Shopes and Ritchie (2004), Townsend (2006), Lincoln and Tierney (2002) and Lincoln and Cannella (2002) observe, is a disciplining of qualitative inquiry which extends from granting agencies to the policing of qualitative research seminars and even the conduct of qualitative dissertations. In some cases, lines of critical inquiry have not been funded and have not gone forward because of criticisms from local IRBs. Pressures from the right discredit critical interpretive inquiry. From the federal to the local levels, a trend seems to be emerging. In too many instances there seems to be a move away from protecting human subjects to an increased monitoring, censuring and policing of projects which are critical of the right and its politics.

Lincoln and Tierney (2002) observe that these policing activities have at least five important implications for critical, social justice inquiry. First, the widespread rejection of alternative forms of research means that qualitative inquiry will be heard less and less in federal and state policy forums. Second, it appears that qualitative researchers are being deliberately excluded from this national dialogue. Consequently, third, young researchers trained in the critical tradition are not being listened to. Fourth, the definition of research has not changed to fit newer models of inquiry. Fifth, in rejecting qualitative inquiry, traditional researchers are endorsing a more distanced form of research that is compatible with existing stereotypes concerning persons of color.

Christians (2007; 2005) summarizes the poverty of this model. It rests on a cognitive model that privileges rational solutions to ethical dilemmas (the rationalist fallacy), and it presumes that humanity is a single subject (the distributive fallacy). It presents the scientist as an objective, neutral observer. Private citizens are coerced into participating in so-called scientific projects, in the name of some distant, public good. The rights-justice-and acts-based system ignores the dialogical nature of human interaction. The model creates the conditions for deception, for the invasion of private spaces, for duping subjects, and for challenges to the subject's moral worth and dignity. Christians calls for its replacement with an ethics based on the values of a feminist communitarianism, an ethic of empowerment, a care-based, dialogical ethic of hope, love and solidarity.

This is an evolving, emerging ethical framework that serves as a powerful antidote to the deception-based utilitarian, IRB system. It allows for an ethical framework that addresses the problems of ethicism outlined by Kvale and Brinkmann. It presumes a community that is ontologically and axiologically prior to the person. This community has common moral values, and research is rooted in a concept of care, of shared governance, of neighborliness, or love, kindness, and the moral good. Accounts of social life should display these values, and be based on interpretive sufficiency. They should have sufficient depth to allow the reader to form a critical understanding about the world studied. These texts should exhibit an absence of racial, class and gender stereotyping. These texts should generate social criticism, lead to resistance, empowerment and to social action, to positive change in the social world.

AAUP Revisions and IRB Mission Creep
The IRB apparatus was initially intended to apply only to federally funded research, namely to

all research on human subjects conducted at, or sponsored by, colleges, universities, hospitals, and nonprofit organizations that is to be supported by any of the federal departments and agencies that have adopted the regulations must be approved in advance by a local IRB (AAUP, 2006, p. 1).

However, on June 23, 2005[7], the federal government extended these regulations to include a second requirement, namely to include IRB supervision, whatever the source of funding:

Institutions at which or under whose auspices federally funded research on human subjects is to be conducted must provide assurance that they will protect the rights of the human subjects of all their research ... whatever its source of funding (AAUP, 2006, p. 1, emphasis added).[8]

The Committee of the AAUP (2006) issued a critical response to this document[9], resisting this expansion of IRB reviews to non-funded research projects. Building on the arguments of the Oral Historical Association (below)[10], the report called for certain methodological exemptions (below) ipso facto. The Committee also supported the move of more than 184 institutions who refuse to submit non-federally funded research for IRB supervision.

This new requirement gives unchecked power to IRBs. It has generated an increasing number of by now familiar complaints: (1) there are no appeal procedures; (2) committees not researchers are defining risk; (3) prior approval must be given, whether or not research poses serious harm. Still, because most universities are risk aversive, the new requirement has been adopted by the majority of institutions (AAUP, 2006, p. 1).

The new requirement supercedes the previous understanding that a waiver could be granted if there was no risk of serious harm. That exclusion seems to have disappeared. Many are now calling for a blanket exemption for interpretive research in the social sciences and the humanities (AAUP, 2006, p. 3).

The lack of an appeal process is critical. An IRB may demand that a change be made in a research protocol as a condition of approval. If the IRB cannot be convinced, the research does not move forward. Difficulties scheduling meetings with an IRB may cause lengthy delays. Requests for change may be unreasonable:

A linguist seeking to study language development in a preliterate tribe was instructed by the IRB to have the subjects read and sign a consent form before the study could proceed (AAUP, 2006, p. 2).

Given this new version of IRB mission creep, the AAUP recommends not a disciplinary exclusion, or exemption, but rather exemptions based on methodology, namely

research on autonomous adults whose methodology consists entirely of collecting data by surveys, conducting interviews, or observing behavior in public places should be exempt from the requirement of IRB review, with no provisos, and no requirement of IRB approval of the exemption (AAUP, 2006, p. 4).

This recommendation creates a space for interpretive, social science inquiry, and recognizes that a single model cannot be made to apply to all forms of research. It eliminates many hardships currently imposed on scholars. It would also eliminate "a considerable amount of totally unnecessary work currently done by IRBs, freeing them to devote attention to seriously risk-imposing research projects" (AAUP, 2006, p. 5).

The AAUP issued a second recommendation regarding the supervision of non-federally funded research, namely, *the blanket application of current federal guidelines to non-funded federal research needs to be re-thought*. If a project is methodologically exempt, and if it is not federally funded, then it should also be exempt from IRB approval. A strong version of this guideline, would endorse the practice of the 184 institutions who refuse to submit non-federally funded research for IRB supervision.

A third guideline, borrowed from the Oral History Association (OHA), can be added to this list; namely, *neither OHRP, nor a campus IRB has the authority to define what constitutes legitimate research in any field, only what research is covered by federal regulations.*

THE EXCLUSION OF ORAL HISTORY
FROM IRB REVIEW

The Oral History Association (OHA) has endorsed the AAUP position. In its October 2006 annual meeting, the executive council of the Oral History Association, following the AAUP, recommended that academic institutions consider as "straightforwardly exempt from IRB review any 'research whose methodology consists entirely of collecting data by surveys, conducting interviews, or observing behavior in public places'" (Howard, 2006, p. 9). This endorsement, builds on previously established exclusions of oral history from IRB review (see below).[11]

The U.S. Office for Human Research Protection (OHRP), working in conjunction with the American Historical Association and the Oral History Association, determined in 2003 that oral history interviewing projects in general *do not involve the type of research defined by HHS regulations and are therefore excluded from Institutional Review Board oversight.*

Federal regulations, as noted above, define research as "a systematic investigation, including research development, testing and evaluation, designed to develop or contribute to generalizable knowledge." The type of research encompassed by the regulations involves standard questionnaires with a large sample of individuals who often remain anonymous, not the open-ended interviews with identifiable individuals who give their interviews with "informed consent" that characterize oral history.

Most oral history interviewing projects are not subject to the requirements of the Department of Health and Human Services (HHS) regulation, and are excluded from institutional review board (IRB) oversight because they do not involve research as defined by the HHS regulations. Only those oral history projects that conform to the regulatory definition of research now need to submit their research protocols for IRB review.[12]

Oral History Exclusions

Oral historians establish their exclusion from IRB review on these grounds:

1. Their version of systematic, qualitative interpretive inquiry does not involve the key assumptions of positivistic science. Their research does not use large samples, nor does it aim at testing hypotheses, or forming statistical generalizations or generalizable knowledge.
2. Unlike biomedical and behavioral science researchers, oral historians do not seek underlying principles of historical or social development, nor do they seek underlying laws or generalizations that have predictive value.
3. Historians explain a particular past, or particular event, or study the life of single individuals.
4. Oral history interviewees and narrators are not anonymous individuals selected as part of a random sample for the purposes of a survey or experiment. Nor do they respond to standard questionnaire items. Oral history narrators engage in dialogues tailored to fit their unique relationship to the topic at hand (see http://www.dickinson.edu/oha).

Since the 2003 understandings (Shopes & Ritchie, 2004), most campus-based oral history projects have been able to proceed with their interviews without submitting protocols for review by a campus-level Institutional Review Board.

Practical, Ethical Implications

These understandings produce the following practical, ethical implications for interpretive inquiry:

1. SUCH WORK IS EXCLUDED, RATHER THAN EXEMPT FROM REVIEW. If oral historians deem that their oral history projects do not meet the regulatory definition of research, they can proceed without consultation with an IRB. If a project does meet the regulatory definition of research, it could still be "exempted" by an IRB, but that must be determined by the IRB. [For the regulatory definitions, see: http://ohrp.osophs.dhhs. gov/humansubjects/guidance/45cfr46.htm]
2. Rather than going to a campus-level IRB, interpretive scholars should take their research protocols to their departmental or college IRB officer or

other administrators responsible for institutional compliance with federal regulations.

3. The policy statement does not say that oral history is "not research." It says that oral history does "not involve research as defined by the HHS regulations."

4. This exclusion does not mean oral history and interpretive inquiry need not be sensitive to ethical issues (see below). Rather, they are freer to act in accordance with ethical and legal standards appropriate to oral history, or interpretive studies, and not biomedical or behavioral research.

For decades, oral historians have promulgated high ethical and professional standards, including their ethical requirement to gain informed consent prior to conducting an interview, and a signed legal release at the conclusion of the interview. These issues are codified in the Oral History Association's *Principles and Standards* and *Evaluation Guidelines*.[13]

The Multi-Track IRB Model

It is clearly necessary to rethink the single-track IRB model. Some United States campuses (Texas A & M, University of Texas at Austin, Purdue, University of South Florida, University of California, Berkeley) are moving to a two-track system, one model for the biomedical sciences, another model for the human sciences and the humanities. A true two- or multi-track IRB model would be based on a new system of regulatory practice. A humanities-based, interpretive inquiry model, based on feminist, communitarian understandings would stand alongside a revised biomedical model. A more traditional, positivistic social science model might represent the third track.

A radical rethinking of the Belmont Principles would produce an inclusive, ethically empowering model that would be applied to all forms of inquiry. Institutional IRBs, as we know them today, would disappear. The regulation and supervision of inquiry would shift from the current top-down, state-sponsored model to the local level entirely. Inquiry would be collaborative, done through the kind of moral give and take outlined by Smith, Bishop and other indigenous and First Nation scholars.

THE ILLINOIS MODEL

I want to extend the AAUP and Oral History Association discourse on what is and what is not research. I want to move the discourse beyond utilitarian ethical models, or out-dated epistemological frameworks (Kvale, 2008). It is not enough to claim IRB exclusions or exemptions on methodological grounds. Ethical discourse needs to be anchored in a moral space, the spaces of decolonization. Critical scholars engage in pedagogical practices that make the world visible. In taking up a critical, interpretive approach to the world, we are aligned with all manner and form of scholarship that seeks not only to understand, but to change the world in positive ways.

I am the IRB officer for the College of Communications, University of Illinois, Urbana-Champaign. In 2004 I asked our campus IRB officer if the oral history exemption was recognized on this campus, and if so, could it be extended to interpretive research in my college.[14] He replied that the UIUC IRB generally upholds the OHA and AHA positions on this. As such, the UIUC typically considers oral histories excluded from IRB review, unless there are severe extenuating factors of some sort (e.g. interactions involving deception) which *may* increase the level of review.

I then argued that interpretive media research involves historical research and open-ended, oral history interviewing. This research does not fit the type of research defined by federal regulations, namely: "A systematic investigation, including research development, testing and evaluation, designed to develop or contribute to generalizable knowledge."

I argued that much of our research is based on case studies, open-ended interviews, life histories and life stories. Each individual case is treated as unique. This category of social science research has historically been called idiographic or emic. Emic studies emphasize stories, narratives, collaborative performances and accounts that capture the meaning persons bring to experience. Nomothetic studies, in contrast, conform to the federal definitions of research. Researchers seek abstract generalizations, test hypotheses, use random sampling techniques, quasi-experimental designs, and so forth.

I requested that the Oral History exclusion apply to interpretive research in the College of Communications, with these provisos:

1. The research is not federally funded;

2. The research does not place subjects at risk or harm;

3. Researchers demonstrate that this exclusion should be granted, because the research in question does not involve research as defined by the HHS regulations. An exemption could be granted, if research does meet the HHS definition.

4. Scholars define their work as scholarship, not research, and locate it within an artistic, humanistic paradigm, including: critical pedagogy, arts-based inquiry, narrative or performance studies (see below).

THE INDIGENOUS ETHICS WATCH

It is against this background that indigenous peoples debate codes of ethics, and issues surrounding intellectual and cultural property rights. In this politicized space "indigenous codes of ethics are being promulgated ... as a sheer act of survival" (Smith, 1999, p. 119). Thus the various charters of indigenous peoples include statements that refer to collective, not individual human rights. These rights include control and ownership of the community's cultural property, its health and knowledge systems, its rituals, and customs, its culture's basic gene pool, rights and rules for self-determination, and an insistence on who the first beneficiaries of indigenous knowledge will be.

These charters call upon governments and states to develop policies that will insure these social goods, including the rights of indigenous peoples to protect new knowledge and its dissemination. These charters embed codes of ethics within this larger perspective. They specify how researchers are to protect and respect the rights and interests of indigenous peoples. These are the selfsame protocols that regulate daily moral and ethical life in the culture.

A Case Study

Marie Battiste (2008), and Battiste and Youngblood (2000) offer a set of ethical practices for ensuring self-determination and the protection of indigenous intellectual property rights. These ethical principles specify institutional and researcher responsibilities. They are based on the guidelines developed by the Mi'kmaq Nation and the Mi'kmaw Ethics Watch (Ethics

Eskinuapimk). Battiste helped write these guidelines. She is a member of this tribal community.

Battiste, like Smith, Bishop and Christians, insists that indigenous people have control over their own knowledge. They must have mechanisms which will inform them when research is being done on, among, or with them. They must train people in protocols for doing research, and this must be research that will benefit, strengthen, and revitalize the community. She is blunt. The challenge is how to create ethical mandates and ethical behavior in a "knowledge system contaminated by colonials and racism. Nowhere is this work more needed than in the universities that pride themselves on their discipline-specific research" (p. 966).

Mi'kmaw Ethics Watch oversees research proposals on behalf of the larger community (see their website: http://mrc.uccb.ns.ca/prinpro.html). Any research done in the community must be reviewed by the Ethics Watch. Their guidelines include the following:

1. Mi'kmaw people are the guardians and interpreters of their culture, knowledge, arts, and lands;
2. Mi'kmaw people have the right and obligation to exercise control to protect their cultural and intellectual properties and knowledge;
3. All research on the Mi'kmaq is to be approached as a negotiated partnership;
4. Participants shall be recognized and treated as equals in the research done instead of as "informants" or "subjects";
5. All research partners must show respect for language, traditions, standards of the communities, and for the highest standards of scholarly research;
6. All research partners shall provide descriptions of research processes in the participant's own language (written and oral), which shall include detailed explanations of usefulness of study, potential benefits and possible harmful effects on individuals, groups and the environment. Researchers must clearly identify sponsors, purposes of the research, sources of financial support and investigators for the research (scholarly and corporate), tasks to be performed, information requested from Mi'kmaw people, participatory research processes, the publication plans for the results, and anticipated royalties for the research;

7. All consent disclosures shall be written in both Mi'kmaq and English, depending on the community norms. All individuals and communities have the right to decline or withdraw from participating at any time without penalties;

8. All research partners shall inform participants in their own language about the use of data gathering devices – tape, video recordings, photos, physiological measurements, and how data will be used. They shall also provide information on the anonymity or confidentiality of their participation, and if not possible, to inform the participant that anonymity is not possible. Participants shall be informed of possible consequences of their choice to remain in the research and their rights to withdraw consent or participation in the research at any time.

9. All research scholars shall invite Mi'kmaw participation in the interpretation and/or review of any conclusions drawn from the research to ensure accuracy and sensitivity of interpretation;

10. The Mi'kmaw Ethics Watch shall increase efforts to educate each community and its individuals to the issues, concerns, benefits, and risks of research involving Mi'kmaq people.

***

These ethical guidelines are typical of the kinds of procedures that now regulate inquiry in indigenous communities. They represent ways of bringing control back into the local community. They also represent ways of decolonizing inquiry.

In the next decade there will be renewed efforts to embed critical and indigenous methodologies in decolonizing discourses. These discourses will interrogate the ways in which power, ethics and social justice intersect. Multiple models of justice will be explored. Feminist, communitarian ethics will be informed by the empowerment ethics of specific indigenous peoples. Indigenous and non-indigenous scholars will refine models of restorative justice that heal the wounds of globalization. They will develop new indigenous methodologies which better address the social and economic concerns of oppressed persons.

IN CONCLUSION; LEARNING NEW ETHICAL BEHAVIOUR[15]

I hope that in the next decade utopian dreams of universal social justice will be better realized. Brinkmann and Kvale (2008, pp. 276-277) suggest that learning a new form of ethical behavior will be a key issue that lies ahead for decolonizing qualitative researchers. The communitarian model anchors this learning process in a moral community of stakeholders and researchers. This must be a dialogical process. It presumes a community where there are shared moral values, such as is the case for Ethics Watch, as described by Battiste.

Thus do Battiste, Kvale, Brinkman, Smith, Bishop and Christians outline a radical ethical path for the future. In so doing they transcend the Belmont Principles, which focus almost exclusively on the problems associated with betrayal, deception, and harm. They call for a collaborative social science research model which makes the researcher responsible not to a removed discipline (or institution), but rather to those studied. This model forcefully aligns the ethics of research with a politics of the oppressed, with a politics of resistance, hope and freedom.

This model directs scholars to take up moral projects that honor and reclaim indigenous cultural practices. Such work produces spiritual, social and psychological healing. Healing, in turn, leads to multiple forms of transformation at the personal and social levels. These transformations shape processes of mobilization, and collective action. These actions help persons realize a radical politics of possibility.

NOTES

1   This essay draws from Denzin and Giardina (2007); Denzin, Lincoln and Giardina (2006), and Denzin (2003, pp. 242-258).

2   Smith (1999, p. 99) presents ten performative ways to be colonized, ten ways that science, technology and Western institutions place indigenous peoples, indeed any group of human beings, their languages, cultures and environments, at risk. These ways include the Human Genome Diversity Project, as well as efforts to scientifically reconstruct previously extinct indigenous peoples, and projects which deny global citizenship to indigenous peoples, while commodifying, patenting and selling indigenous cultural traditions and rituals.

3   The TESTIMONIO has a central place in Smith's list of projects. She begins her discussion of the testimonio with these lines from Menchu (1984, p. 1): "My name is Rigoberta Menchu, I

am twenty-three years old, and this is my testimony." The testimonio presents oral evidence to an audience, often in the form of a monologue. Indigenous testimonios are "a way of talking about an extremely painful event of series of events. The testimonio can be constructed as "a monologue and as a public performance" Smith, 1999, p. 144).

4   I thank Bob Stake for this insight.

5   Federal protection of human subjects has been in effect in the United States since 1974, now codified in Title 45 Part 46 of the U. S. Code of Federal Regulations. Title 45, Part 46 was revised November 13, 2001, effective December 13, 2001. IRBs review all federally funded research involving human subjects to ensure their ethical protection.

6   The Family Education Rights and Privacy Act, the Protection of Pupil Rights Amendment and the Parental Freedom of Information Amendment extend additional privacy rights to children (See Shavelson & Towne, 2002, pp. 152-153).

7   http//www.hhs.gov/ohrp/humansubjects/guidance/45cfr46.htm

8   On non-federally funded research, it is perhaps of interest to note that 80 % of all research projects reviewed by the University of Chicago's Social Science IRB are personally funded, privately funded or unfunded. To date, 164 institutions, including Harvard, Princeton, Chicago and Berkeley, have explicitly declined to commit themselves to imposing on research that is not federally funded. The AAUP hesitates to formulate policy for unfunded research, except for the recommendation below.

9   http// www.aaup.org/AAUP/About/committees/committee+repts/CommA/

10 See Shopes, 2000; Shopes & Ritchie, 2004; Townsend, 2006; Chronicle of Higher Education, 2006. This appeal echoes previously established understandings that waivers could be given (as noted above) if the research involves normal educational practice, the use of interviews, previously collected materials, research on cultural beliefs, or the observation of public behavior.

11 The following section draws directly from Shopes (2000).

12 To clarify, while some oral history scholarship clearly involves research that lends itself to generalizations, oral historians' standard operating procedures do not fit the type of research defined by federal regulations: "A systematic investigation, including research development, testing and evaluation, designed to develop or contribute to generalizable knowledge." Individually-tailored interviews with a narrator's informed consent do not meet this definition of "research." Nor do they contribute to "generalizable knowledge," even if conducted with people identified with a common group, theme or event, and whether or not the interviewer or other researchers might draw some historical generalizations from multiple interviews. The interviews must be *designed* specifically to produce generalizable knowledge

in the scientific sense. Interview projects that meet the above federal definition should be submitted for IRB review. Those that do not are not subject to review.

13 Oral history involves interviews for the record, explicitly intended for preservation as a historical document. Informed consent means that those being interviewed fully understand the purposes and potential uses of the interview, as well as their freedom not to answer some questions, and their identification in research and writing drawn from the interview. Legal releases are linked to issues of evidence and copyright. If a researcher makes explicit use of an interview in written work (both in direct quotation and paraphrase), the interview should be cited in a footnote, so that others can identify and locate that information within the framework of extant evidence. Recorded interviews involve copyright, and interviewees must sign an agreement that establishes access for those who use the interview in any way. If the interviews are deposited in a library or archives, legal releases will establish ownership of the copyright and the terms of access and reproduction. If the interviews are published, legal releases will satisfy publishers' concerns over copyright.

14 There are four research paradigms or streams in my College: (1) experimental and survey-based research; (2) oral history, interpretive inquiry that does not require IRB review; (3) standard behavioral research that qualifies for expedited review within the College IRB; (4) journalist inquiries involving investigative, narrative and public affairs reporting. Such work is routinely exempted from review under the First Amendment.

15 I take this phrase from Brinkmann and Kvale, 2008, p. 276.

Steinar Kvale
University of Aarhus, Denmark

Carsten Østerlund
Syracuse University, United States

HOW DO YOU ADVISE GRADUATE STUDENTS ON QUALITATIVE RESEARCH PROJECTS? AN INTERVIEW WITH STEINAR KVALE BY CARSTEN ØSTERLUND

Abstract:

Carsten Østerlund has interviewed Steinar Kvale about advising, and in particular the advising of qualitative research projects carried out by graduate students. The interview explores how Steinar Kvale's own work on evaluation, dialogue, qualitative interview, and apprenticeship influences his advising practices. The interview pursues issues such as the selection of PhD students, navigating institutional requirements, helping students build and conduct a qualitative research, the advising dialogue and power dynamics, mentor motivation, advising as compensation for a dynamic research environment, access to research networks, and long-term relationships with advisees.

Steinar Kvale is Professor of Educational Psychology and Director of the Centre of Qualitative Research at the University of Aarhus, and adjunct faculty at Saybrook Institute, San Francisco. Drawing on continental philosophies such as phenomenology, hermeneutics, and dialectics he explores issues of learning and knowing in education and psychology (Kvale, 1992). Three empirical themes stand out as central to his authorship. First, the role of examinations and grading has been a long-term interest (Kvale, 1972; 2007). Second, an interest in the dialogue or dyadic conversation shows up in his work on the qualitative interview (Kvale, 1996; Kvale & Brinkmann, 2008) and articles on advising (Kvale, 2000; 2006; Kvale, 2007). Third, Kvale has explored the role apprenticeship and professional practices play in knowing and the structure of learning environments (Kvale, 1997; 2003; Nielsen & Kvale, 1997; Nielsen & Kvale, 1999). Together with Klaus Nielsen, for instance, he has edited *Mesterlære – Læring som social praksis* (*Apprenticeship – Learning as Social Practice*, 1999) and *Praktikkens læringslandskab – At lære gennem arbejde* (*The learning landscape of practice – Learning through work*, 2003).

The present interview explores how Kvale reconciles these three areas of interest in his own advising practices of numerous undergraduate, Masters, and PhD students. The overarching question for the interview becomes: how does Kvale's empirical and theoretical work on evaluation, the dialogue as a research tool, qualitative research, and apprenticeship inform his day-to-day advising of students?

The interviewer, Carsten Østerlund is an Assistant Professor at the School of Information Studies at Syracuse University. Among other things he studies learning in workplace settings (Østerlund & Carlile, 2005; Østerlund, 1996). Like Kvale, he conceives of research as an intellectual craft ideally honed through apprenticeship. At the same time he is coming to terms with his role as a scholar within a university system where individual advising sessions play an important part.

The interview took place in the course of two meetings over the summer of 2007. The conversation was conducted in English, taped, and transcribed. The interviewer edited the interview for repetitions, flow, and language. Subsequently, the interviewee made some retrospective clarifications in collaboration with the interviewer.

I help them get through the system

CØ: I would like for us to talk about your advising of PhD students; how you establish an advising relationship, how you carry it through, and how you end it. Taking it from the top: how do you select new PhD students and establish a relationship with them?

SK: They come to me. Most of them know my profile.

CØ: How do you help them develop the project?

SK: I help them define the project and develop their PhD application. One that is likely to get through the department's PhD committee. In the Danish system you apply and get admitted based on a five-page dissertation proposal; equivalent to the dissertation prospectus that US PhD students submit after their first two years of coursework. I help them get through the system and develop the best possible project description.

CØ: In these early phases how do you structure your meetings?

SK: I tell them to prepare a draft proposal describing their main research area, research questions, and method. On that basis we talk.

CØ: Do you have a format for those conversations?

SK: No. It is not that often I have them and it depends on the situation. Some topics fall within my area, but not always. One student, Svend Brinkmann, for instance, wanted to study ethics in social science research. It doesn't fall within my area of expertise but I wanted to support the research. He knows more about philosophy and ethics than I do. In that case our discussion focused on the clarity of the questions, the relevance of the topic for psychology, and whether the PhD committee would accept it. Actually, they didn't. As it often happens here, the local PhD review board preferred quantitative hypotheses-testing research designs. He was rejected twice by the PhD committee. In the end the department chair overruled the committee and accepted the student. As a PhD student he then published in more international venues a year than most of our tenured faculty.

The readers of this interview should probably also know that you were not as lucky when you applied to our PhD program with me as your advisor some years earlier. The PhD committee didn't rate your qualitative research proposal high enough to secure you a scholarship. You then applied with the same project to the PhD programs at UC Berkeley and MIT. As I recall, you were accepted both places but chose MIT.

CØ: That's right... So, you are not so much advising prospective students on the content of their project but rather helping them manage their relationship to the institution?

SK: Yes. At the university we have a Center for Qualitative Research. Still, we find it difficult to get students through the PhD admission committee. They may request that the student add more interview subjects to the research design. High numbers of subjects easily become a problem in qualitative interview projects. To ensure manageable and high-quality research projects I often find myself helping the student cut down the number of interview subjects and themes that the review board demands.

I like to think of research training as an apprenticeship

cø: Your PhD student is accepted, how do you help them structure the process – the three-year study?

sk: I regard the students as adults who can manage themselves, who can plan and organize their activities. I don't structure it for them.

Now that I think of it, most of my PhD students have already participated in my seminars or been assistants at my PhD level qualitative research courses. Before they apply they know the steps of doing qualitative research.

cø: Ah – this changes everything: You already have a relationship with your future PhD students. How do they become part of your interview courses?

sk: I like to think of research training as an apprenticeship. In apprenticeship you start at the periphery and do simple tasks. My assistants at the method courses do literature searches; make coffee, copy handouts, set-up tables. Otherwise, they take part in the course on a close to equal footing with everybody else. They are, with an expression from Lave and Wenger "legitimate peripheral participants". They participate and learn from the course at the same time. They learn about research stages and their pitfalls. Their participation equips them to carry out a study on their own.

At a social level they learn from engaging with current PhD students. Through their participation in group meetings, meals and parties, they learn about the PhD process and the sufferings, loneliness and the positive, fun aspects. They get the war stories. All things an advisor would find hard to put in words. They peek into the PhD process and what it means to be a PhD student. Some will apply to the PhD program; others decide that it is not for them.

cø: How do they become assistants?

SK: These Masters students volunteer and in some cases I may invite a student to participate. I don't pay them, but they never seem to regret the time they invested.

CØ: Do you have ethical concerns about not paying them?

SK: No, why.....? It's an issue of motivation. If they are motivated enough, they will do it for free. I feel confident about it because there is so much learning involved. I do not exploit their time. They pay for their "tuition" with their work. You have it in other fields too, in the film industry, for instance. When the Danish director Lars von Trier shoots a movie, young people line up to become gofers.

CØ: Do the students navigate the PhD process more or less spontaneously?

SK: It depends very much on where they are in the process and how confident they feel about what they are doing. Some of my best students I hardly advise. They just come and ask me very specific questions about literature for instance, and go on doing their thing. Sometimes they don't bother having me read their writings.

Otherwise, I know the critical phases. With interviews for instance, I know that the written instructions for the interviewees are critical for the interpretation. I make sure to go through these instructions with the student.

CØ: How do you structure those conversations?

SK: Normally, I'll ask them to give me the interview instructions and questions in advance. Then there are some standard hazards. Most students use a very academic language and I help them turn the text into colloquial Danish. For every phase of the project one finds typical roadblocks that I can help them navigate, if needed.

Advising compensates for students not being part of active research communities

CØ: You have nimbly avoided my questions about the advising dialogue.

SK: Too often people focus on the advising situation in isolation. If you work in the same part of the building and have lunch together, people find ample opportunities to discuss their ongoing research projects and learn from others' successes and failures. If needed, they can drop by my office and ask specific questions. The everyday activities overshadow the formal meetings.

You learn the tricks of the trade through observing and participation. You learn research by doing research and participating with more experienced researchers. Research is a craft with limits to what can be verbalized. The advising dialogue rarely suffices.

I have had students living out of town, coming by every other month. Those advising sessions tend to become too dense. There is too much to do during those brief meetings. All the nooks and crannies of doing research rarely get sufficient attention. When people share the same daily environment the new students learn from the slightly more advanced students. If you see each other daily the advising situation becomes less overburdened. You can focus on one or two issues and spend an hour sifting through the questionnaire together or hammer out the research topic. If the student comes in from out of town for a two-hour meeting it becomes too high pressure.

CØ: Does none of your work on the dialogue and interviews fit into this picture?

SK: For many years I have written much about dialogue, interviews, and interview as dialogue. Recently it started to dawn on me that dialogue was a dangerous concept. If your boss asks for a dialogue these days most people know to tread carefully. Open dialogue between equals seeking a common and true knowledge is an ideal situation. Advising is not a conversation between equals. One is trying to learn from the other and you don't want them to be equal.

The ideal advising situation is a learning environment where advising becomes hardly necessary. I think advising is too overburdened today – at least the formal advising situations. It compensates for students not being part of active research communities.

Students are often not given access to the community or faculty members use advising to compensate for their own lack of an active research agenda. A formalized advising system may in some cases offer a refuge, if instructors cannot or dare not take responsibility for a disciplinary program. The advisor slips into a parasite-like existence living off the topics and literature selected by students. Advising can easily become a dignified intellectual retirement.

People rarely recognize the power at play in advising

SK: Likewise people rarely recognize the power at play in advising. When you teach undergraduate and Masters students the power of the exam table looms in the background. The advisee may not agree with the advisor, but feels that he or she must pay lip service to the advisor's perspective. Otherwise it may affect their grade. To counterbalance, some advisors, in psychology at least, may personalize the whole situation by focusing on the student's emotions. The student may feel great in the situation but often wake up abruptly when facing a critical external examiner at the exam table. Advising should not be called a dialogue. There is no equality or leveled playing field in sight.

A lecture or seminar is not as context dependent. In those more formal settings people can discuss and disagreements become public. You can allow dissonance and agnostic positions and actively confront viewpoints. Students can leave if they don't like what they hear. Advising is so closely tied to the interpersonal dynamics and power relationship. If you have different viewpoints things tend to defuse more in a working environment. Divergent methodological or theoretical perspectives become more apparent to all. When they become public in a work situation, seminar or lecture it seems easier to accept those differences.

When I advise Masters students, I prefer a seminar format where I give advice to students in front of their peers. They give short presentations on the thesis work and we all comment. I don't have to say the same things 12 times to 12 students. Often these peer groups also have a better feel for when their friends need encouragement and support. If I don't like a specific project or approach the other students will counterbalance my critique. I feel safer to just say what I think, compared to facing a lone student behind a closed office door.

With PhD students the power dynamics are slightly different compared to undergraduate and Masters students. In the Danish PhD system the advisor serves as a member of the exam committee but does not have a vote. In those situations I usually feel like the defense attorney working on behalf of the student. The foundation for the advisor-advisee relationships takes another form.

CØ: You don't use seminars to the same extent with your PhD students?

SK: Seminars can still be helpful. My colleague Klaus Nielsen found his PhD students to be rather weak theoretically. They did strong empirical work but their theory sections lacked quality. He organized a PhD seminar series and invited his colleagues. We read Lave & Wenger's book on situated learning for the first session. The next session we read and discussed one of his student's chapters and related it to Lave and Wenger's concepts. In this way the sessions oscillated between the reading of an important book and student presentations. Some of the faculty members endorsed a situated learning perspective; others built their work on activity theory. The pedagogical intention was to help the students pay closer attention to the theoretical framing of their research. An unintended consequence was that they got to see the different faculty members' divergent theoretical stands play out against each other. We, the faculty members, enjoyed the discussions as well. It is much easier to create such dynamics if you have 10 people than two people around a desk.

CØ: How do you motivate your colleagues to attend?

SK: We wanted to do it. It was texts we worked with, wanted to read and discuss. It was entirely voluntary.

Advising is much more context dependent compared to classroom teaching

CØ: Would you give me an example of an advising situation that didn't work?

SK: My own Masters thesis from the early 60's may be an example. It was an experimental study on how people form concepts. I was working as a paid research assistant for a professor with a strong cognitive orientation – Ragnar Rommetveit. On my part, I was deep into the phenomenological and existential literature and wanted to use Sartre and Merleau-Ponty to understand learning.

When it came to writing my Masters thesis it turned out that we couldn't reconcile our views on psychology. We had several heated discussions about our differences in a seminar. Finally, we agreed to disagree. No more advising. I still worked for him daily conducting the experiments, but wrote the thesis on my own. He was one of the examiners and ended up giving me a rather high grade for the thesis.

Another example, a Norwegian philosopher, Hans Skjervheim, studied phenomenological and existential psychology in the 60s. He couldn't get a tenured university position in Norway. His work was deemed outside the reigning analytical philosophy. Instead he got a full professor position in Denmark in the 70s Roskilde University Center, where all teaching was organized around the advising of student-led projects. There were no lectures or seminars – only the advising of small student groups. At the time all the students worked within competing fractions of Marxist theory. The professor had published critiques of Marx and wanted to discuss these with the students. However, the advising situation, which was the primary mode of contact between students and professor, left no room for the professor to question the students' basic assumptions. He resigned after a couple of years.

CØ: The advisor sounds nearly powerless?

SK: Again, it depends. At that university in the 70s the students were in power. Today most advisors hold a stronger position. Advising is much more context dependent compared to classroom teaching. You don't want to approach advising like some Robinson Crusoe educating a primitive Friday on some isolated island. The institutional context matters. Is the faculty member advising lone individuals behind a closed office door, or small groups of students as Hans Skjervheim did back in the 70s? The power dynamics are very different. You can go on: Is advising the main mode of student contact or a mere supplement? Is it part of an active and engaging research environment or does the student solely define the project? Do you serve simply as a consultant or do you also evaluate at judgment day? You learn little from looking at advising in isolation.

The conversation often turns into an interview

CØ: So you do not have any method for advising PhD students?

SK: It depends on the situation, whether it is to help someone plan a research project or work through their interview guide. In the former case, the conversation often turns into an interview. I probe the student about their basic research question. Often they want to do a qualitative study but need to specify the research topic. They need to develop their ideas in order to operationalize them into specific forms of interviews and observation. I ask those types of clarifying questions.

CØ: After all, you do use your interview experience in those advising situations?

SK: Well yes, not that deliberately. Only after a session do I often realize that I just conducted an interview to help the student find out what she really wanted to study before I can add any sensible advice.

In those cases it is much easier if it is my own project and they work for me. I can ask them to focus on specific aspects and come back and write a proposal or an interview guide. The responsibility is clear. I want specific problems investigated and I know what way I want to do it. If it is their own project it is easier if they know what they want. If not, the responsibility easily becomes muddled.

There is much research on the topic of "student motivation." What about "teacher motivation"?

CØ: Do you introduce your PhD students to your professional network?

SK: Whenever possible we attend conferences together or submit symposia where we present at joint sessions. We work together preparing the sessions spending much time discussing their papers, sometimes only in the last minute on the plane to the conference. I guess this is a form of advising but different. It is real work and my primary motive is to get the best possible products. It is real work.

In some cases we coauthor papers. For instance, when Klaus Nielsen was a PhD student we organized a session on apprenticeship learning at a Nordic conference where we got a lot of interesting papers. We contacted additional people in the field and ended up editing a journal issue on apprenticeship. He did most of the work with me on the sideline supporting his effort.

People often talk about the "burden of advising." But if you work together on a project it is no longer a burden. I'm not just advising to get them through their PhD. We have a common research problem. We struggle together figuring out how to approach it theoretically, methodologically, and how to best present our findings. It is much more fun working together on approximately equal terms.

There is much research on the topic of "student motivation." What about "teacher motivation"? If you can create a good working environment there is high teacher motivation. What motivates is coming to grips with an issue, developing new knowledge, publishing the results and making an impact. We re-introduced in the 1990s a debate about apprenticeship into Danish vocational education, went to conferences with vocational teachers, organized workshops and conference panels; all things that I would not have been able to accomplish on my own. I have had such a group for the past 10 years. Before that, advising rarely offered the same pleasure and productivity.

I don't end the relationship

CØ: How do you end the relationship?

SK: I don't end the relationship. The formal process comes to an end when they submit their dissertation. It is then my responsibility to suggest a list of possible exam committee members to the department chair, who will make the final choices. It has to be committees which will understand the premise of the study and at the same time offer a critical perspective. In a sense I strive towards as critical a committee as the student can handle. The stronger the committee, the stronger will be their stamp of quality for the candidate's dissertation.

CØ: They defend their dissertation successfully, then what?

SK: Some get a position in the department and others move on to other institutions. There is no formal process. I don't have all that many students at a time – maybe three or four at the most.

CØ: Do you maintain a relationship beyond this point?

SK: With some. Today I was in an editorial meeting with former PhD and Masters students editing a book on what they call "action carried knowledge". I am contributing a chapter. I am also working on a chapter for a book on professional learning among psychologists edited by two other former students. And you as my former Masters student are interviewing me on advising right now. I was late for your interview because the editorial meeting for the first book ran over time. My former students wanted me to reframe my chapter on learning the interview craft!

CØ: Did they use dialogue to muscle you into shape?

SK: Yes indeed! It was friendly fire but the power relations were not all that transparent. I ended up accepting their suggestions.

REFERENCES

Abbott, A. (2001). *Time Matters. On Theory and Method*. Chicago: University of Chicago Press.

American Association of University Professors (1981). Regulations Governing Research on Human Subjects: Academic Freedom and the Institutional Review Board. *Academe, 67*, 358-370.

American Association of University Professors (2001). Protecting Human Beings: Institutional Review Boards and Social Science Research. *Academe, 87* (3), 55-67.

American Association of University Professors (2002). Should All Disciplines Be Subject to the Common Rule? Human Subjects of Social Science Research. *Academe, 88* (1), 1-15.

American Association of University Professors, Committee A. (2006). Report on Human Subjects: Academic Freedom and the Institutional Review Boards (AAUP, 2006 – see http/www.aaup.org/AAUP/About/committees/committee+repts/CommA/.)

Argyrus, C. & Schön, D. (1996). *Organizational learning II*. USA: Addison-Westley Publishing Company.

Aristotle (1994). *Nicomachean Ethics* (Loeb Classical Library edition). Cambridge, MA: Harvard University Press.

Austin, J.L. (1975). *How to do things with words* (2nd ed.). Cambridge, MA: Harvard University Press.

Bakan, P. (1956). The collection and use of retrospective data. *Journal of Psychology, 41*, 396-379.

Bakhtin, M.M. (1981). *The Dialogic Imagination. Austin*, TX: University of Texas Press.

Bakhtin, M.M. (1984). *Problems of Dostoevsky's Poetics*. Minneapolis, MN: University of Minnesota Press.

Bakhtin, M.M. (1986). *Speech Genres and Other Late Essays*. Austin, TX: University of Texas Press.

Bakhtin, M.M. (1993). *Toward a Philosophy of the Act*. Austin: University of Texas Press.

Barbour, R.S. (2001). Checklists for improving rigour in qualitative research: a case of the tail wagging the dog? *BMJ 322*, 1115-1117.

Battiste, M. (2008). Research Ethics for Protecting Indigenous Knowledge and Heritage: Institutional and Researcher Responsibilities. In N.K. Denzin, Y.S. Lincoln & L.T. Smith (Eds.). *Handbook of Critical Indigenous Methodologies*, pp. 600-625. Thousand Oaks: Sage Publications.

Battiste, M. & Henderson, J. [Sa'ke'j] Youngblood. (2000). *Protecting Indigenous Knowledge and Heritage*. Saskatoon, Saskatchewan, Canada: Purich Publishing Ltd.

Bergstedt, E. (2005). *LiU-nytt, no. 6*, p. 6/7.

Bernstein, R. J. (1971). *Praxis and action: Contemporary philosophies of human action*. Philadelphia: University of Pennsylvania Press.

Biesta, G. (2005). Against Learning. Reclaiming a language for education in an age of learning. *Nordisk Pedagogik, 1*, 54-66.

Bishop, R. (1998). Freeing Ourselves from Neo-Colonial Domination in Research: A Maori Approach to Creating Knowledge. *International Journal of Qualitative Studies in Education, 11*, 199-219.

Bishop, R. (2005). Freeing Ourselves from Neocolonial Domination in Research. In N.K. Denzin & Y.S. Lincoln (Eds.). *Handbook of Qualitative Research*, 3/e, pp. 109-139. Thousand Oaks, CA: Sage.

Bjørgen, I., A. (1995). *Ansvar for egen læring. (Responsibility for One's Own Learning)*. Trondheim: Tapir Publishers.

Bottrup, P. (2001). *Læringsrum i arbejdslivet – et kritisk blik på Den lærende Organisation*. Copenhagen: Forlaget Sociologi.

Bourdieu, P. (1977). *Outline of a Theory of Practice*. Cambridge: Cambridge University Press.

Bourdieu, P. et al. (1999). *The Weight of the World – Social Suffering in Contemporary Society*. Stanford, CA: Stanford University Press.

Bracci, S.L. & Christians, C.G. (2002). Editor's Introduction. In S.L. Bracci & C.G. Christians (Eds.). *Moral Engagement in Public Life*, pp. 1-15. New York: Peter Lang.

Brinkmann, S. (2005). "Det kompetente menneske", (The Competent Human Being). *Nord Nytt: Nordisk Tidsskrift for Etnologi og Folkloristik, 96*, 5-17.

Brinkmann, S. & Kvale, S. (2005). Confronting the Ethics of Qualitative Research. *Journal of Constructionist Psychology, 18*, 2, 157-181.

Brinkmann, S. & Kvale, S. (2008). Ethics in Qualitative Psychological Research. In C. Willig & W. Stainton-Rogers (Eds.), *Handbook of Qualitative Research in Psychology*, pp. 261-279. London: Sage.

Cahan, E.D. & White, S.H. (1992). Proposals for a Second Psychology. *American Psychologist, 47*(2), 224-235.

Cannella, G.S. & Lincoln, Y.S. (2007). Predatory vs. Dialogic Ethics: Constructing an Illusion or Ethical Practice as the Core of Research Methods. *Qualitative Inquiry, 13,* 3 (April), 315-335.

Chaiklin, S. & J. Lave (Eds.) (1993). *Understanding Practice: Perspectives on Activity and Context.* Cambridge: Cambridge University Press.

Chamberlain, K. (2000). Methodolatry and qualitative health research. *Journal of Health Psychology, 5,* 285-296.

Cheek, J. (2006). The challenge of tailor made research quality: The RQF in Australia. In N.K. Denzin & M.D. Giardina (Eds.). *Qualitative inquiry and the conservative challenge: Contesting methodological fundamentalism,* pp. 109-126. Walnut Creek, CA: Left Coast Press.

Christians, C. (2000). Ethics and Politics in Qualitative Research. In N.K. Denzin & Y.S. Lincoln (Eds.). *Handbook of Qualitative Research,* 3/e, pp. 133-155. Thousand Oaks, CA: Sage.

Christians, C.G. (2002). The Social Ethics of Agnes Heller. *Qualitative Inquiry, Vol. 8,* No. 4, 411-428.

Christians, C. (2005). Ethics and Politics in Qualitative Research. In N.K. Denzin & Y.S. Lincoln (Eds.), *Handbook of Qualitative Research,* 3/e, pp. 139-164. Thousand Oaks, CA: Sage.

Christians, C. (2007a). Cultural Continuity as an Ethical Imperative. *Qualitative Inquiry, 13,* 3 (April), 437-444.

Christians, C. (2007b). Neutral Science and the Ethics of Resistance. In Norman K. Denzin & M.D. Giardina (Eds.). *Ethical Futures in Qualitative Research: Decolonizing the Politics of Knowledge,* pp. 33-52. Walnut Creek, CA: Left Coast Press.

Christians, G.C. (1995). The Naturalistic Fallacy in Contemporary Interactionist-Interpretive Research. *Studies in Symbolic Interaction, 19,* 125-130.

Christians, G.C. (1997). The Ethics of Being in a Communications Context. In C. Christians & M. Traber (Eds.). *Communication Ethics and Universal Values,* pp. 3-23. Thousand Oaks: Sage.

Christians, G.C. (1998). The Sacredness of Life. *Media Development 2,* 3-7.

Chronicle of Higher Education. (2006). Live Discussions: Getting to Interview Grandma. Http://chronicle.com/live/2006/11/townsend/

Clare, J. & Lewandowsky, S. (2004). Verbalizing facial memory: Criterion effects in verbal overshadowing. *Journal of Experimental Psychology: Learning, Memory and Cognition, 30,* 739-755.

Collins, P.H. (1991). *Black Feminist Thought.* New York: Routledge.

Comte, A. (1830). *Introduction to Positive Philosophy*. (This edition 1988). Indianapolis, In: Hackett Publishing Company.

Dash, L. (2007). Journalism and Institutional Review Boards. *Qualitative Inquiry, 13*, 6 (September), 871-874.

Davis, J. & Lambert, J. (1974). Affective arousal and energization properties of positive and negative stimuli. *Journal of Experimental Psychology, 103*, 196-200.

de Certeau, M. (1984). *The practice of everyday life* (S. Rendall, Trans.). Berkeley: University of California Press.

Deloria, V. Jr. (1969). *Custer Died for Your Sins: An Indian Manifesto*. New York: Macmillan.

Denzin, N.K. (2003). *Performance [Auto] Ethnography: Critical Pedagogy and the Politics of Culture*. Thousand Oaks and London: Sage.

Denzin, N.K. & Giardina, M.D. (2007). Introduction: Decolonizing the Politics of Knowledge. In N.K. Denzin & M.D. Giardina (Eds.). *Ethical Futures in Qualitative Research: Decolonizing the Politics of Knowledge*, pp. 1-32. Walnut Creek, CA: Left Coast Press.

Denzin, N.K., Lincoln, Y.S. & Giardina, M.D. (2006). Disciplining Qualitative Research. *International Journal of Qualitative Studies in Education, 19* (Nov-Dec), 769-782.

Denzin, N.K. & Giardina, M.D. (Eds.). (2006). *Qualitative inquiry and the conservative challenge: Contesting methodological fundamentalism*. Walnut Creek, CA: Left Coast Press.

Denzin, N.K. & Lincoln, Y.S. (2005). Introduction: The discipline and practice of qualitative research. In N.K. Denzin & Y.S. Lincoln (Eds.). *Handbook of qualitative research, third edition*, pp. 1-32. Thousand Oaks, CA: Sage Publications.

Denzin, N.K., Lincoln, Y.S. & Giardina, M.D. (2006). Disciplining qualitative research. *International Journal of Qualitative Studies in Education, 19*(6), 769-782.

Dewey, J. (1956). *The school and Society*. Chicago & London: The university of Chicago Press.

Dewey, J. (1984). *The Quest for Certainty*. Carbondale, IL; Southern Illinois University Press.

Dewey, J. (1991). *How we think*. N.Y.: Prometheus Books.

Dickens, C. (opr.1859). *A Tale of Two Cities*. Ware: Wordsworth.

Dreier, O. (1999). Læring som ændring af personlig deltagelse i sociale kontekster. In: K. Nielsen & S. Kvale (Eds.) *Mesterlære – Læring som social praksis*, 76-99. Copenhagen: Hans Reitzels Forlag.

Dreier, O. (2003). Learning in Personal Trajectories of Participation. In N. Stephenson, L.H. Radtke, R.J. Jorna & H.J. Stam (Eds.), *Theoretical Psychology. Critical Contributions*, pp. 20-29. Concord, Canada: Captus University Publications.

Dreier, O. (2007). Generality and Particularity of Knowledge. In V. van Deventer, M. Terre Blanche, E. Fourie & P. Segalo (Eds.) *Citizen City. Between Constructing Agent and Constructed Agency*, pp. 188-196. Concord: Captus University Publ.

Dreier, O. (2008). *Psychotherapy in Everyday Life*. New York: Cambridge University Press.

Dreier, O. (in press). Persons in Structures of Social Practice. *Theory & Psychology*.

Durkheim, W. & Mauss, M. (1963). *Primitive Classification*. R. Needham (ed. and trans.). Chicago: University of Chicago Press.

Ebbinghaus, H. (1964). *Memory: A Contribution to Experimental Psychology*. New York: Dover.

Elkjær, B. (1999). In Search of a Social Learning Theory. In M. Easterby-Smith, J. Burgoyne & L. Araujo (Eds.). *Organizational learning and the Learning Organisation – Developments in theory and practice*, pp. 75-911. London: Sage Publications.

Elmholdt, C. (2003). Metaphors for Learning: Cognitive acquisition versus social participation. *Scandinavian Journal of Educational Research, 47*, 115-131.

Elmholdt, C. & Brinkmann, S. (2006). Discursive practices at work. In: D. Boud, P. Cressey, P. Docherty (Eds.), *Productive reflection at work*, pp. 170-180. London: Routledge.

European Commission (2000). *Memorandum on Lifelong Learning*. Brussels: European Commission.

European Commission (2001). *Making a European Area of Lifelong Learning a Reality*. Brussels: European Commission.

Feenberg, A. (1986). *Lukacs, Marx and the sources of critical theory*. Oxford University Press.

Fejes, A. (2006). New wine in old skin: changing patterns in the governing of the adult learner in Sweden. *Int. J. of Lifelong Education, Vol. 24*, 1, 71-86.

Foucault, M. (1980). *Power/Knowledge: Selected Interviews and Other Writings*, 1972-1977. Edited by C. Gordon; translated by L. Marshall, J. Mepham, and K. Soper. New York: Pantheon.

Foucault, M. (1982). The subject and power. *Critical Inquiry 8*, 777-795. University of Chigaco.

Freud, S. (1901). The Psychopathology of Everyday Life, in J. Strachey (Ed.), *The Standard Edition of the Complete Psychological Works of Sigmund Freud, Vol. 21*. London: Vintage, The Hogarth Press and the Institute of Psycho-Analysis.

Gadamer, H.-G. (1988). *Truth and Method*. Tuebingen: J.C.B. Mohr.

Giorgi, A. (1967). A phenomenological approach to the problem of meaning and serial learning. *Review of Existential Psychology and Psychiatry, VII*, 106-118.

Giorgi, A. (1975). An application of phenomenological method in psychology, in A. Giorgi, C. Fischer & E. Murray (Eds.). *Duquesne Studies in Phenomenological Psychology II*. Pittsburgh, PA: Duquesne University Press.

Giorgi, A. (1994). Foreword: The psychology of Georges Politzer, in G. Politzer, *Critique of the Foundations of Psychology: The Psychology of Psychoanalysis.* Pittsburgh, PA: Duquesne University Press.

Gould, C.C. (1978). *Marx's social ontology: Individuality and community in Marx's theory of social relations.* Cambridge, MA: MIT Press.

Grandy, S. (2000). American Indian Identity and Intellectualism: The Quest for a New Red Pedagogy. *Qualitative Studies in Education, 13,* 343-360.

Graveline, F.J. (2000). Circle as Methodology: Enacting an Aboriginal Paradigm. *International Journal of Qualitative Studies in Education, 13,* 361-370.

Gregory, P. (2007). Downloaded 16th April 2007. http://www.spanishguitars.co.uk/pages/players. htm.

Gunsalus, C.K. (2002). Point of View: Rethinking Protections for Human Subjects. *Chronicle of Higher Education, 49* (Issue 12, 15 November), B24.

Gunsalus, C.K., Brunmer, E.M., Burbules, N.C., Dash, L., Finkin, M., Goldberg, J., Greenough, W., Miller, G., Pratt, M., Iriye, M. & Aronson, D. (2007). The Illinois White Paper: Improving the System for Protecting Human Subjects: Counteracting IRB 'Mission Creep' *Qualitative Inquiry, 13,* 5 (July), 617-649.

Hacking, I. (1995). The Looping Effect of Human Kinds. In: D. Sperber, D. Premack & A.J. Premack (Eds.). *Causal Cognition: A Multidisciplinary Debate,* pp. 351-383. Oxford. Clarendon Press.

Haugeland, J. (1981). Semantic engines: An introduction to mind design. In J. Haugeland (Ed.), *Mind design: Philosophy, psychology, artificial intelligence,* pp. 1-34. Cambridge, MA: MIT Press.

Hebdige, D. (1988). *Hiding in the light: On images and things.* London: Routledge.

Hellige, J.B. & Grant, D. (1974). Response rate and development of response topography in eyelid conditioning under different conditions of reinforcement. *Journal of Experimental Psychology, 103,* 574-582.

Holland, D. & Lachicotte, W. Jr. (2007). Vygotsky, Mead, and the New Sociocultural Studies of Identity. In H. Daniels, M. Cole, and J.V. Wertsch (Eds.) *The Cambridge Companion to Vygotsky.* Cambridge: Cambridge University Press.

Holland, D., Lachicotte, W., Skinner, D. & Cain, C. (1998). *Identity and Agency in Cultural Worlds.* Cambridge, MA: Harvard University Press.

Holland, D. & Lave, J. (2001). *History in Person: Enduring Struggles, Contentious Practice, Intimate Identities.* Santa Fe, New Mexico: The School of American Research Press.

Holmes, D., Murray, S., Perron, A. & Rail, G. (2006). Deconstructing the evidence-based discourse in health sciences: Truth, power and fascism. *International Journal of Evidence Based Healthcare, 4*, 180-186.

Holzkamp, K. (1983). *Grundlegung der Psychologie*. Frankfurt am Main: Campus Verlag.

Holzkamp, K. (1993). *Lernen. Subjektwissenschaftliche Grundlegung*. Frankfurt am Main: Campus Verlag.

Holzkamp, K. (1996). Manuskripte zum Arbeitsprojekt 'Lebensführung'. *Forum Kritische Psychologie 36*, 7-112.

Houellebecq, M. (1999). *Whatever*. London: Serpent's Tale.

Houellebecq, M. (2001). *Atomized*. London: Vintage.

Howard, J. (2006). Oral History Under Review. *Chronicle of Higher Education, 10* November: http:///chronicle.com/free/v53/112/12a01401.htm.

Illeris, K. (1981). *Modkvalificeringens pædagogik. (Education as Counter Qualification)*. Copenhagen: Unge Pædagoger.

Illeris, N. (2005). Erfaringspædagogik og projektarbejde. (Experience-based Education and Project work). In: N.J. Bisgaard & J. Rasmussen (Eds.). *Pædagogiske teorier. (Educational Theories)*. 4th edition. Værløse: Billesø & Baltzer.

Ingholt, L. (2007). *Fællesskaber, vaner og deltagelse. Et studie af unge på to gymnasier*. PhD Thesis, Department of Psychology, University of Copenhagen.

Janesick, V. (2000). The choreography of qualitative research design: Minuets, improvisations and crystallization. In N.K. Denzin & Y.S. Lincoln (Eds.). *Handbook of qualitative research*, third edition, pp. 379-400. Thousand Oaks, CA: Sage Publications.

Jay, M. (1984). *Marxism and totality: The adventures of a concept from Lukacs to Habermas*. Berkeley: University of California Press.

Kant, I. (1787/1965). *Critique of pure reason*. New York: St. Martin's Press.

Koch, S. (1959). Some trends of study I, Epilogue in S. Koch (Ed.) *Psychology: A study of a science, Vol. 3*, pp. 729-788. N.Y. Mcgraw-Hill.

Kraft, G. (1997). Review of I.A. Bjørgen "Ansvar for egen læring" (Responsibility for One's Own Learning). In *Newsletter for Centre of Qualitative Research Methods, no. 22*, Aarhus: Department of Psychology. University of Aarhus.

Kuhn, T. (1970). *The Structure of Scientific Revolutions* University of Chicago Press.

Kvale, S. (1972). *Prüfung und Herrschaft*. Weinheim, Germany: Beltz.

Kvale, S. (1974). The temporality of memory. *Journal of Phenomenological Psychology, 5*, 7-31.

Kvale, S. (1975). Memory and dialectics: Some reflections on Ebbinghaus and Mao Tse-tung, *Human Development, 18*, 205-222.

Kvale, S. (1976). The Psychology of Learning as Ideology and Technology. *Behaviorism 4*, 97-116.

Kvale, S. (1977). Dialectics of Remembering. In N. Datan & H.W. Reese (Eds.), *Life-span Developmental Psychology: Dialectical Perspectives on Experimental Research*. New York: Academic Press.

Kvale, S. (1992). *Psychology and postmodernism* London: Sage.

Kvale, S. (1992). Postmodern psychology: A contradiction in terms? In S. Kvale (Ed.), *Psychology and Postmodernism*. London and Thousand Oaks, CA.: Sage.

Kvale, S. (1993). En pædagogisk rehabilitering af mesterlæren? *Dansk Pædagogisk tidsskrift, 41*(1), 9-18.

Kvale, S. (1996). *InterViews: An Introduction to Qualitative Research Interviewing*. London and Thousand Oaks, CA.: Sage.

Kvale, S. (1997). Research apprenticeship. *Nordisk Pedagogik [Nordic Journal of Educational Research], 17*, 186-194.

Kvale, S. (2000). Å bli veiledet i en speillabyrint i tåke. In: K. Skagen (Ed.). *Kunnskap og handling i pedagogisk veiledning*. Bergen: Fagbokforlaget.

Kvale, S. (2003). The church, the factory and the market: Scenarios for psychology in a postmodern age. *Theory & Psychology, 13*(5), 579-603.

Kvale, S. (2003). The Psychoanalytic Interview as Inspiration for Qualitative Research. In P. Camic, J. Rhodes, & L. Yardley (Eds.). *Qualitative Research in Psychology: Expanding Perspectives in Methodology and Design*, pp. 275-297. Washington, DC: American Psychological Association Press.

Kvale, S. (2003). Danish Ph.D.-education between schooling and apprenticeship. *Nordisk Pedagogik, 23*, 184-96.

Kvale, S. (2004). Frigørende pædagogik som frigørende til forbrug. In J. Krejsler (Ed.). *Pædagogikken og kampen om individet*. Copenhagen: Hans Reitzels Forlag.

Kvale, S. (2006, May). *Interviewing between method and craft*. Paper presented at the Second International Congress of Qualitative Inquiry, Urbana-Champaign, Illinois.

Kvale, S. (2006). Dominance through interviews and dialogues. *Qualitative Inquiry, 12*(3), 480-500.

Kvale, S. (2007). Contradictions of assesment for learning in institutions of higher learning. In: D. Boud & N. Falchikov (Ed.). *Rethinking Assessment in Higher Education: Learning for the Longer Term*, pp. 57-71. London: Routhledge.

Kvale, S. (2008). Qualitative Inquiry Between Scientistic Evidentialism, Ethical Subjectivism and the Free Market. *International Review of Qualitative Research, 1*, 1, pp. 5-18.

Kvale, S. (Ed.) (1992). *Psychology and postmodernism*. London: Sage.

Kvale, S. & Grenness, C.E. (1967). Skinner and Sartre: Towards a radical phenomenology of behavior? *Review of Existential Psychology and Psychiatry, 7*, 128-150.

Kvale, S. & Nielsen, K. (1999). Landskab for læring. In K. Nielsen & S. Kvale (Eds.). *Mesterlære – Læring som social praksis*. Copenhagen: Hans Reitzels Forlag.

Kvale, S. & Brinkmann, S. (2008). *InterViews. Second Edition. Learning the Craft of Qualitative Research Interviewing*. Thousand Oaks, CA: Sage Publications.

Lather, P. (2007). *Getting Lost: Feminist Efforts toward a Double (d) Science*. Albany: SUNY Press.

Lave, J. (1988). *Cognition in Practice. Mind, Mathematics and Culture in Everyday Life*. New York: Cambridge University Press.

Lave, J. (1992). Word Problems: A Microcosm of Theories of Learning. In P. Light & G. Butterworth (Eds.). *Context and Cognition: Ways of Learning and Knowing*, pp. 74-92. Hemel Hempstead, Hertfordshire, England: Harvester Wheatsheaf.

Lave, J. (1993). The practice of learning. In S. Chaiklin & J. Lave (Eds.). *Understanding Practice: Perspectives in Activity and Context*, pp. 3-32. New York: Cambridge University Press.

Lave, J. & Wenger, E. (1991). *Situated learning – Legitimate Peripheral Participation*. Cambridge University Press.

Lefebvre, H. (1947, trans. 1991). *Critique of Everyday Life*. Vol. 1 (Trans. J. Moore). London: Verso.

Lefebvre, H. (1971). *Everyday life in the modern world* (S. Rabinovitch, Trans.). London: Penguin.

Levy-Bruhl, L. (1910). *How Natives Think*. (Reprinted, New York: Washington Square Press 1966).

Light, L. & Berger, D. (1974). Memory for modality: Within-modality discrimination is not automatic. *Journal of Experimental Psychology, 103*, 854-860.

Lincoln, Y. (1995). Emerging Criteria for Quality in Qualitative and Interpretive Inquiry. *Qualitative Inquiry. 1*, 275-289.

Lincoln, Y.S. & Cannella, G. (2002). *Qualitative Research and the Radical Right: Cats and Dogs and other Natural Enemies*. Presented to the 2002 Annual Meetings of the American Education Research Association, New Orleans, April, 1-5.

Lincoln, Y.S. & Tierney, W.G. (2002). What We Have Here is a Failure to Communicate. *Qualitative Research and Institutional Review Boards (IRBS)*. Presented to the 2002 Annual Meetings of the American Education Research Association, New Orleans, April, 1-5.

Lukács, G. (1923/1988). *History and class consciousness: Studies in Marxist dialectics*. Cambridge: MIT Press.

Lukács, G. (1978a). *The ontology of social being: Vol. 1. Hegel's false and his genuine ontology* (D. Fernbach, Trans.). London: Merlin Press.

Lukács, G. (1978b). *The ontology of social being: Vol. 2. Marx's basic ontological principles* (D. Fernbach, Trans.). London: Merlin.

Lykes, M.B. (1997). Activist participatory research among the Maya of Guatemala: Constructing meanings from situated knowledge. *Journal of Social Issues, 53*, 725-746.

Lyotard, J.-F. (1984). *The Postmodern Condition: A report on Knowledge* (G. Bennington & B. Massumi, Trans.). Manchester: Manchester University Press.

Lyotard, J.-F. (1996). *Viden og det postmoderne samfund*. Aarhus: Slagmarks Skyttegravsserie.

Lyotard, J.-F. (2001). *The Inhuman*. California: Stanford University Press.

Mao Tse-tung (1968). *Four Essays on Philosophy*. Peking: Foreign Languages Press.

Maxey, I. (1999). Beyond boundaries? Activism, academia, reflexivity and research. *Area, 31*(3), 199-208.

McKenzie, C., Wixted, J. & Noelle, D. (2004). Explaining purportedly irrational behavior by modeling skepticism in task parameters: An example examining confidence in forced-choice tasks. *Journal of Experimental Psychology: Learning, Memory and Cognition, 30*, 947-959.

Menchu, R. (1984). *I, Rigoberta Menchu: An Indian Woman in Guatemala*. London: Verso.

Merleau-Ponty, M. (1955/1974). *Adventures of the dialectic* (J. Bien, Trans.). London: Heinemann.

Michell, J. (2003). The Quantitative Imperative: Positivism, Naive Realism and the Place of Qualitative Methods in Psychology. *Theory & Psychology, 13*, 5-31.

Mishler, E.G. (1999). *Storylines. Craftartists' Narratives of Identity*. Cambridge, MA: Harvard University Press.

Mishler, E.G. (1986). *Research interviewing: Context and narrative*. Cambridge, MA: Harvard University Press.

Musaeus, P. (2005). *Crafting Persons. A Sociocultural Approach to Recognition and Apprenticeship Learning*. PhD Thesis Aarhus: Department of Psychology, University of Aarhus.

Nielsen, K. (1997). Musical apprenticeship: Trajectories of participation at the academy of music. *Nordisk Pedagogik. 17*, 160-169.

Nielsen, K. (1999). *Musical Apprenticeship – Learning at the Academy of Music as Socially Situated*. Department of Psychology, University of Aarhus.

Nielsen, K. (2005). *Håndværkslæring. Kundskab, magt og køn i bageriet*. Aarhus: Department of Psychology, University of Aarhus.

Nielsen, K. (2006). Learning to do things with things: apprenticeship learning in a bakery as economy and social practice. In A. Costall & O. Dreier, *Doing Things with Things. The Design and Use of Everyday Objects*. Aldershot: Ashgate.

Nielsen, K. & Kvale, S. (1997). Current issues of apprenticeship. *Nordic Journal of Educational Research, 17*(3), 130-139.

Nielsen, K. & Kvale, S. (Eds.) (1999). *Mesterlære – Læring som social praksis*. Copenhagen: Hans Reitzels Forlag.

Nielsen, K. & Kvale, S. (Eds.) (2003). *Praktikkens Læringslandskab. At lære gennem arbejde*. Copenhagen: Akademisk Forlag.

Nielsen, K. & Kvale, S. (2006), The workplace – a landscape of learning. In E. Antonacopoulou, P. Jarvis, V. Andersen, B. Elkjaer, S. & Høyrup (Eds). *Learning, working and living*, p. 119-135. Palgrave Macmillan.

Omrod, J. (1999). *Human Learning*. Upper Saddle River, NJ: Prentice-Hall.

Ormgod, J.E. (2003). *Educational Psychology – Developing Learners*. 4th Edition. Pearson Prentice Hall.

Parker, I. (2005). *Qualitative Psychology – Introducing Radical Research*. Buckingham: Open University Press.

Packer, M. (1993). Away from internalization. In E.A. Forman, N. Minick & C.A. Stone (Eds.), *Contexts for learning: Sociocultural dynamics in children's development*, pp. 254-265. New York: Oxford University Press.

Packer, M. (2001). The problem of transfer, and the sociocultural critique of schooling. *The Journal of the Learning Sciences, 10*, 493-514.

Packer, M. (2008). Is Vygotsky relevant? Vygotsky's Marxist psychology. *Mind, Culture, and Activity, 15(1)*.

Packer, M.J. & Goicoechea, J. (2000). Sociocultural and constructivist theories of learning: Ontology, not just epistemology. *Educational Psychologist, 35*, 227-241.

Piaget, J. (1937/1955). *The construction of reality in the child*. London: Routledge & Kegan Paul.

Piaget, J. (1970/1988). *Structuralism* (C. Maschler, Trans.). New York: Harper & Row.

Piaget, J. (1976/1972). *The child and reality: Problems of genetic epistemology* (A. Rosen, Trans.). Penguin.

Piaget, J. (1977). *The development of thought: Equilibration of cognitive structures*. New York: Viking.

Plato (1997). *Symposium and the Death of Socrates*. Ware, Herts: Wordworth Editions Limited.

Politzer, G. (1994). *Critique of the Foundations of Psychology: The Psychology of Psychoanalysis*. Pittsburgh, PA: Duquesne University Press.

Usher, R. & Edwards, R. (2001). Lifelong Learning: A postmodern condition of education? *Adult education quarterly, 51*, 4, 273-287.

Van der Veer, R., & Valsiner, J. (1991). *Understanding Vygotsky. A quest for synthesis*. Oxford: Basil Blackwell.

Varsava, J.A. (2005). Utopian Yearnings, Dystopian Thoughts: Houellebecq's The Elementary Particles and the Problem of Scientific Communitarianism. *College Literature, 32*(4), 145-167.

Watson, J.B. (1919). *Psychology from the standpoint of a behaviorist*. Philadelphia, PA. J.B. Lippincott.

Wertsch, J.V. (1991). *Voices of the Mind. A Sociocultural Approach to Mediated Action*. Cambridge, MA: Harvard University Press.

West, C. (1993). *Keeping the Faith: Philosophy and Race in America*. New York: Routledge.

Willis, P. (1977/1981). *Learning to labor: How working class kids get working class jobs*. New York: Columbia University Press.

Wundt, W. (1883). *Logik Vol. II Methodenlehre*. Stuttgart. Verlag Ferdinand von Enke.

Østerlund, C. & Carlile, P. (2005). Relations in practice: Sorting through practice theories on knowledge sharing in complex organizations. *The Information Society, 21*, 91-107.

Østerlund, C. (1996). Sales apprentices on the move: A multi-contextual perspective on situated learning. *Nordisk Pedagogik, 17*, 169-78.

LIST OF AUTHORS

Svend Brinkmann, Assistant professor
Department of Psychology, University of Aarhus

Julianne Cheek, Professor
Institute of Nursing and Health Sciences, Section for Nursing Science, University of Oslo
Director: Centre for Research into Sustainable Health Care, University of South Australia

Norman K. Denzin, Professor
Institute of Communications Research, University of Illinois at Urbana-Champaign

Ole Dreier, Professor
Department of Psychology, University of Copenhagen

Hubert L. Dreyfus, Professor Emeritus
Department of Philosophy, University of California, Berkeley

Stuart E. Dreyfus, Professor Emeritus
Industrial and Engineering Operation Research, University of California, Berkeley

Claus Elmholdt, Consultant
Udviklingskonsulenterne